# TOWN GOVERNMENT IN
# MASSACHUSETTS

# TOWN GOVERNMENT IN MASSACHUSETTS

## (1620–1930)

BY

JOHN FAIRFIELD SLY

ARCHON BOOKS
HAMDEN, CONNECTICUT
1967

**TO**

MY FATHER AND MOTHER

# PREFACE

THE steady and continuous unfolding of a local institutional pattern contains within it the historic facts from which spring many of those generalizations which form the fibre of political thought. There is a new understanding that comes with a long perspective; there is a judicious tolerance towards contemporary institutions that grows from a grasp of past usefulness; and there is an impetus to orderly progress in the description and analysis of those present-day adjustments through which perplexed communities aim to regulate the rapid and often extreme transitions that are a phenomenon of modern life. Broadly, the application of these observations to one of America's most distinguished political experiments — the Massachusetts town meeting — forms the purpose of this brief study.

There are those to whom I owe a great personal debt. The acknowledgment of the vision and guidance of William Bennett Munro carries with it everywhere the assurance of student years well spent and of counsel wisely given. This book would neither have been undertaken nor published without his aid and encouragement, and while such admission is no unusual privilege among scholars, it marks an obligation that must always remain.

Others have given freely of their time and thought. Professor Arthur Norman Holcombe and Professor Samuel Eliot Morison read critically portions of the manuscript and advised me on many important points.

vii

Dr. Miller McClintock, Director of the Albert Russel Erskine Bureau for Street Traffic Research, Harvard University, and Henry S. Dennison, President of the Dennison Manufacturing Company, Framingham, did much to expedite publication. The late John H. Edmunds, Director of the Division of Archives of the Commonwealth, and Joseph Wright, Librarian of the Bureau for Municipal Research, Harvard University, called my attention to valuable historical materials, and William G. Grundy, Second Deputy Secretary of the Commonwealth, Clarence A. Bingham, Town Manager of Norwood, and James E. Pendergast, Town Clerk and Accountant of Norwood, placed their wide experience in local affairs at my disposal by reading contemporary chapters.

J. F. S.

CAMBRIDGE, MASSACHUSETTS
November, 1929

# CONTENTS

In town meeting the great secret of political science was uncovered and the problem solved — how to give every individual his fair weight in the government, without any disorder from numbers.

EMERSON

Still more salutary is the moral part of the instruction afforded by the participation of the private citizen, if even rarely, in public functions. He is called upon, while so engaged, to weight interests not his own, to be guided, in case of conflicting claims, by another rule than his private partialities; to apply, at every turn principles and maxims which have for their reason of existence the general good.

J. S. MILL

C'est pourtant dans la commune que réside la force des peuples libres. Les institutions communales sont à la liberté ce que les écoles primaires sont à la science; elles la mettent à la portée du peuple; elles lui en font goûter l'usage paisible et l'habituent à s'en servir. Sans institutions communales une nation peut se donner un gouvernement libre, mais elle n'a pas l'esprit de la liberté.

DE TOCQUEVILLE

Das Studium des Gemeindewesens in Amerika, dem Sie sich jetzt widem, wird sicher sehr fruchtbar werden. In der Gemeinde ist die grosse Mehre der Bürger mehr als im Stadt veranlasst, an öffentlichen Angelegenheiten und gemeinsamen Interessen zu betheiligen. Die Gemeinde ist überdem auch die Vorschule für den Stat. Der Bau der Republiken hat seine Grundlage in der Selbständigkeit der Gemeinden.

BLUNTSCHLI

# TOWN GOVERNMENT IN
# MASSACHUSETTS

# I

## SETTLEMENT

PLYMOUTH is a symbol of national origins and the voyage of the *Mayflower* an American epic. The years have failed to match the glory of being the first to maintain a precarious foot-hold on a lonely and unknown coast, while the Pilgrim story has softened the hard realities of history, and assured enduring favor to everyone connected with the venture. Yet in the cold light of historical fact there can be little doubt that had the settlement vanished as others about it, the main streams of political development in New England would quite probably have been unaltered. There were rugged virtues in plenty — courage, fortitude and religious fervor — which give a strong and unbending fibre to community life; but there were also poverty, sparse population and political insecurity which undermine the sturdiest efforts toward institutional development.

Surviving records give ample evidence of limited opportunities. The patent obtained by John Peirce and his associates was meager and restricted — a hundred acres of land to each colonist at a yearly rental of two shillings an acre after seven years.[1] The devastations of the first winter left only fifty-one persons. A year later there were barely double that number.[2] In 1624

[1] "The First Plymouth Patent" (1621), *Mass. Hist. Soc. Coll.*, 4th series. II, 159, 160.
[2] J. B. Felt, "Statistics of Population in Massachusetts," *Amer. Stat. Assn. Coll.*, I (pt. 2), 143.

3

Captain John Smith reported something less than two hundred,[1] and even a decade after landing the numbers had increased slightly enough, the most hopeful estimate being in Bradford's charter commending the growth of the plantation "to neere three hundred people."[2] Strenuous efforts, moreover, failed to obtain a secure definition of political powers. As late as 1636 the General Court of the colony could do no better than base its authority on a heterogeneous array of documents including the Mayflower compact, the league of peace with Massasoit, the subsequent land grant from the Indians, and "sundry commissions" chiefly represented by the charters of Peirce and Bradford.[3]

The necessary civil regulation was obtained through a governor, numerous assistants and a constable — simple, probably unpremeditated and thoroughly practical. Questions of public interest were discussed by the adult male population, each case, generally, being referred to the governor and council for approval. There are fragmentary references to action "by the most voices," or "the consent of the body of the company," or "at a general meeting."[4] But legislation was scant — for ten years the surviving records occupy only a little over two pages. There is no doubt that to the end of its separate existence the colony of Plymouth remained a humble

[1] "Advertisements for the Unexperienced Planters of New-England" (1631), *Mass. Hist. Soc. Coll.*, 3d series, III, 27.

[2] William Brigham (ed.), *The Compact with the Charter and Laws of the Colony of New Plymouth* (Boston, 1836), p. 22.

[3] Massachusetts General Court, *Records of the Colony of New Plymouth in New England* (N. B. Shurtleff and David Pulsifer, eds., 12 vols., Boston, 1855–1861), XI, *Laws* (1623–1686), 150–151. Hereafter cited *Ply. Col. Rec.*

[4] "Mourt's Relation" (1622) in Alexander Young's *Chronicles of the Pilgrim Fathers of the Colony of Plymouth* (1602–1625) (Boston, 1844), pp. 167, 173, 331, 347.

community in numbers, wealth and political influence,[1] but that nevertheless like ancient Bethlehem, though "little among the thousands of Judah," a favored position made its name immortal.

This is in no way to disparage the service of the first permanent settlement in New England, it is rather to emphasize the stern character of the venture, and to indicate the difficulties of contributing effectively to institutional history. Whatever may be the vigor that hardships engender, political insecurity is more likely to result in efforts towards preservation than improvement, and it remained for a wealthier, more numerous and more cosmopolitan immigration, free alike from undue hardships and restraints to respond to the liberalizing effects of a frontier. During the obscure years of the southern colony, "There were," wrote Cotton Mather, "more than a few attempts . . . to people and improve the parts of New-England which were to the northward,"[2] with the result that when John Winthrop arrived in the summer of 1630, the "old planters" were occupying many favorable sites. As early as 1622, Weymouth (then known as Wessagusett) was held by Thomas Weston, formerly a merchant and citizen of London, and although he soon abandoned the settlement, a son of the distinguished Ferdinando Gorges reoccupied the site and gave permanence to the undertaking.[3] By 1625, Mount Wollaston (now Braintree)

---

[1] J. A. Goodwin, *The Pilgrim Republic* (Boston, 1888), pp. 159–160.

[2] *Magnalia Christi Americana* (Thomas Robbins, ed., 2 vols., Hartford, Conn., 1855), I, 65.

[3] Ferdinando Gorges, "A Briefe Narration" (1658), *Mass. Hist. Soc. Coll.*, 3d series, VI, 74; Thomas Prince, *A Chronological History of New England, in the Form of Annals* (1602-1730) (Boston, 1826), pp. 213–214,

was settled. The sponsor of this venture was one Captain Wollaston, whose disappointment with the community caused his early departure to fairer prospects in Virginia. It was then that Thomas Morton — dubiously described as a "kind of pettifogger at Furnival's Inn" — obtained control of the colony, only to follow a notorious course of dissipation, symbolized by his infamous "May Pole," and completed by temporary deportation to Old England.[1]

It was in the summer of 1624 that Nantasket was occupied by discontented members of the Plymouth colony, who managed a rather unsatisfactory existence near a temporary habitation that Miles Standish had built for trade with the Indians a year or two before. Among them was Roger Conant,—"a pious, sober, and prudent gentleman,"— who impressed John White and his associates of Dorchester sufficiently to be chosen governor of their proposed colony at Cape Ann. A year's trial on this new site, however, brought dissatisfaction, and the settlement was moved "down a little lower towards the bottom of the Bay" (soon to be called Salem) — "the first foundation on which the next colonies were built."[2]

221–222, 230; Edward Winslow, "Good News from New England" (1625), Mass. Hist. Soc. Coll., VIII, 245–248.

[1] "Dudley's Letter to the Countess of Lincoln" (1630), in Alexander Young's Chronicles of the First Planters of the Colony of Massachusetts Bay (1623–1636) (Boston, 1846), pp. 309, 321 (note 2); Prince, Chronological History, pp. 231, 240.

[2] "Hubbard's Narrative" (ca. 1680), in Young's Chronicles of Massachusetts Bay, pp. 20–21; H. B. Adams, "Origin of Salem Plantation," Essex Inst. Hist. Coll., XIX, 153–156; G. D. Phipper, "The Old Planters of Salem," ibid., I, 99; Prince, Chronological History, 231. The charter granted to the Dorchester adventurers is found in J. W. Thornton's The Landing at Cape Anne (Boston, 1854), together with a complete discussion of the whole

There were, moreover, individual adventurers who came to the new world at unknown times and for obscure reasons, and occupied more or less permanent sites in the vicinity of Massachusetts Bay. There was Samuel Maverick — "a man of loving and curteous behaviour . . . yet an enemy to the Reformation in hand" — who with the help of David Thompson (sent out by Gorges as early as 1623) built a fort on Noddle's Island — a site now widely known as East Boston. On a small creek "about one mile distant upon the River" (probably the vicinity of Charlestown) there lived Edward Gibbons — a one-time member of that "church of misrule" at Mount Wollaston — while to the south on Blaxton's Point (near the present juncture of Charles and Pinckney streets) lived the well-known William Blaxton who came to America in an unknown ship, at an uncertain time and for an undiscovered cause and "sat down, alone, on the peninsula now the chief part of Boston." Southeast of him, near Thompson's Island (now part of Quincy) there lived "some few planters more." [1]

This was, indeed, a slender beginning. For almost ten years the Plymouth settlement had led its mercurial existence, and there had been little in its history to attract others to so rigid an adventure. But James I was not a king to watch a continent go by default, and one of his famous land companies, the New England

episode. Conant was probably chosen governor of the colony near the close of the first year of its settlement — 1624.

[1] Francis Baylies, *An Historical Memoir of the Colony of New Plymouth,* 2 vols. (Boston, 1866), I (pt. 1), 197–198; Edward Johnson, *Wonder-Working Providence of Sions Saviour in New England* (1654) (W. F. Poole, ed., Andover, 1867), p. 37.

Council,[1] while eking out a somewhat spasmodic and turbulent existence, quite unwittingly prepared for the realization of the princely hopes. In March, 1627/8, six gentlemen living in the vicinity of Dorchester purchased from this company a strip of land on Massachusetts Bay the use of which was destined to alter the character of settlement in the new world.[2] The six conveyed to others an interest in the purchase,[3] and the proprietors showed every desire to take immediate advantage of their investment.

The grant gave title to the soil but of course no rights of government, and while it was almost a year before a charter was secured from Charles I creating a corporation under the title of the "Governor and Company of Massachusetts Bay in New England,"[4] three months after the grant had been obtained, a group of emigrants was sent to America with John Endicott, one of the original purchasers, as governor. At the site of Salem this company met Roger Conant with the survivors of his community, and while the older settlers seemed disposed to question the claims of the new arrivals to possession of the territory, sober counsel prevailed, and Endicott was allowed to join the two groups into a united colony of some fifty or sixty persons.[5]

The company in England was, however, still far

[1] Brigham, *Compact with the Charter and Laws*, pp. 1–18.

[2] This grant is not known to be extant, but is recited in the subsequent charter.

[3] Massachusetts General Court, *Records of the Governor and Company of the Massachusetts Bay in New England* (1628–1686) (N. B. Shurtleff, ed., 5 vols. in 6, Boston, 1853–1854), Cradock to Endicott (Feb. 16, 1628/9), I, p. 383. Hereafter cited *Mass. Col. Rec.*

[4] I *Mass. Col. Rec.* 10–11.

[5] "White's Brief Relation" (1630) in Young's *Chronicles of Massachusetts*, p. 13.

enough removed from the rigorous needs of a new continent to indulge in legal apprehensions for the future.
The presence of the "old planters" to the south as well
as the activities of others known to be interested in the
soil caused uneasiness, and in the first general letter of
instructions to Endicott and his council, directions were
issued designed to prevent any misunderstandings that
might arise:

> And because wee would not omitt to doe any thinge which
> might strengthen our right, wee would have you (as soone as
> these [shipps, or any] of them, arrive [with you, whe]reby
> [you may have men to do it]) send 40 or 50 [persons] to
> Mattachusetts [Bay to inhabite there, which we] pray you
> not to protract, but to doe it with [all] speede.[1]

Endicott appears, however, to have anticipated this
suggestion, for, in the fall of 1628, he had given his
approval to Ralph Sprague, his brothers, Richard and
William, and several more who had subsequently arrived in Salem, to secure a foothold on Massachusetts
Bay. Thus authorized, the small company traveled
twelve miles to the southwest and came to a place on
the north side of the Charles River. There was only
one Englishman residing on the site — Thomas Walford, a smith — but conditions were hopeful enough
to encourage the group to remain. Within the next few
months, they were joined by others, and the new settlement was raised to "the denomination of an English
town." Within a short time it was agreed that this place,
formerly called *Mishawum*, should henceforth "from the
name of the river, be called Charlestown; which was

---

[1] I *Mass. Col. Rec.* 390 (April, 1629).

also confirmed by Mr. John Endicott, Governor." [1]
The new communities prospered. The fall of 1629
found perhaps two hundred colonists at Salem and
probably well over half as many at Charlestown; [2] but a
movement of great importance was being undertaken
by the company in England which was to give an
unprecedented impetus to settlement. At a General
Court held in London, July 28, 1629, Governor Cradock
proposed that the interest of the plantation demanded
the transfer of the government to the New World [3] —
a plan that for the first time was to bring the spirit of
enterprise into complete grips with colonization. As
revolutionary as such a suggestion must have appeared,
it was nevertheless favorably received, and given
definite expression in the famous Cambridge agreement of August 8, 1629. [4]  Three days later a General
Court gave final approval to the proposal, [5] new officers
were chosen, and in April of the following year, company and charter set sail from old England with four
staunch ships — a vanguard of some seventeen vessels
destined to arrive in America before the following October had elapsed.

[1] "Early Records of Charlestown" (ca. 1664) in Young's *Chronicles
of Massachusetts*, pp. 375, 376. There is some confusion as to just when
this episode happened. See Richard Frothingham's *The History of Charlestown* (Boston, 1845–1849), p. 14, and Prince's *Chronological History*, pp. 250
and 261 (note).

[2] Francis Higginson, "New-Englands Plantation" (1630) in Young's
*Chronicles of Massachusetts*, p. 259: "There are in all of us, both old and
new planters, about three hundred, whereof two hundred of them are settled
at Nehum-kek, now called Salem, and the rest have planted themselves at
Masathulets Bay, beginning to build a town there, which we do call Cherton
or Charles town."

[3] I *Mass. Col. Rec.* 49.

[4] Young's *Chronicles of Massachusetts*, pp. 281–282.

[5] I *Mass. Col. Rec.* 51.

It was natural that a large part of the ships should land at Salem — the first settlement and colonial headquarters of the company; and it was also natural that the newly arrived immigrants should be displeased with the site.[1] Not only was it remote from other settlements and away from what had always been regarded as the attractive and promising littoral of Massachusetts Bay, but the Winthrop colonists found the inhabitants close to destitution, and while they arrived in time to prevent approaching famine, provisions were inadequate for more than a temporary relief. No time was lost, accordingly, in sending some of their number to "the Bay" to search for more propitious sites, and suitable places were soon found — one on the Mystic (near the present Malden), and another some "three leagues up Charles river" (probably where Cambridge now stands);[2] but because Mr. Blackstone (the Blaxton of Johnson's narrative), who lived in a cottage on the other side of the river at a place which the Indians called *Shawmut*, told the governor of a highly superior spring there His Excellency "with Mr. Wilson and the greatest part of the church, removed thither . . . and this place was called Boston."[3] Thomas Hutchinson tells the story simply:

The governor, and some of the principal persons, left Salem the 17th of June, and travelled through the woods to Charlestown, about twenty miles, to look out for a convenient place for their chief town, which they had determined

[1] Prince, *Chronological History*, p. 308.
[2] "Dudley's Letter to the Countess of Lincoln," pp. 310–312; John Winthrop, *The History of New England* (1630–1649) (2 vols., Boston, 1825), I, 27.
[3] "Early Records of Charlestown," pp. 380–381.

should be in some part of the bay or harbor between Nantasket and Cambridge.   At first they pitched upon the northside of Charles River, or rather northwest, by the major voice; but a number of the principal gentlemen having fixed their cottages, shelters intended for one winter only, upon the opposite side of the river, the governor and most of the assistants removed to them in November.[1]

About a fortnight before the landing of Governor Winthrop with the passengers and crew of the *Arbella*, another ship, the *Mary and John*, brought an additional load of colonists to Massachusetts.   The captain, it seems, had undertaken to disembark his passengers on the banks of the Charles, but either unwillingness or misunderstanding caused a landing on "Nantasket Point," where, writes one of the company, he "left us to shift for ourselves on a forlorn place in this wilderness."   But a party of the ablest men obtained a boat from some "old planters" and started for their original destination.   They stopped at Charlestown, where they found some wigwams and a house (probably the home of Walford, the smith), and then continued upstream until the river grew narrow and shallow.   Here, after much labor, for the banks were steep, they landed their goods and prepared to erect a permanent settlement. Within a few days, however, word was received from their companions "to come away from that place, which was about Watertown, unto a place called Mattapan [now Dorchester], because there was there a neck of land fit to keep our cattle on," and the painstaking Clap concludes "we removed, and came to Mattapan." [2]

[1] Thomas Hutchinson, *The History of Massachusetts* (2 vols., 3d ed., Salem, 1795), I, 26.

[2] "Memoirs of Capt. Roger Clap" (*ca.* 1676) in Young's *Chronicles of*

In such a manner the earliest towns of Massachusetts
came into existence and the steady arrival of new colonists led to the establishment of many others. Watertown began "by occasion of Sir *Richard Saltingstall*, who
at his arrivall, having some store of Cattell and servants,
they wintered in those parts;"[1] Roxbury owed its settlement to the continued dispersal of the Winthrop colonists when "Mr. Pincheon and several others planted
betwixt Boston and Dorchester; which place was called
Roxbury;" while still others "issued out to a place between Charlestown and Salem, called Saugust, since ordered to be called Linn."[2] Cambridge was the result of
much deliberation on the part of the governor and
assistants concerning a suitable site for a fortified town.
It was finally agreed to build such a place on the"Charles
river, about three miles west from Charlestown," and
practically all pledged themselves to erect houses there
the following spring and to "remove their ordnance and
munition thither."[3]

Neither definite land policy nor formal legal sanction
marked their establishment, and the exigencies that determined the choice of sites were highly practical ones.
"We could not have a town in the place aforesaid"
[Roxbury], wrote Winthrop, "Because men would be
forced to keep two families. . . . There was no running
water; and if there were any springs, they would not
suffice the town. . . . The most part of the people had

*Massachusetts*, pp. 348–350; W. D. Orcutt, *Good Old Dorchester* (Cambridge,
1893), pp. 28–29.

[1] Johnson, *Wonder-Working Providence*, p. 46.
[2] "Early Records of Charlestown," p. 381.
[3] "Dudley's Letter to the Countess of Lincoln," p. 320; Prince, *Chronological History*, p. 326.

built already, and would not be able to build again." [1] Save for the expedient advice contained in the company's first letter of instructions to Endicott relative to what later became Charlestown and Boston, the communities were settled with little authority or guidance. They were due to the spontaneous action of settlers in a new world impelled principally through motives of comfort, security, and economic promise. About ten weeks after landing, the first court of assistants was convened at Charlestown (August 23, 1630), and at that time the colonists of Massachusetts Bay were scattered throughout at least eleven settlements. Dudley in his letter to the Countess of Lincoln — the most complete contemporary account that has come down to us — enumerated what he evidently intended to be a complete record:

We were forced . . . to plant dispersedly, some at Charlestown, which standeth on the north side of the mouth of Charles river; some on the south side thereof, which place we named BOSTON, (as we intended to have done the place we first resolved on;) some of us upon Mistick, which we named Medford [Malden], some of us westwards on Charles river, four miles from Charlestown, which place we named Watertown; others of us two miles from Boston, in a place we named Rocksbury; others upon the river of Saugus, between Salem and Charlestown [Lynn]; and the western men four miles south from Boston, at a place we named Dorchester.[2]

But if these early communities were of somewhat

---

[1] Winthrop, *History of New England*, p. 38.

[2] "Dudley's Letter to the Countess of Lincoln," pp. 313–314. In addition there was of course, Salem, besides the older settlements of "Wessaguscus" and "Nantascett" mentioned in the first tax list of September 28, 1630 (I *Mass. Col. Rec.* 77).

haphazard origin, they were so very largely because of political necessity. As soon as the government of the company was organized, a regulation began that promised close supervision. Indiscriminate settlement was no longer allowed. The second Court of Assistants meeting in Charlestown (September 7, 1630) ordered that no person should settle within the limits of the patent without permission from the Governor and Assistants. A subsequent regulation provided that no authority but the General Court should have power to dispose of lands, and a few months later it was required that only a majority of the magistrates should have the power to regulate from time to time "the sitting downe of men in any newe plantation, & that none shall goe without leave from them."[1] Subsequently a definite method was arranged under which lands were to be distributed, by requiring that a committee of five, named in the order, have the power to receive requests from interested settlers. With due regard to their shares in the common stock, their ability to make use of the land, as well as the extent of grants previously made in their favor, the committee was to make what allowance seemed expedient, and certify such action to the General Court. It was made plain, however, that while fifty acres a person was allowed the first planters, such generosity could hardly be permitted to all applicants, and the committee was cautioned to remember that everyone could not be expected to receive his full proportion at that time.[2]

Under such a policy various methods of settlement

[1] I *Mass. Col. Rec.* 76, 117, 167.
[2] *Ibid.*, p. 240.

were undertaken. At times the General Court would
award certain grants to individuals for their personal
use: "There is a necke of land lyeing about 3 myles
from Salem, contain[ing] aboute 300 acre of land,
graunted to Captain Jo: Endicott, to enioy to him & his
heires for euer." [1] On other occasions existing towns
would receive additional tracts: as, "Shawshin is
granted to Cambridge, provided they make it a village,
to have 10 families there setled within three yeares."
More directly, the General Court would definitely provide for a new community: "It is ordered, that there
shalbe a plantation setled, aboute two myles above the
falls of Charles Ryver, on the north east syde thereof,
to have ground lyeing to it on both sydes the ryver, both
upland & meadowe, to be layde out hereafter, as the
Court shall appoynct"; and at times further migration
to certain localities would be restricted,[2] or permission
be granted the inhabitants of an established town (as in
the case of Thomas Hooker and his restless congregation) to seek a new locality more suited to their needs.[3]

Committees were frequently appointed to assist
petitioners in laying out the proposed plantation, or in
determining the boundaries of old ones; [4] and occasionally encouragement was given to individuals to

---

[1] *Ibid.*, pp. 97, 100, 114.

[2] *Ibid.*, pp. 330, 156, 103.

[3] *Ibid.*, p. 119:"Thereis leaue graunted to the inhabitants of Newe Towne
to seeke out some convenient place for them, with promise that it shalbe
confirmed unto them, to which they may remove their habitations, or haue
as an addition to that which already they haue, provided they doe not
take it in any place to prejudice a plantation already setled."

[4] *Ibid.*, p. 102 (Dorchester and Roxbury), 146 (Newbury), 173 (Newton).
The best account of the whole movement is Melville Egleston's "The Land
System of the New England Colonies," *Johns Hopkins University Studies
in Historical and Political Science,* IV, nos. 11, 12,

"looke out ffermes for themselues, with promise to accommidate them." [1] Plantations were even formally established on the modern promotion basis of three years immunity from public charges and a guarantee of adequate means for taking the necessary property to the new location; [2] or more naturally a town would grant independence to a portion of its inhabitants, and the General Court would be called upon to add its sanction. Marblehead was so incorporated, "Salem haveing granted them to be a towne of themselues, & appointed them the bounds of their towne, which the Courte doth graunt." [3]

The terse record of the General Court is aptly supplemented and summarized by the contemporary account of Captain Edward Johnson. This gentleman probably came to America with the Winthrop colonists in 1630, and began what was destined to be a long career of public life in church and colony with service on a committee to found the new town of Woburn. He was, therefore, in an excellent position to see the various steps of community building, and in his famous *Wonder-Working Providence of Sions Saviour in New England*

---

[1] I *Mass. Col. Rec.* 121.

[2] *Ibid.*, p. 157 (Concord); 179–180 (Dedham); III *Mass. Col. Rec.* 388 (Groton).

[3] II *Mass. Col. Rec.* 266. Under various conditions land was even leased to responsible parties. "The Ileland called Conant's Ileland" was disposed of to Winthrop for the term of his life with renewal to his heirs, subject to a payment of forty shillings, a small yearly rent, and a promise to plant a vineyard and orchard on the property. This was subsequently changed to a "hogshead of the best wyne that shall grow there, to be paide yearely"; and again in 1640, to an annual rental of "onely two bushels of apples every year — one bushell to the Governor, & another to the Generall Court in winter — the same to bee of the best apples there growing" (I *Mass. Col. Rec.* 94, 139, 293).

outlined the manner in which he observed the establishment of a large part of these early settlements:

But to begin, this Town [Woburn], as all others had its bounds fixed by the General Court, to the contenese of four miles square, (beginning at the end of *Charles Town* bounds) the grant is to seven men of good and honest report, upon condition, that within two year they erect houses for habitation thereon, and so go on to make a Town thereof, upon the Act of Court; these seven men have power to give and grant out lands unto any persons who are willing to take up their dwellings within the said precinct, & to be admitted to al comon priviledges of the said Town, giving them such an ample portion, both of Medow and Upland, as their present and future stock of cattle and hands were like to improve, with eye had to others that might after come to populate the said Town; this they did without any respect of persons, yet such as were exorbitant, and of a turbulent spirit, unfit for a civil society they would reject, till they come to mend their manners, such came not to enjoy any freehold: These seven men ordered and disposed of the streets of the Town, as might be best for the improvement of the Land, and yet civil and religious society maintained; to which end those that had land neerest the place for Sabbath Assembly, had a lesser quantity at home, and more farther off to improve for corn, of all kinds; they refused not men for their poverty, but according to their ability were helpful to the poorest sort, in building their houses, and distributed to them land accordingly; the poorest had six or seven acres of Medow, and twenty-five of Upland, or thereabouts: Thus was this Town populated, to the number of sixty families, or thereabout, and after this manner are the Towns of *New England* peopled.[1]

If the General Court were solicitous as to the methods by which new towns were to be established, it became mildly paternal in an endeavor to compel ade-

1 Johnson, *Wonder-Working Providence*, p. 176.

quate provisions to insure local security and prosperity.
Even before the first meeting of the freemen (October
19, 1630), several Courts of Assistants prescribed minor
regulations of a local character. It was early ordered
that "Trimountaine shalbe called Boston; Mattapan,
Dorchester; & the towne upon Charles Ryver, Water-
ton." [1] Constables were selected for Salem and Dorchester to hold office for one year and thereafter until
a successor be chosen, and a subsequent entry dis-
ciplined the Dorchester officer "for takeing upon him
to marry Clement Briggs & Joane Allen, & to be imprisoned till hee hath paid his ffyne."[2] A group of
colonists were ordered to pay for certain cattle according
to a commercial agreement to which they were a party,
and a tax was levied on the several plantations for the
maintenance of the local pastors, Mr. Patrick and
Mr. Underhill.[3]

With the development of the colony, this policy continued with vigor. The first General Court held at
Boston in the autumn chose constables for Charlestown, Roxbury and Watertown.[4] Every plantation was
directed to provide common weights and measures, to
maintain a suitable pound, to survey and record its

[1] I *Mass. Col. Rec.* 75.
[2] *Ibid.*, pp. 76, 83.
[3] *Mass. Col. Rec.* 76, 77. At first the plantations were taxed repeatedly
by the Court of Assistants for public purposes (*ibid.*, pp. 77, 82, 89, 93, etc.).
But in May, 1634, the General Court ordered that it only had the power
to grant lands and levy taxes (*ibid.*, p. 117). Although it seems that the
Massachusetts Bay Company had no legal justification for such action,
the explanation may be found in financial necessity, in the existing political
practices of the mother country, and in the precedent of earlier contributions within the colony (E. E. Day, *The History of the General Property
Tax in Massachusetts Prior to 1690*, MS. Thesis, Harvard University,
1909, p. 5).
[4] *Ibid.*, p. 79.

land allotments, and to provide a proper place to store powder and ammunition.[1] Each town was given the liberty to make such orders as it deemed expedient concerning the restriction of swine, new plantations were forbidden to build houses more than half a mile from the meeting-house without permission of the General Court, and specified training days for the local militia were ordered.[2] Few meetings passed without similar directions, until at a General Court held at "Newe Towne," March 3, 1635/6, there was enacted the first organic law for the regulation of towns in Massachusetts — indeed, the first grant of local self-government in America. In simple phrases the order provided the flexible, elementary requirements of a pioneer community — to dispose of its common property, to order its civil affairs, and to choose its "owne particular officers."[3]

Originating in a nucleus of "old planters," sponsored by a great commercial company, of uncertain legal status and ill-defined local powers, the Massachusetts town came into existence. In its relation to the colonial government there is little evidence of extreme autonomy on the one hand or of irksome paternalism on the other. Rather there is apparent a community consciousness rapidly broadening from a commercial interest to wide social requirements — a condition less susceptible to formal regulation than to voluntary coöperation. It was in such an environment that democracy met its fullest expression, not only because of the absence of

[1] *Ibid.*, pp. 87, 150, 116, 138.
[2] *Ibid.*, pp. 119, 157, 90.
[3] *Ibid.*, p. 172.

restraints, remoteness from settled areas, the rigors of a frontier, and the natural propensities of Englishmen for self-government, but because there was the most urgent need for an extreme personal coöperation that required each man to find his station in the local public service. Whatever may be subsequently concluded by a puzzled court or zealous antiquarian as to the remote physical and legal origins of these early settlements, the fact remains that by 1640 official recognition had been extended to twenty communities, within whose early records are concealed the institutional beginnings of local self-government in America. They are as follows:

| Town | Cited | Mass. Col. Rec. | |
|------|-------|------|------|
| Salem | First mentioned | 8–23–1630 | I, 73 |
| Charlestown | First mentioned | 8–23–1630 | I, 73 |
| Watertown | Named | 9– 7–1630 | I, 75 |
| Dorchester | Named | 9– 7–1630 | I, 75 |
| Boston | Named | 9– 7–1630 | I, 75 |
| Roxbury | First mentioned | 9–28–1630 | I, 77 |
| Medford | First mentioned | 9–28–1630 | I, 77 |
| Marblehead | First mentioned | 7– 2–1633 | I, 106 |
| Ipswich | Named | 8– 5–1634 | I, 123 |
| Newbury | Named | 5– 6–1635 | I, 146 |
| Weymouth | Named | 9– 2–1635 | I, 156 |
| Hingham | Named | 9– 2–1635 | I, 156 |
| Concord | Named | 9– 3–1635 | I, 157 |
| Cambridge | Named | 9– 8–1636 | I, 180 |
| Dedham | Named | 9– 8–1636 | I, 179–180 |
| Lynn | Named | 11–20–1637 | I, 211 |
| Rowley | Named | 9– 4–1639 | I, 271 |
| Sudbury | Named | 9– 4–1639 | I, 271 |
| Colechester | Named | 9– 4–1639 | I, 271 |
| Hampton | Named | 9– 4–1639 | I, 271 [1] |

[1] This table is based on an examination of the *Massachusetts Colony Records*. The date is the one on which the town is either first mentioned or named under its present title with the exception of Colchester, which in October, 1640, was named Salisbury (I *Mass. Col. Rec.* 305). Hampton was lost to New Hampshire in 1680. Many of the areas are, however, mentioned previously under other titles (see pp. 70–71). In the case of

As has been indicated, the early period of Plymouth furnished little of importance in the field of political origins. The smallness of its population, the dominance of the governor and council, and the embarrassments of financial entanglements, retarded development. The geographical extent of the colony, moreover, was not large. The patent obtained by Peirce in 1621 gave no definite grant of territory, and was likewise silent on other essential points. The bounds of the colony, defined in Bradford's charter as generally co-extensive with the present counties of Plymouth, Bristol, and Barnstable with a small part of Rhode Island included,[1] were meager enough beside the imperial domains of the Massachusetts Bay colony — three miles north of the Merrimac to three miles south of the Charles "from the Atlantick . . . on the east parte, to the south sea on the west" [2] — and coming moreover from the Council of Plymouth and not from the king, there was an uncertainty to its political powers that was always a cause of anxiety.[3]

Such conditions coupled with an added apprehension of the natives caused a reluctant expansion. But when congestion finally made demands for other settlements, a desire to be close to the strong communities of the north turned migration in that direction, and it seems

Cambridge, there are two citations in the records: "Thomas Cheesholme is licensed to keepe a house of intertainment at Newe Towne, now called Cambridge" (I Mass. Col. Rec. 180 [9–8–1636]), and "It is ordered, that Newetowne shall henceforward be called Cambridge" (Ibid., 228 [5–2–1638]). The first is accepted for the above purpose.

[1] Goodwin, The Pilgrim Republic, p. 337; Brigham, Compact with the Charter and Laws, pp. 22–23.

[2] I Mass. Col. Rec. 5.

[3] William Brigham, "The Colony of New Plymouth and Its Relations to Massachusetts," Lowell Institute Lectures (Boston, 1869), p. 168.

that as early as 1627 members of the colony moved as far as Duxbury and probably the next year to Scituate.[1] About the same time a feeble extension was made westward by planting an outpost on Manomet River near Buzzards Bay.[2] Such separations, however, were not regarded with favor. Bradford regretted the tendency because "the towne, in which they lived compactly till now, was left very thine, and in a short time allmost desolate," and he saw in it "the ruine of New-England, at least of the churches of God ther," and a provocation for "the Lords displeasure against them."[3] The General Court apparently shared this view, for in October, 1633,

it was by full consent agreed upon & enacted, that the chiefe government be tyed to the towne of Plymouth, and that the Governor for the time being be tyed there to keepe his residence & dwelling; and there also to hold such Courts as concerne the whole.[4]

The expansion, however, persisted. Occasional reference is found to "our dispersion so far asunder and the inconvenience that may befall," or to the requirement that every "Cunstablericke have a sufficient pound to impound cattle," or to the vacant acres in Plymouth, "the ancient inhabitants being for the most part removed from thence."[5] In March, 1635/6, it was proposed to reunite the people of Duxbury and Plymouth; but during the delay in bringing the matter to a conclusion, Scituate was given the privileges of an inde-

[1] Baylies, *Historical Memoir*, I (pt. 1), 277, 279.

[2] Goodwin, *The Pilgrim Republic*, p. 290.

[3] William Bradford, *History of Plymouth Plantation* (Charles Deane, ed., Boston, 1856), pp. 303, 304.

[4] I *Ply. Col. Rec.* 16.

[5] Brigham, *Plymouth Colony Laws*, pp. 31, 34, 32.

pendent town — "to make such orders in their towne-
ship for their convenient & comfortable living as they
shall finde necessary," with the single proviso that for
the administration of justice the inhabitants were to
have recourse to Plymouth.[1]   On June 7 of the following
year, the negotiations with Duxbury having still come
to nothing, that community was declared to have the
privileges of a town with the single qualification that
the bounds be established by the General Court.[2]

Barnstable was subsequently settled from Scituate.
Lynn, by an overflow of population, established Sandwich and Yarmouth. Taunton was settled from Boston.
Rexhame (soon named Marshfield)[3]—the result of lands
granted at Green River to retard a more serious dispersal[4] — was given a new church in 1640 and became,
thereby, the eighth separate settlement in the colony.
The latter town, with Duxbury, had been accepted by
the General Court with regrets as tending to diminish
the population and prestige of the parent settlement;
but the other communities were incorporated promptly,
and were evidently regarded as unalloyed assets.[5] They
were in 1640:

| Town | Cited | Ply. Col. Rec. | |
|------|-------|---------------|---|
| Plymouth | Settled | 12–11–1620 | |
| Scituate | First mentioned | 7– 1–1633 | I, 13 |
| Duxbury | First mentioned | 1–5–1635/6 | I, 36 |
| Sandwich | First mentioned | 3–6–1637/8 | I, 80 |
| Yarmouth | First mentioned | 1–7–1638/9 | I, 108 |
| Barnstable | First mentioned | 6–4–1639 | I, 125 |
| Taunton | First mentioned | 3–3–1639/40 | I, 141 [6] |

[1] I *Ply. Col. Rec.* 44.
[2] *Ibid.*, p. 62.
[3] Brigham, *Plymouth Colony Laws*, p. 69.
[4] Bradford, *History of Plymouth*, p. 303.
[5] Goodwin, *The Pilgrim Republic*, p. 363.
[6] These data are based on an examination of the *Plymouth Colony*

The General Court names these towns (with the addition of Rexhame), in a tax list of June 1, 1641,[1] and over a year later still refers to them as comprising a complete enumeration.[2] But their comparatively late beginnings (with the exception of Plymouth) make them of small use in the search for traces of early political developments. The surviving records of town proceedings, moreover, are inadequate for the opening years. Even Plymouth was not a town as distinct from the colony until after the order directing that the government "be tyed there to," and the town records do not begin until three years later.[3] There are only fragmentary records for Taunton before 1804 — those prior to that time were burned.[4] The Duxbury records begin with 1686 — one volume for the years 1640 to 1688 is lost.[5] Marshfield (Rexhame) records start with

---

*Records* and the same view is represented as in the Massachusetts Bay colony settlements (*supra*, p. 00). The date for Plymouth is as given by Bradford (*History of Plymouth*, pp. 87–88), and the same source enumerates the towns settled throughout the colony by 1640 (p. 372): as, "Plimoth, Duxberie, Sityate, Tanton, Sandwich, Yarmouth, Barnstable, Marchfeeld, and not longe after, Seacunke (called afterward, at the desire of the inhabitants, Rehoboth) and Nawsett." "Sicquncke" is mentioned for the first time in the records of the Court of Assistants for July 6, 1641 (II *Ply. Col. Rec.* 23) and "Nossett," as a dwelling place in March, 1644/5 (*ibid.*, p. 81), and as a town in the next year (*ibid.*, 102).

[1] II *Ply. Col. Rec.* 18.

[2] XI *Ply. Col. Rec.* 38: "It is enacted by the Court that all the Townes within thee Government shall make woolfe trapps and bayte them and looke unto them dayly vpon the penalty of Xs a trap that shalbe neglected. the number that eich Towne is to make is as followeth.

Plymouth fiue Duxborrow fiue Scittuate Foure Sandwich three Taunton two Barnestable three Yarmouth three & Marshfeild two."

[3] Town of Plymouth, *Records of the Town of Plymouth* (W. T. Davis, ed., 3 vols., Plymouth, Mass., 1889–1903), I, x.

[4] S. H. Emery, *History of Taunton* (Syracuse, N. Y., 1898), pp. 128*ff.*

[5] Town of Duxbury, *Copy of the Old Records of the Town of Duxbury* (1642–1770) (George Etheridge, ed., Plymouth, Mass., 1893), p. 175.

1643,[1] Barnstable with 1640, Sandwich with 1650, Scituate with 1665,[2] and Yarmouth with 1677 — the early records of the latter town having been destroyed by fire.[3] The twilight of institutional development is eight years long — between the unpreserved actions of Endicott and his council after the arrival of the company at Salem (1628), and the famous ordinance of March 3, 1635/36 giving an organic law to firmly established communities. For this period, the records of the towns in Plymouth colony are almost silent. It is, therefore, within the Massachusetts Bay settlements that the early unfolding of local political institutions is to be sought.[4]

[1] L. S. Richards, *History of Marshfield* (Plymouth, Mass., 1901), p. 24.

[2] Samuel Deane, *History of Scituate* (Boston, 1831), p. 111.

[3] C. F. Swift, *History of Old Yarmouth* (Yarmouth Port, Mass., 1884), p. 107.

[4] C. D. Wright, *Report on the Custody and Condition of the Public Records of Parishes, Towns and Counties* (Boston, 1889), p. 259 (Plymouth); 174 (Taunton); 254 (Duxbury); 258 (Marshfield); 149 (Barnstable); 153 (Sandwich); 261 (Scituate); 155 (Yarmouth).

# II

## INSTITUTIONAL BEGINNINGS

THE charter of the Massachusetts Bay Company was primarily commercial. Cotton Mather tells the story of a minister preaching to a congregation in the "northeast regions" who urged his listeners to be religious, "otherwise they would contradict the main end of planting this wilderness"; but a prominent member of the assembly cried out, "Sir, you are mistaken . . . our *main end* was to *catch fish*." [1] Whatever may have been the social, theological or political motives and aspirations of the adventurers, the provisions for government were plainly designed to give effective control of an investment. Matthew Cradock was named by the charter, itself, as the first Governor of the company. At a General Court held in London (April 30, 1629) Captain John Endicott was chosen "to the place of present Gouernor in our . . . plantation." [2] There was, therefore, to be a governor of the *company* as well as one of the *colony*. When Endicott arrived in Salem, he was probably fully instructed as to the regulation of affairs of which, however, there are no extant records,[3] but at all events, implicit directions were received by letter during the spring of 1629.[4] The order investing him with the governorship created, at the same time, a council of twelve

[1] *Magnalia Christi Americana*, I, 66.
[2] I *Mass. Col. Rec.* 11, 361.
[3] "Hubbard's Narrative" in Young's *Chronicles of Massachusetts*, p. 30.
[4] I *Mass. Col. Rec.* 386–407.

to hold office for one year: seven named by the company, three chosen by the seven in conjunction with the governor, and two additional members to be selected by the "old planters" — that they might "have no just occasion of exception." Collectively, these were to form the political authority of the colony, and were intrusted with ample power to make laws, to administer justice, and otherwise to establish an orderly government.[1]

There are no definite records of gatherings that might even remotely resemble town meetings for civil purposes, although Thomas Morton in his *New English Canaan* (with due allowance for his Philistinian proclivities) gives testimony that at least one such occasion took place:

This man [Endicott], thinking none so worthy as himselfe, tooke upon him infinitely: and made warrants in his owne name . . . . and summoned a generall apparance at the worshipfull towne of Salem: there in open assembly was tendered certaine Articles, devised betweene him and theire new Pastor . . . .

To these Articles every Planter, old and new, must signe, or be expelled from any manner of aboade within the Compas of the Land contained within that graunt then shewed.[2]

Perhaps such direct methods resembling more the fiat of military leadership than popular approval could have continued indefinitely had not the seat of the corpora-

[1] Specifically, "to make, ordaine, and establish all manner of wholesome & reasonable lawes, orders, ordinances, & constitutions, (soe as the same bee noe way repugnant or contrary to the lawes of the realme of England,) for the administering of justice upon malefactors, and inflicting condigne punishment upon all other offendors, and for the furtherance and propagating of the said plantation, and the more decent & orderly gouerment of the inhabitants resydent there" (I *Mass. Col. Rec.* 362–363, 387).

[2] *New English Canaan* (1637) (C. F. Adams, Jr., ed.), Boston (Prince Soc. Pub.), 1883, p. 306.

tion been summarily moved from London to New England. Whatever may be the legal questions involved, the fact remains that the change was made, and that no serious objections appear to have been raised when the political framework at Salem with Endicott at its head was superseded by the corporation itself, with John Winthrop as governor,[1] a situation that not only assumed a new order but that altered the character of settlement throughout the social structure.

Within a few weeks the members of the company exercised the right of suffrage given to them by the charter;[2] and when the inconvenience of assembling became increasingly evident, the General Court made provision for its members to vote through deputies.[3] But there appears to be no early record whereby the inhabitants of the several plantations were instructed to meet for any particular purpose. The orders of the company requiring local action seem to have been directed to the communities with confidence that the initiative of the townsmen would attend to their execution, and in the presence of conditions unprovided in the charter it is probable that from the earliest days the planters took civil affairs into their own hands, each group meeting together to discuss matters of common concern, to decide the proper action to be taken, and to appoint men to give such decisions effect.[4] At a very early period, regularity in the time and attendance

---

[1] A. C. Goodell, "The Origin of Towns in Massachusetts," *Mass. Hist. Soc. Proc.*, 2d series, V, 325–326.

[2] I *Mass. Col. Rec.* 16.

[3] *Ibid.*, pp. 166, 188.

[4] A. B. MacLear, "Early New England Towns," *Col. Uni. Stud. in Hist., Ec. and Pub. Law*, XXIX, 107.

of such gatherings was recognized as necessary, and under the first dated page of the Cambridge town records (December 24, 1632) is found "Ann Agreement made by A Gennerall Conf[erence] for a mounthly meeting" in which every person "under subscribed" is ordered, under penalty of a fine, to appear "Every second Monday in Every mounth within [the] meeting-house In the Afternoon within half [an] ouer after the ringing of the bell." [1]

In Dorchester, the first local records commence in January, 1632/33, and they are probably the oldest extant in Massachusetts.[2] The affairs of the plantation were at first under the control of the clergymen, aided by the advice of the magistrates;[3] but by the spring of 1631, a large number of the inhabitants had become freemen, and in May of that year a meeting took place to make more adequate arrangements for the control of local affairs. Yet it seems no formal action was taken until some two years later, when the first extant provisions for a town meeting were agreed to by "the whole consent and vote of the Plantation." This entry of October 8, 1633, is probably the earliest "home rule" document in American institutional history, and is a clear example of the pragmatic elements that moved the colonists in determining their local po-

---

[1] City of Cambridge, *The Records of the Town of Cambridge* (1630–1703) (Cambridge, 1901), p. 4.

[2] There are items in the Charlestown records that seem to be at least contemporaneous, but they appear to have been inserted some time after the occurrences took place (*New Eng. Hist. and Gen. Reg.*, XXI, 163). The town meeting records of Salem begin December 26, 1636 (*Essex Inst. Hist. Coll.*, IX, 4), and land records October 1, 1634 (*Ibid.*, IV, 89).

[3] Committee of the Dorchester Antiquarian and Historical Society, *History of the Town of Dorchester, Massachusetts*, Boston, 1859, pp. 29–31.

litical organization. It is provided that on every Monday morning at eight o'clock, the occasion to be announced by the beating of the drum, a general gathering of the inhabitants was to take place at the meetinghouse, to record such orders as might seem necessary for the good government of the community. Twelve men were to be selected as a sort of "steering committee," but were otherwise to have no additional authority, and all matters concluded at the gathering were to hold until the next monthly meeting. A possible reluctance to attend to civil affairs as regularly as once a week is expressed in the hope that in spite of the special responsibilities of the "Twelve" that "most of the Plantation will keep the meeting constantly," as well as in the suggestion of a monthly gathering that seems to have been given an importance not accorded to the others.[1]

Additional communities were quick to make formal provision for similar arrangements. Under date of February 1, 1634 an entry in the Cambridge records announces that,

Att a Gennerall Meeting of the whole Towne Itt was Agreed vppon by a Joynt Consent that 7 menn should bee Chossen to doe the whole bussines of the Towne and soe to Continew vntell the ffirst Monday in November next and vntell new be Chossen in their Room soe ther wars then Elected and Chosen John Haynes Esqr mr Symon Bradstreet John Taylcott William Westwood John White. William Wadswoorth James Olmsted Constable.[2]

Here the seven men appear to be regarded as an execu-

---

[1] City of Boston, Registry Department, *Records Relating to the Early History of Boston* (variously edited and hereafter cited as Report of the Record Commissioners, etc.), 39 vols., Boston, 1876–1909, *Dorchester Town Records* (1632–1687), IV (1880), p. 3.

[2] *Cambridge Town Records*, 11.

tive committee to carry on the affairs of the community during the interim between town meetings, but the first page of the Watertown records dated in the summer of the same year (August 23, 1634) authenticates still another step in their evolution:

Agreed by the consent of the Freemen, that there shalbe Chosen three persons to be [    ] the ordering of the civill affaires in the Towne One of them to serve as Towne Clark, and shall keep the Records and Acts of the Towne. The three chosen are William Jennison, Briam Pembleton, John Eddie.[1]

It remained, however, to the inhabitants of Charlestown to give additional impetus to the development. In January 1633/4, a committee had been selected "to lay out any lots and make any rates" for the ensuing year, and a few months later a committee of three was appointed "to be at town meetings to assist in ordering their affairs." But this expedient did not, apparently, prove to be sufficient, for on February 10, 1634/5, because "by reason of many men meeting, things were not so easily brought unto a joynt issue," an order was passed providing the first official record of a board of selectmen, to be eleven in number, and to serve for one year. Their powers were far broader than in previous records — "to entreat of all such business as shall conscerne the Townsmen, the choise of officers excepted" —and their authorized decisions were to have the same effect as orders of the town meeting.[2]

---

[1] Town of Watertown, *Watertown Records* ("Prepared for publication by the Historical Society"), 4 vols., Watertown (Mass.), 1894–1906, I, 1.

[2] Frothingham, *History of Charlestown*, pp. 50–51. A facsimile of the manuscript record is inserted.

These officers easily became the most important local officials. Early records call them by various names. In Boston they were referred to as "the 10 to manage the affaires of the towne," "the 9 men," or the "Selectmen for the Townes affaires."[1] The Salem records mention "the towne representative viz. the 13 men."[2] Braintree describes them as "those that are chosen to dispose of the towns affaires," or simply as "the selectmen of Brantree."[3] The records of Rowley announce those "chosen to order the affaires of the Towne for this yeare," or "the Prudential men," or "the Select then chose for this yeare."[4] The Ipswich records speak of "the seven men . . . chosen to order Towne business for these three months next following,"[5] and the Cambridge proceedings refer to the "Townsmen."[6] They are not designated in the records of the colony until May, 1642, when it is declared "that the selected townes men haue power to lay out particular & private wayes concerning their owne towne onely," and the next month, because the General Court became alarmed at the educational neglect of parents and masters in the early training of children, it ordered that "in euery towne the chosen men appointed for managing the pru-

[1] Report of the Record Commissioners, *Boston Town Records* (1634–1661), vol. II (1877), pp. 2, 65, 99.

[2] "Town Records of Salem" (1634–1659), *Essex Inst. Hist. Coll.*, 2d series, I, 15, 17.

[3] Towns of Braintree, Quincy, Randolph, and Holbrook, *Records of the Town of Braintree* (1640–1793) (S. A. Bates, ed.), Randolph (Mass.), 1886, pp. 2, 5.

[4] Town of Rowley, *The Early Records of the Town of Rowley* (1639–1672) (B. P. Mighill and G. B. Blodgette, committee), Rowley (Mass.), 1894, pp. 52, 55, 70.

[5] Town of Ipswich, *The Ancient Records of the Town of Ipswich* (1634–1650) (G. A. Schofield, ed.), Ipswich (Mass.), 1899. See under Feb. 13, 1636.

[6] *Cambridge Town Records*, 99.

dentiall affajres of the same" be charged with the duty of redressing this evil.[1]

The selectmen met frequently — once a month or oftener. Their proceedings are given every prominence that is accorded the records of the town, and in many cases they are hardly to be distinguished.[2] At first it was customary to describe their duties in a widely inclusive phrase, but under formal regulation they assumed a much more precise character. Rowley gave them full power to transact all "comon affaires" of the town, but forbade them to dispose of land for inheritance, to lease town land beyond the current year, or to increase the minister's rate above sixty pounds, without the consent of the town.[3] Cambridge on the contrary ordered that anything they should do "in the Compas of ther tyme" should be as if the whole town had taken action,[4] while Dorchester was more detailed in their responsibilities, and gave them

all accustomed liberty concerninge comon landes in Fence also our towne lotts that they shall haue power to inioyne the seuerall p'prietors to make and Repaire such Fence as is due unto them by p'portion and upon default therin to chardge such penalty upon them as they see meet. Item that they order the Ringeinge and youkeinge of Hogges: the keepeinge of our Cowes in the pen stintinge the Cowe Walke baringe the woods in season and that they carefully p'vide

---

[1] II *Mass. Col. Rec.* 4, 6.

[2] Town of Dedham, *The Early Records of the Town of Dedham* (1636–1706) (D. G. Hill, ed.), 5 vols., Dedham (Mass.), 1886–1899, III (1636–1659), pp. 55–75; Town of Manchester, *Town Records of Manchester* (1636–1736), Salem (Mass.), 1889–1891, pp. 17, 31, 38, etc. The *Salem Town Records* offer particularly good examples of the close resemblance between the two.

[3] *Rowley Town Records*, 55.

[4] *Cambridge Town Records*, 11.

for the safety of our Comons: in the wood and Timber.[1]

Yet their greatest powers arose (as so many political powers do) through general acquiescence in the need, and confidence in the officers. The selectmen became largely responsible for the local financial administration. At times they determined, assessed, and abated town taxes,[2] and granted respites "untill farther consideration may be had about it." It became customary, indeed, to afford them increasing power in this direction. In 1652, Cambridge gave the "Townesmen" formal authority to make the tax rates.[3] Even earlier (1645) Dorchester established a similar practice, and in 1667 ordered that the selectmen should "make such rates for the towns use as they in their descretion shall think fitt not exceeding fortie pounds for this yeer." [4] Even before such orders were enacted, however, it is quite likely that their recommendations were practically conclusive.[5] They were, moreover, the towns'

[1] *Dorchester Town Records*, 289–290. Every order was, however, subject to the approval of the town. Provision was made that regulations of the selectmen should "upon the next Lecture Day after Lecture" be read "to the Company of free men who are to be warned at present to stay. And then all acts and conclusions that shall not be contradicted by the major p'ts of the freemen present, shall stand for orders and bind the Plantation and euery inhabitant thereof" (*ibid.*, 21).

[2] *Boston Town Records* (1634–1661), pp. 95, 96, 97, 132.

[3] *Cambridge Town Records*, 100.

[4] *Dorchester Town Records*, 290, 220.

[5] In the early days before the advent of a treasurer (Dorchester elected one in 1672) (MacLear, "Early New England Towns," 69), the rate was both collected and at times expended by the constable (*Dorchester Town Records*, 111, 115), or the duty was divided among several of them (*Salem Town Records*, 227). The rate for the ministry was often made and administered by the aid of the deacons (*Dorchester Town Records*, 63, 138), but the sum was reported by the town raters to the selectmen (*ibid.*, pp. 124, 131), and warrants issued to the constables to collect delinquent assessments (*ibid.*, pp. 115, 131). The rate was levied as a general property tax, based upon a careful valuation of the items familiar to the community (MacLear,

legal representatives, and in this capacity let public contracts, sold town property, conducted suits,[1] determined the admission of new members to the community, and regulated the sojourn of strangers.[2] The use of the common lands was one of their most frequent problems and innumerable entries deal with the cutting of timber, the control of swine, and the condition of the common pastures.

A vast amount of administrative work was supplemented by additional duties that the General Court from time to time imposed,[3] and the records teem with scores of minor permissive requirements of the most diverse character, allowing them to build wharves, to set up windmills, to remove oyster shells from the public highway, and to regulate the building of cellar doors [4] — the latter a matter of some importance as obstructions to public ways. There are prescriptions for felling trees, for regulating the height of fences,[5] for repairing the meeting-house, and orders appointing dozens of minor officers.[6] In addition, not the least part of the selectmen's functions were judicial, and the proceedings of some of their meetings read very much like the rec-

"Early New England Towns," 60–61; *Dedham Town Records*, 77–78). But the town meeting never entirely relinquished control over finances.

[1] *Watertown Town Records*, I, 67; *Boston Town Records* (1634–1661), pp. 92, 93, 98; *Rowley Town Records*, 129.

[2] *Boston Town Records* (1634–1661), pp. 36, 43; *Dorchester Town Records*, 124–125, 131. But Dedham in the case of "Townsmen" seems to have considered it a matter for a general meeting (*Dedham Town Records*, 5), and in Cambridge the town meeting retained the control over the admission of inhabitants (MacLear, "Early New England Towns," 124).

[3] G. E. Howard, *An Introduction to the Local Constitutional History of the United States* (Baltimore, 1889), p. 82.

[4] *Boston Town Records* (1634–1661), pp. 78, 108, 98, 146.

[5] *Cambridge Town Records*, 196, 152.

[6] *Dorchester Town Records*, 111.

ords of a court of petty jurisdiction — which, indeed, they frequently were:

Att a meeting of Tho. Marshall, James Olliver, Peter Olliver, Sam. Cole, Wm. Paddy and Wm. Davis.

Isacc Walker, Sam. Norden, Robt. Nanny, and Xofer Gibson are fined 10s. a man for their Chymnyes being on fire, which the Constables are to leavy.

Samson Shore is fined 10s for the like offense.

The Constables are to allow to Walter Merry eight shillings in lieu of a debt due to him from the towne in ('44).

Sam. Jewell is admitted an inhabitant and Mark Hames is bound in a bond of 40*l*. to save the town from charge.

Deacon Johnston hath liberty to sett up a porch before his house doore foure foote into the streete.

Robert Wyatt and Wm. Lane are appointed to sweepe chimneyes and to cry aboutt streetes that they may bee knowne.

Sam. Norden hath 5s. of his fine remitted.[1]

But as wide and varied as their powers were, there are at times restrictions. The selectmen were not to dispose of the town lands, nor, indeed, "to alter any p'cell . . . without the consent of p'prietors."[2] They were

---

[1] *Boston Town Records* (1660–1701), p. 127. Very early the magistrates (*i.e.*, members of the Court of Assistants) could try cases within the town in which they resided, and in addition "Commissioners of Small Claims" were used (selected by the town and approved by the Court of Assistants or the County Court) either in conjunction with the magistrate or solely within a town where no magistrate resided. The selectmen were also allowed to try civil cases in which the local magistrate or commissioners might be personally interested, or that concerned the by-laws of the town. For a complete account with citations to the records see Emory Washburn's *Sketches of the Judicial History of Massachusetts* (Boston, 1840), ch. II, W. T. Davis' *History of the Judiciary of Massachusetts* (Boston, 1900), ch. I (Plymouth), ch. II (Massachusetts Bay), and C. J. Hilkey's "Legal Development in Colonial Massachusetts" (1630–1686), *Col. Univ. Stud. in Hist., Ec. and Pub. Law*, XXXVII, no. 2, pp. 29–50. The latter study is the most complete account of the movement.

[2] *Dorchester Town Records*, 289.

warned to do nothing contrary to the orders of the General Court, nor to lease land for more than a year's time, nor "dispose noe land for Inheritance without the consent of the Towne." [1] In theory, at least, every order was subject to the approval of the town and this was quite likely the practice as well. Indeed, as has been indicated, special provision was often made to check the action of selectmen by submitting current decisions to the freemen (and quite possibly all churchmen, as well) at the close of each Sabbath's "Lecture." All acts that stood this scrutiny were summarily declared binding upon the plantation and every inhabitant thereof; [2] and while the towns occasionally exercised their prerogative to set aside unpopular orders, such action was infrequent, and it appears that the selectmen usually enjoyed to a high degree the confidence and support of the community.

The selectmen thus represented a culmination of leadership and publicity — they were (as they still remain) the "first men" of the community, held to an exacting responsibility that only the public criticism of neighbors can compel. A recital of their powers rings with the broad finality of dictatorship in local matters, but the spirit of their service resembles the humblest agent. It is probable that since *Prytaneis* of the ancient Athenian *Boulé* there has been no such breadth of authority so confidently granted nor so thoroughly and publicly checked as in the executive services of the early New England town. However nebulous may be the "phan-

[1] *Rowley Town Records*, 55; for complete regulations see *Dedham Town Records*, 5; *Dorchester Town Records*, 289–290; *Cambridge Town Records*, 99–100.

[2] *Dorchester Town Records*, 21.

tom public" of the modern state, there can be no doubt that the community impulses emanating from the early town meeting were severe realities.

With the administrative duties that brought the selectmen into existence, there became necessary a group of minor officials that took over a great diversity of tasks pertaining to the affairs of the town. The most important, perhaps, was the constable. He was, at least, the oldest. Miles Standish has been called the first. "There have been Towns in New England" wrote Herbert Baxter Adams "without Selectmen, without Ministers, without a Church or a Common School, but there never was a Town without a Constable."[1] From time to time his duties embraced the most varied functions. He warned town meetings, had charge of highways, levied fines, apprehended Quakers, collected rates, assisted tithingmen, acted as water bailiff (a kind of shore police),[2] and was even ordered to "attend funerals of any, that die with the small pox, and walk before the corpse to give notice to any, who may be in danger of the infection."[3] He was the first colonial officer to have his duties codified by the General Court,[4] and as early as May, 1658, they were various enough to require twenty-six descriptive clauses. So numerous, indeed, did they become, that both Plymouth and the Massachusetts Bay Colony found it necessary to compel acceptance of the office under penalties of respectable fines — even as high as ten pounds in Boston.[5]

[1] H. B. Adams, "Norman Constables in America," *Johns Hopkins University Studies in Historical and Political Science*, I, no. 8, p. 21.

[2] Brigham, *Compact with Charter and Laws*, 190.

[3] I *Ply. Col. Rec.* 190. — Also index under CONSTABLE.

[4] IV *Mass. Col. Rec.* (pt. 1), 324–327.

[5] Brigham, *Compact with Charter and Laws*, 99, 127–128, 264; W. H.

Possibly the next local officer in point of prominence was the tithingman — a constable whose duties began on Sunday. He was to preserve order in the meeting-house, and the selectmen later coöperated to the extent of providing him "at the Town-Charge with Staffs two Feet long, black, and tipt at one End with Brass, about *three* Inches."[1]   In addition, he was a sort of an ecclesiastical whip, largely responsible for church attendance, and appointed every Sunday.

to walke forth in the time of Gods worshippe, to take notice of such as either lye about the meeting howse without attending to the word or ordinances, or that lye at home or in the fields, without giuing good account thereof, and . . . . to take the names of such persons & to present them to the Magistrate, whereby they may be accordinglie proceeded against.[2]

In addition there were fence viewers, poundkeepers, herdsmen, raters and "surveyors of highways;"[3] hog-reeves, town drummers, and perambulators; sealers of leather,[4] procurers of wood and "overseers of the fences."[5]   There was a "clark to call town meeting," a judge to judge delinquents at town meeting,[6] and

Whitmore (ed.), *Colonial Laws of Massachusetts* (Boston, 1889), pp. 55, 148. Selectmen were formally introduced into the Plymouth colony in 1662 (XI *Ply. Col. Rec.* [pt. 2], 143).

[1] *The County and Town Officer*, "By a Gentleman" (Boston, 1768), pp. 99, 129, 131.

[2] *Salem Town Records*, 131; H. B. Adams, "Saxon Tithingmen in America," *Johns Hopkins University Studies in Historical and Political Science*, I, no. 4, 1–2; G. H. Moore, *Notes on Tithingmen and the Ballot*, Worcester (Mass.), 1884.

[3] *Dorchester Town Records*, 33, 42, 35.

[4] *Manchester Town Records*, 166–167.

[5] *Salem Town Records*, 137.

[6] *Rowley Town Records*, 95.

additional special officers for still more special duties. A typical record of a little later period reads:

Braintree ye 1st.  March 1708.

The inhabitants of the Town of Braintree Regularly Assembled, then chose Coll. Quincy Esqr. moderator for that day.

The Selectmen then chosen for ye year ensuing were,

Coll. Edmund Quinsey Esq Capt. John Mills, Serjeant Joseph Neall Serjeant Nehemiah Hayden Mr. John Webb.

Then voted that ye present Selectmen be Assessors for ye year ensuing.

Joseph Parmenter was then chosen Town Clerk.

The Constables then chosen were Benjamin Webb, and Moses Curtis.

Town Treasurer then chosen was Joseph Bass Junior.

The Titheing men were Ensign Peter Adams, Ensign Samuel Baxter Peter Webb and Jonathan Hayward.

Surveyors, Moses Penniman   Joseph Bracket
            Josiah Hobart       Benjamin Allen

Haward or Field Drivers  James Penniman & William Savel.

The meet pursons to look after ye act relating to Horses, were John Thayer and Joseph Crosbye.

Fence Viewers  Deacon Moses Payne  Nathaniel Spear
            Josiah Faxon, Samuel White Junior.[1]

\* \* \* \* \* \* \*

The records very frequently describe the duties of these officers. The town drummer was instructed "to doe all Common service in drumming for the Town on Trayning dayes and watches;"[2] the surveyor of highways "shall ouer see and p'cure the makeing or amend-

---

[1] *Braintree Town Records*, 67. For the "climax of petty officialdom" see F. T. Waters, "The Development of Our Town Government and Common Lands and Commonage," *Ipswich Hist. Soc. Pub.*, VIII, 10; and "Boxford Town Records" (1685–1706), *Essex Inst. Hist. Coll.*, XXXVI, 99.

[2] *Boston Town Records* (1634–1661), 76.

ing such high wayes as are defectiue within the plantation"; [1] and the bell ringer was also "to digge the
graues to interr the dead & to haue for his payns 18d:
per graue for digginge." [2] The fence viewers were en-
joined to view all the fences and if they found any defect
were empowered to make the necessary repairs, and to
demand adequate compensation for their services from
the owners. [3] When a town rate was ordered, the appor-
tionment was made by the raters to be collected by the
constable, and the Dorchester records announce that:

Robert Deeble is chosen Baylif for halfe a yeere or till an
other be chosen and it is ordered that he shall levy all fines
rates and amercements for the Plantation by impounding
the offenders Goods, and then to deteyne them till satis-
faction be made. . . . . It shall be lawful for the sayd Baylif
to recouer any rates or amercements by way of destresse on
any goods. [4]

The formation of the administrative branch of the
government caused the general gatherings of the inhabitants to be less frequent. While there were undoubtedly many special occasions upon which the townsmen
came together, definite arrangements for one annual
meeting were generally made, which undertook as its
principal function the election of town officers for the
ensuing year and "the Redressinge of any greauance
that maie be discouerd." [5] The town was notified of
the meeting. This was usually done by the selectmen,
who gave notice to the people on "a lecture day," or by

[1] *Dorchester Town Records*, 42.
[2] *Salem Town Records*, 190.
[3] *Dorchester Town Records*, 36.
[4] *Ibid.*, pp. 32, 35.
[5] *Ibid.*, p. 289; *Cambridge Town Records*, 45; *Watertown Town Records*,
I, 78.

"sendinge a special messenger from house to house," or at times through warnings in designated precincts.[1] If, however, the meeting was a regular one, it seems that a clerk might call the gathering:

It is ordered that the Clarke who is to Call towne meetings shall attend as other men and shall Call the houre apoynted if the day be Cleare otherways att the discretion of the selectmen or a maior pt of them.[2]

Attendance was compulsory, and fines for absence were frequently imposed.[3] In "the agitation of . . . publicke matters" it was very early found necessary to restrict discussion to certain prearranged subjects — the "first . . . brought to the 7 men or to som tow or more of them"; for aside from the fact that important affairs were often introduced in the meeting without previous warning and much time expended on irrelevant topics, some members were often considerably disturbed when projects of interest to them received no hearing at all.[4] The meeting was presided over by the moderator.[5]

---

[1] *Boston Town Records* (1634–1661), 128, 129, 152, 154; *Dorchester Town Records*, 293.

[2] *Rowley Town Records*, 57.

[3] *Dedham Town Records*, 30.

[4] *Dorchester Town Records*, 50–51: "Whereas it hath beene obserued diuerse tymes, in our general Towne meetinge, that some Confusion and disorder hath happened in the agitation of our publicke matters and Plantation affaires, by reason that men haue used thier libertye to p'pound theere matters to the Plantation without any fore knoledge of the seauen men, and theere matters haue beene so followed that diuerse things haue beene spoken of and fewe matters haue beene issued by reason that new matters haue beene vpsterted whyles a former hath beene in heeringe and so much tyme spent and lytle worke don, and moreover the spirits of som men trobled and offended by reason that thier matters could not be hearde. . . . "

[5] The moderator was first mentioned by the colonial government in the Body of Liberties (sec. 71): "The Governor shall have a casting voice whensoever an Equi vote shall fall out in the Court of Assistants, or general

He was occasionally chosen by the selectmen from their own number, but otherwise, by the town meeting.[1] The procedure was simple. In Dorchester, the Directory — a set of rules for the political guidance of the townsman — was read.[2] It was usually received without objection but occasionally amendments would be moved, and these would be disposed of before other business was taken up. In Dedham, the minutes of the previous meeting were first approved,[3] and the selectmen would then present various items for the consideration of the town.[4] It is probably true that they had nominal control of the procedure, and that even in the early days much of the business was determined beforehand. Voting was evidently, at first, largely a matter of acclamation, but at least as early as 1645 the necessity for more precise methods was recognized, and Dorchester ordered that all "elections be by papers and not p'pounded by their predicessors,"[5] while Dedham, influenced perhaps by colonial practice, required that all votes pertaining to the admittance of townsmen should be given in kernels

assembly. So shall the president or moderator have in all Civill Courts or Assemblies" (*Mass. Hist. Soc. Coll.*, VIII, 228).

[1] *Manchester Town Records*, 142, 143, 149, etc.; *Watertown Town Records*, I, 64, 91; *Rowley Town Records*, 155. The latter method became universal.

[2] *Dorchester Town Records*, 136, 162, 180, 187, etc.: "After the directory was orderly read ther was some adjetation about changing a day of the Select mens meeting: viz. Whereas the Second Month by the directory is exempted as one of the fower months; It is now agreed unto by Voate that the theird month is exempted from meeting, and instead they are to meet the Second Month for the time to come and it shalbe soe ordered in the directory."

[3] *Dedham Town Records*, 32, 38, 41, etc.

[4] Selectmen's meetings are frequently interspersed with notes and memoranda of matters to be brought up in some future town meeting. See *Dedham Town Records*, 190–191.

[5] *Dorchester Town Records*, 289.

of wheat and Indian corn — the wheat to signify the affirmative and the corn the negative.[1]

In spite of a regard for uniformity in general matters, the General Court placed few restrictions on the local legislative powers of the towns. Local communities could, of course, pass no ordinances incompatible with the regulations of the colony. They were restricted, also, in the amount of fines to be imposed, the method of disposing of their lands, and the duties and choice of minor officials.[2] On the contrary, the Body of Liberties (1641) — the first code of laws established in New England — granted them certain privileges. Definite provision was made for selectmen; all jurors were to be chosen by the freemen of the town wherein they lived; and every town was to have the authority to send deputies to the General Court. The sixty-sixth section[3] provided in addition that

The Freemen of every Township shall have power to make such by laws and constitutions as may concerne the wellfare

[1] *Dedham Town Records*, 18. Thomas Lechford (1642) in his "Plain Dealing" (*Mass. Hist. Soc. Coll.*, 3d series, III, 82), speaks of the manner of elections in the Company: "At first, the chiefe Governour and Magistrates were chosen in *London*, by erection of hands, by all the Free-men of this *Society*. Since the transmitting of the Patent into *New-England*, the election is not by voices, nor erection of hands, but by papers." Here follows a careful description of the procedure. This account is substantiated in part by the records (I *Mass. Col. Rec.* 79), but the year following the publication of Lechford's account the General Court ordered: "that for the yearly choosing of Assistants for the time to come, in steed of papers the freemen shall use Indian beanes, the white beanes to manifest election, the black for blanks" (II *Mass. Col. Rec.* 42, Sept. 7, 1643). Later both papers and beans were evidently utilized, for provisions were enacted to provide penalties for fraudulent use (*ibid.*, p. 48). See also W. C. Ford's "Voting with Beans and Corn" (*Mass. Hist. Soc. Proc.*, LXVII, 230–239).

[2] *Mass. Col. Rec.* 172.

[3] "Early Laws of Massachusetts," *Mass. Hist. Soc. Coll.*, 3d series, VIII, 196; Body of Liberties (pp. 216–237), secs. 50, 62, 66, 74.

of their Towne, provided they be not of a Criminall, but onely of a prudentiall nature, and that their penalties exceed not 20 sh. for one offense. And that they be not repugnant to the publique laws and orders of the Countrie. And if any inhabitant shall neglect or refuse to observe them, they shall have power to levy the appointed penalties by distresse.

The term "prudentiall" appears here, it seems, for the first time in a Massachusetts public record. It was used again by the General Court in 1642 [1] in referring to the selectmen appointed "for managing the prudentiall affajres," and subsequently passed into the law of the Province and Commonwealth.[2] The term was probably coined by Nathaniel Ward, the "Simple Cobbler of Agawam" (supposed author of the Body of Liberties),[3] and aside from denoting the antithesis of "criminal," merely seems to recognize that many unauthorized acts were necessary to effective government in the new communities, and such acts were to be handled with prudence — a kind of local "police power." [4]

Yet democracy in the sense that every resident enjoyed an equal voice in the town's affairs was not always

[1] II *Mass. Col. Rec.* 6.

[2] C. W. Ernst, *Constitutional History of Boston* (Boston, 1894), pp. 21–27.

[3] "Early Laws of Massachusetts," 106.

[4] The term still remains in the statutes, and appears to denote municipal interests as opposed to affairs of the Commonwealth. The court has said: "After all, the question recurs, what are the prudential concerns of a town; and perhaps no better approximation to an exact description can be made, than to say that it embraces that large class of miscellaneous subjects affecting the accommodation and convenience of the inhabitants, which have been placed under the municipal jurisdiction of towns, by statute or by usage. Many such subjects will probably occur to the recollection of those conversant with the proceedings of towns, as unquestionably within the jurisdiction of towns, in respect to which there are no statute provisions; such as public hay scales, burying grounds, wells and reservoirs, and many others." (Willard *v.* Newburyport (1831), 12 *Pick.* (Mass.) 231; Spaulding *v.* Lowell (1839), 23 *Pick.* (Mass.) 77–78.)

intended as an attribute of seventeenth-century politics in Massachusetts. There were, on the contrary, a few who assembled on occasion to settle certain matters pertaining to the well ordering of the community, and the record headings of early town meetings plainly indicate a difference in personnel. Some read "At a towne meeting of the ffreemen" [1] or "Granted by the freemen of Salem"; [2] others, "At a publique meeting of the Inhabitants of the Towne"; "At a Generall meeteing of the whole towne"; [3] "At a generall and legall Towne meetinge"; or simply "At a legall Towne meeting." [4] It will be observed that the Body of Liberties, moreover, was specific that it is the "Freemen of every Township" who have the power to make local laws, and the "Freemen" who are to choose "out of themselves" the men to order "the prudentiall occasions of that Towne." [5] There were, therefore, politically, two classes: first, the freemen — those entitled under the charter and subsequent laws to vote in charter elections and to hold office under that document. These were the body of *electors*. It was early determined (May, 1631) that they must be members of a church within the colony, that admittance to the freedom of the colony (May, 1634) was to be effected only by action of the General Court, and that

[1] *Salem Town Records*, 142.

[2] *Ibid.*, pp. 13, 14.

[3] *Cambridge Town Records*, 48, 81, 72.

[4] *Rowley Town Records*, 108, 118.

[5] The status of freemen was provided in the charter itself (I *Mass. Col. Rec.* 10, 12), and they were plainly given the political authority of the community. For a complete discussion of the relation of the freemen to the suffrage both in the Plymouth and Massachusetts Bay colonies see G. H. Haynes' "History of Representation and Suffrage in Massachusetts" (1620–1691), *Johns Hopkins University Studies in Historical and Political Science*, XII, nos. 8–9.

none but freemen (September, 1635) should vote in any town "in any action of auethoritie, or necessity . . . as receaving inhabitants, & layeing out of lotts."[1] A similar situation prevailed in Plymouth — the laws of the colony were to be made by ".ffreemen of the Corporacion" and "no other."[2]

There were, on the other hand, the inhabitants — those permitted to dwell permanently within the limits of the town. They might or might not enjoy the status of freemen, own property, or belong to the established church. Their electoral privileges were strictly limited, and although it appears that they attended all town meetings, they had a positive voice in the proceedings only at specified times. This was, at least, the legal situation. Just what the practice was, is difficult to say. It seems probable, however, that even in the early meetings the adult male population assembled, and with little formality disposed of its communal affairs.[3] At all events, the Body of Liberties in 1641 tended to legalize a wider participation by requiring that,

Every man whether Inhabitant or fforreiner, free or not free shall have libertie to come to any publique Court, Councel, or Towne meeting and either by speech or writing to move any lawfull, seasonable, and materiall question, or

---

[1] I *Mass. Col. Rec.* 87, 117, 161. Lechford, *Plain Dealing,* 81: "None may now be a *Freeman* of that Commonwealth . . . unlesse he be a Church member amongst them. None have voice in elections of Governours, Deputy, and Assistants; none are to be Magistrates, Officers, or Jurymen, grand or petite, but *Freemen.*"

[2] XI *Ply. Col. Rec.* 11 (1642).

[3] The symposium of Messrs. C. F. Adams, A. C. Goodell, Mellen Chamberlain and Edward Channing (*Mass. Hist. Soc. Proc.,* 2d series, VII, 174–263) is perhaps the ablest discussion of the theory of New England town origins. As to the political character of the community see especially *223ff.* and *239ff.*

to present any necessary motion, complaint, petition, Bill
or information, whereof that meeting hath proper cognizance,
so it be done in convenient time, due order, and respective
manner.[1]

A few years later (May, 1647) the General Court —
probably in recognition of conditions generally existing
— made still more generous provisions that remained in
force throughout the life of the colony:

This Courte, taking into consideration the usefull partes
& abilities of divers inhabitants amongst us, which are not
freemen . . . . doth hereby declare that henceforth it shall
& may be lawfull for the freemen within any of the said
townes to make choyce of such inhabitants . . . . to have
their votes in the choyce of the select men for towne affaires,
asseasment of rates & other prudentials proper to the selectmen of the severall townes.[2]

Henceforth the only restrictions on full participation of
qualified inhabitants were that the majority of all boards
of selectmen should be freemen, no non-freeman was to
vote until he had reached the age of twenty-four, and
to enjoy the privilege of suffrage he must, further, have
no record of court conviction. Such action amounted,
it seems, to making certain of the inhabitants freemen
of the town as distinct from the freedom enjoyed in a
colonial sense,[3] and gave thereby a far broader basis to
local politics.

[1] Body of Liberties, sec. 12.

[2] II *Mass. Col. Rec.* 197.

[3] In 1647 (II *Mass. Col. Rec.* 208) there is an order aimed at certain
church members who "to exempt themselues from all publike service in ye
commonwealth will not come in to be made freemen," to the effect that if
such men are chosen by the "*freemen of the severall townes*" (the italics are
mine) to certain town offices, "they shall not be exempted from such public
service."

It was because of these distinctions that the towns held two kinds of meetings:

5:1. 1659–60.
Att a meeting of the Freemen upon publick notice Capt. Tho. Savage and Mr. Anthony Stodard are chosen Deputyes for the Gen. Court for the yeare ensuing.
Mr. Edward Tynge was chosen Commissioner to carry in the votes for magistrates and County Treasurer.

A few days later, this entry is made:

12:1: 1659–60.
Att a generall Townes-meeting upon publick notice from house to house, were chosen for the yeare ensuing . . . .

Here follows a detailed list of the town officers chosen — moderator, selectmen, clerks of market, surveyors of highways, sealers of leather, water bailiff, packer of meat and fish, and constables. A contract made by the selectmen was voted to be perpetual, instructions previously given to them were confirmed, and they were secured from damage while acting as administrators of a certain legacy — all matters within the scope of local electors.[1]

The legal situation seems clear, but it is hard to say just what procedure was followed. At present, the law provides that none but qualified voters may take part in a town meeting, but every moderator in a large community is familiar with the hopelessness of determining such a status, and anyone who has participated in a gathering when matters of great local interest are

---

[1] *Boston Town Records* (1634–1660), 154; *ibid.*, p. 100 (to choose a deputy to the General Court), 148 (to petition the General Court), 149 (provision for separate meeting of the freemen to be arranged by the selectmen "distinct from the general townes meetings"), 159 (instructions to the deputies to the General Court), etc.

under consideration is only too familiar with the indiscriminate voting of everyone in attendance.[1] If the future investigator is to depend upon the account of the town meeting that is published in the annual reports of the various present-day communities to reconstruct contemporary procedure, he is quite likely to find his task a difficult one. Many towns, it is true, keep stenographic accounts that are almost verbatim but that give few details of personnel. The terse phrases of an unimaginative clerk is the record generally published. Some of the smaller towns, indeed, publish no records — not even a copy of the warrant. Even under favorable conditions the points that would enable the observer to reconstruct this political pattern as a realistic study of composition and procedure are exceedingly meager, and they are far less numerous in the records of Colony and Province. There are legal distinctions in plenty, but every political observer is aware of the acute divergencies that mark the law and practice of every period, and while such may be evidence of laxity of enforcement or disregard for public authority, they are far more likely to be mainly the result of social pressures that make institutional history a story of perpetual compromise.

[1] This, however, is not true in small towns.

# III

## A CRITIQUE OF TOWN ORIGINS

THE brief account of the beginning of local government contained in the preceding chapters, has been subject to extensive interpretation. When the "new historical school" of the later years of the last century evinced so keen an interest in source materials, the accessible but little used records of the Massachusetts town offered American scholars an attractive field. Not only did they promise a kind of intellectual exercise in the use of what some writers were inclined to call "new methods," but they formed a fascinating and in some respects final link in the unity of institutional development that was the historical hypothesis of the new group. If at times too well-defined *a priori* views attempted to wring from scanty records proofs that were not there, the result was nevertheless a systematic statement of local origins that broke sharply with surmises of the preceding generation.

Almost every writer of the middle period who dealt with Massachusetts history had presented brief conclusions concerning the origin of Massachusetts towns. Francis Baylies [1] admitted that the subject was involved in some obscurity, but seemed to find its basis in the independent churches, which, passing through the customary ecclesiastical and proprietary influences,

---

[1] Baylies, *Historical Memoir*, I, 240–243.

subsequently assumed the names of towns and became in effect, political corporations. Jared Sparks [1] was of the opinion that the colonists of Plymouth were politically in a state of nature, and for both convenience and protection they agreed on a system of regulations which had the effect of laws. The example of the parent settlement was readily followed, remoter communities acted similarly, and soon acquired the knowledge and habits necessary to local government from which was subsequently derived the municipal system of New England. Alexis de Tocqueville [2] went into spiritual fields. He saw in the formation of the early town a law of social existence. Of all political associations, the village and township were the only units so natural that wherever a number of men collected they seemed to constitute themselves. Within them, indeed, were aspects of divine guidance, for the town or tithing existed in all nations whatever their laws or customs might be, and while men might be credited with sufficient human ingenuity to make monarchies and republics, the township seemed to come directly from the hand of God.

Richard Frothingham sought remoter historical origins that were destined to become increasingly attractive to future investigators. He called attention to close precedents for town government in "those little independent nations, the free cities of the twelfth century; or in the towns of the Anglo Saxons, where every office

---

[1] Jared Sparks, "Observations of Jared Sparks on the Government of Towns in Massachusetts," *Johns Hopkins University Studies in Historical and Political Science*, XVI, 579, 580.

[2] Alexis de Tocqueville, *Democracy in America* (Henry Reeve, trans., Francis Bowen, ed., 2d ed., 2 vols., Cambridge, 1863), I, 74–75.

was elective."[1] John Stetson Barry[2] disposed of the subject briefly: the local institutions of New England were in a measure peculiar to America, and the idea of founding such communities was probably derived from long experience with the parish governments of England. Joel Parker[3] was emphatically pragmatic — like most useful machinery the Massachusetts town had its origin in the wants of the time, and came into existence by a gradual progress from imperfect beginnings. He neglected the influence of earlier institutions, denied that the church polity determined the political organization, and saw no more mystical an explanation in town origins than the secular needs of new communities.

It was about this time that a new impetus was given to the problem. In 1881 Edward Augustus Freeman came to America and in a paper prepared for the first volume of the *Johns Hopkins University Studies in Historical and Political Science* presented a principle of remote origins that was to change the channels of local constitutional investigation. It was not new. English and German scholars — Kemble, Green, Stubbs, Maine and Freeman himself, von Maurer, Hanssen, Metizen, Nasse, and George Waitz — had written approvingly and at times extensively on the unity of local institutions, and with patience and ingenuity had shown evidence of "survivals" and "revivals" of Aryan, Teu-

---

[1] Frothingham, *History of Charlestown*, pp. 49–50.

[2] J. S. Barry, *The History of Massachusetts* (3 vols., Boston, 1855–1857), I (Colonial Period), 215.

[3] Joel Parker, "The Origin, Organization, and Influence of the Towns of New England," *Mass. Hist. Soc. Proc.*, IX, 20; also, *An Address delivered at the Centennial Celebration, in Jaffrey, August 20, 1873* (Winchendon, 1873), p. 15, Appendix B, 43ff.

tonic, and Anglo-Saxon methods.[1] But the application was nevertheless impressive. To say that the local polities of Massachusetts (and these offered the most ready comparisons) were part of the institutions of the English people, and these again merely part of more remote continental and even Asiatic precedents, was to give new importance to an institution that had, until the Jackson period at least, received no more than passing comment. Enough work had been done, moreover, to make com-

---

[1] John Richard Green saw in the early Britain political attributes of the Germanic race — in the ancient Teutonic village "lay ready formed the social and political life which is found round us in the England of to-day" (*History of the English People*, 4 vols., London, 1887, I, 8). To William Stubbs the Germanic institutions of England were even freer from foreign influence than those remaining in Germany, for the proof of which he looked not only to historical analogy, but to "the progressive, persistent development of English constitutional history from the primeval polity of the common fatherland" (*The Constitutional History of England*, 6th ed., Oxford, 1873, I, 11). Henry Sumner Maine found the origin of village communities "in remote barbarism" and added that the "earliest settlers in New England appear to have planted themselves in townships having a strong resemblance to village communities" (*Dissertations on Early Law and Custom*, London, 1883, p. 331). The Mark was thoroughly described by Georg Ludwig von Maurer in his *Einleitung zur Geschichte der Mark-, Hof-, Dorf-, und Stadt-Verfassung und der Öffentlichen Gewalt* (München, 1854), and ten years earlier George Waitz had stressed the continuity of European institutions in his *Deutsche Verfassungsgeschichte* (8 vols., Kiel, 1844–78), I, 53–54:

"Wie aber die Eintheilungen des Volks, der Völkerschaft verschieden waren, so auch die Versammlungen in denen sie erschienen. Jede Hundertschaft hatte ihr eigenes Thing, in dem die Angelegenheiten derselben behandelt und erledigt wurden. Aber auch der Gau hatte seine Versammlung. Neben dem Heradsthing bestand in Norwegen das Fylkithing, in Danemark das Sysselthing, in England neben der Versammlung der Hundrede der Shiregemot; in Deutschland gab es eine Malstatt wie in jeder Centene so im Gau. Ja wir sehen, wie unter den Friesen, im Brokmerlander, die vier Distrikte — Bura', Bauerschaften, heissen sie — aus denen es bestand, jeder seine besondere Versammlung hielt, zugleich aber zweimal im Jahr alle sich vereinigten und die gemeine Gemeinde bildeten." For further citations to contemporary writings see Fustel de Coulanges' *Recherches sur Quelques Problèmes d'Histoire* (Paris, 1885; 2d ed., Paris, 1894), pp. 319–322.

parisons, if not continuity, fairly definite; and, even admitting modifications because of a strange environment and new events, there were still interesting similarities in the New England town and the local institutions of Athens, Rome, Switzerland and England.[1]

American writers had for some time expressed like theories, but largely as plausible generalities or as echoes of foreign influence. There was one scholar, however, who approached the question with a vigor and acuteness worthy of the best European methods. A few months preceding Freeman's visit to America, Herbert Baxter Adams made public what has remained the classic study of the Germanic origins of the New England town. Here was the first systematic attempt to bring the local political institutions of Massachusetts into the oneness of universal history. Their spontaneous growth was presented as impossible — wherever organic life was found, there was a seed, and

Town institutions were propagated in New England by old English and Germanic ideas, brought over by Pilgrims and Puritans, and as ready to take root in the free soil of America as would Egyptian grain which had been drying in a mummy-case for thousands of years.[2]

[1] E. A. Freeman, "An Introduction to American Institutional History," *Johns Hopkins University Studies in Historical and Political Science*, I, no. 1, p. 13: "The institutions of Massachusetts or Maryland, such at least among them as have been handed down from the foundation of those colonies, are not simply the institutions of Massachusetts and Maryland. They are part of the general institutions of the English people, as those are again part of the general institutions of the Teutonic race, and those are again part of the general institutions of the whole Aryan family. There I must stop; some of my friends are able to go further; and, if they can prove that something which I am satisfied with showing to be English, Teutonic, Aryan, is really common to all mankind, they do me no wrong."

[2] H. B. Adams, "The Germanic Origin of New England Towns," *Johns Hopkins University Studies in Historical and Political Science*, I, no. 2, p. 8.

Green, Freeman and Stubbs were quoted as recognizing in "their older fatherland" the basis of English institutions. In the works of distinguished German scholars (as well as in the *Germania* of Tacitus) was found ample evidence of Teutonic precedents. The Black Forest of modern Germany offered surviving features of the ancient village — land systems, agrarian laws, village moats, town gates, stockades and common fields — and these in turn were found reproduced in the towns of Massachusetts Bay, uniting the old world forever to the new. Vestiges of remote origins were thought to be in almost every old town in New England, and especially the numerous incidents of common lands still surviving, gave added color to the conclusion that beneath the surface of national institutions there reposed a vast and far-reaching country of common historical worth.[1]

Not the least effect of this essay was to stimulate Edward Channing, then an instructor in history at Harvard University, to write a short monograph on *Town and County Government in the English Colonies of North America*, with the result that a refreshing realism was introduced into the discussion. The exact form that local institutions in the English colonies assumed, was due far less to Teutonic and Aryan precedents than to local economic conditions, previous political experience, and the form of church government and land system that was found to be expedient. Beginning with a brief statement of the political in-

[1] *Ibid.*, p. 38. Other monographs by Mr. Adams further supported his theory. See "Saxon Tithingmen in America," *Johns Hopkins University Studies in Historical and Political Science*, I, no. 4; "Norman Constables in America," *ibid.*, no. 8; "Village Communities of Cape Anne and Salem," *ibid.*, nos. 9-10.

fluences of economic conditions, the essay continued
with an examination of local institutions in seventeenth-
century England — particularly the parish government, its composition, officers, and procedure. There
followed a short statement of the ecclesiastical organization and land systems of the colonies, as well as a
thorough examination of local government in Massachusetts and Virginia.[1] While corroborating the theories of H. B. Adams, Channing was of the opinion that
both town and county government in the English colonies were survivals of the English common-law parish
of 1600, and that any modifications were due to the
causes first described.[2] But however significant these
may have proved to be, the constitutional history of
Massachusetts and of Virginia before their settlement,
was one history — "the continuous history of the English people." [3]

The next few years brought additional monographs,
each emphasizing the local or historical influence that
impressed the various authors as of predominating
importance. Alexander Johnston attempted to show
that in Connecticut the state was the product rather
than the source of its local communities, and pictured
the town as a tiny embryo steadily expanding into
larger units, and thus what Adams had done for the

[1] Edward Channing, "Town and County Government in the English
Colonies of North America," *Johns Hopkins University Studies in Historical
and Political Science*, II, no.10, pp. 5–57.

[2] *Ibid.*, p. 5: "—the exact form which the local organization of each colony
should assume depended on, (1) the economic conditions of the colony;
(2) the experience in the management of local concerns which its founders
brought from the mother country; and (3) the form of church government
and land system which should be found expedient."

[3] *Ibid.*, p. 53.

"Germanic theory" and Channing had done for the "parish theory," Johnston did for the theory of the "primordial cell." [1] John Fiske was a staunch supporter of "survivals," but felt, nevertheless, the practical effects of ecclesiastical influences,[2] a view that Noah Porter took occasion to express:

> Out of the church grew the town; or rather the town was evolved or developed along with the church. Whether church members, as in Massachusetts and New Haven, were at first the only voters, or whether, as in Connecticut, the town voted into its commonwealth, those men, and those only, who were fit to be freemen, it was all the same, as the church was the germ and the meeting house was the center of the self-governed commonwealth, and became the scene of all those public transactions which should connect man with his fellow man, and with his God, in an organized and common life.[3]

The year following the publication of Johnston's essay (1883) a reaction set in. P. Emory Aldrich denied that there were any pre-existing models for New England

[1] Alexander Johnston, "The Genesis of a New England State," *Johns Hopkins University Studies in Historical and Political Science*, I, no. 11, pp. 5–29. The essay was practically incorporated in the author's *Connecticut: A Study of a Commonwealth Democracy* (Boston, 1887), ch. 6.

[2] John Fiske, *American Political Ideas* (New York, 1885), pp. 37, 49; *ibid., Civil Government in the United States Considered with Some Reference to its Origins* (Cambridge (Mass.), ca., 1890), pp. 34–37, 38; *ibid., The Beginnings of New England* (New York, 1897), pp. 27–28.

[3] Noah Porter, "The New England Meeting House," *The New Englander*, XLII, 305. Probably J. S. Clark in *A Historical Sketch of the Congregational Churches* (1620–1858) (Boston, 1858), set forth the classical expression of this view. After outlining the establishment of the earliest churches in New England before 1630 (Plymouth, Salem, Dorchester, Charlestown (Boston), and Watertown) which he described as "the foundation work of the whole superstructure, civil and religious, that has since risen up among us" (p. 11), it is concluded that the United States "sprang up spontaneously from the system of church polity which our New England fathers deduced from the Bible." See also Leonard Bacon's *The Genesis of the New England Churches* (N. Y., 1874), ch. 16.

towns, asserting that they were original creations, formed
to meet conditions peculiar to settlers in a new and vir-
gin country.  They were, moreover, completely subordinate to the legislature and always had been — "built
according to no archaic or mediaeval patterns, but established institutions as original in their character as their
own situation was novel."[1] At the January meeting
(1890) of the Massachusetts Historical Society, Mellen
Chamberlain criticised the recent work "of young men
mainly of scholastic training, unacquainted with affairs,
and without opportunities for observing how the elementary facts that make history are colored and even trans-
formed in legislative assemblies, by judicial decisions,
and in the tumultuous proceedings of the crowd." He
warned that analogies did not constitute identities, nor
could he see that similarities or adaptations necessarily
showed even relationships.  The colonists brought with
them the instincts, habits and traditions of their race,
but they did not bring English towns, churches or vestries.  On the contrary, they built for themselves the institutions that were needed, as Englishmen had always
done and as they continued to do — as it was, indeed,
quite probable that their ancestors who came from the
forests of Germany had done.  And with a critical statement of Johnston's theory, he concluded that the town
was not the "primordial cell" that later became the state,
but that the state was the mother of the towns within
her borders.[2]

[1] *Amer. Antiq. Soc. Proc.*, III (pt. 1), 118, 124.
[2] Mellen Chamberlain, "The New Historical School," *Mass. Hist. Soc.
Proc.*, 2d series, V, 265, 267, 268–269, 276: They did not bring "English
towns . . . nor English churches, nor vestries, nor British institutions. But
on occasion they builded for themselves, as Englishmen always and every-

At the next meeting of the society, Abner C. Goodell entered an additional protest. He expressed little sympathy with those who having adopted the naive theories of de Tocqueville, endeavored with ingenuity; industry, and enthusiasm, to trace the township back to remote ancestries;[1] and while evincing reluctance to disparage the followers of Freeman and Adams, he felt, nevertheless, that prepossession of a theory detracted from the value of its conclusions, and frequently caused a strained interpretation of otherwise simple events. In the fall of the same year, Charles McLean Andrews expressed further doubts of ancient survivals.[2] In October he published *The Beginnings of the Connecticut Towns*, and the next year, *The Theory of the Village Community*,[3] denying that the local organizations of New England were "the reversion to a type two thousand or so years old," and refusing to subscribe to a view that considered the town the primordial unit of the body politic.

The controversy did not, however, confine itself to condemnation and criticism. In January, 1892 Charles Francis Adams injected a new and novel explanation into this medley of theories. He had previously pre-

where had done and still do, according to the exigencies of their situation, and after the manner of their race, just as the seeds they brought with them produced, each after its kind, but modified by the differences of soil, climate, and situation. And so doubtless was it with their ancestors, and ours, who came from the forests of Germany to England; but it is questionable whether they brought German towns into England."

[1] *Ibid.*, pp. 322–323.

[2] C. M. Andrews, "The River Towns of Connecticut: A Study of Wethersfield, Hartford, and Windsor," *Johns Hopkins University Studies in Historical and Political Science*, VII, nos. 7-9, p. 31 (note).

[3] *Ibid.*, "The Beginnings of the Connecticut Towns," *Ann. of Amer. Acad.*, I, no. 2, pp. 165–191; "The Theory of the Village Community," *Amer. Hist. Assn. Papers*, V (pts. 1-2), pp. 47–60.

pared a paper tracing the evolution of the New England town from the common-law vestry and the congregational society. But becoming dissatisfied with these conclusions, he suppressed the paper and prepared another wholly at variance with his former view. In it he presented what has since received prominence as the "Massachusetts charter theory." Following a careful analysis of the early records of Braintree, Dorchester, Dedham, Hingham, Weymouth, Cambridge, and Boston, he concluded that the government of the Massachusetts town was of purely secular origin, and had no connection with the church, except that certain members of the church were freemen and inhabitants of the town. The basis of these communities, moreover, was purely economic — a joint interest in the tract of land upon which the town was situated — and the inhabitants, therefore, were in the nature of stockholders in a modern corporation. Through efforts to meet necessary political requirements, the analogy of the company charter was followed very closely and

— the body of freemen or inhabitants constituted the General Court of the town, subsequently called the general town-meeting; and the townsmen, later on the selectmen, were the board of assistants, or, as they would now be called, directors.[1]

Such had, in a general way, been the story of the search for historical origins and early influences of town government in New England. From the writings of two generations it is difficult tó select the thoughts that en-

[1] C. F. Adams, "The Genesis of the Massachusetts Town, and the Development of Town-Meeting Government," *Mass. Hist. Soc. Proc.*, 2d series, VII, 174–211, 196.

dured to form the principal theories; but the various conclusions may, in part, be summarized:

(1) The towns were indigenous — planted by Englishmen possessing all the attributes that determined the political methods of their race; but under an environment utterly dissimilar to their native land, there developed an institution new to political history.

(2) They were more or less conscious imitations of English prototypes, which, in turn had been derived in large part, at least, from Germanic and even Aryan regions.

(3) There was the view that minimized the more remote continental precedents, but saw in the New England town a reproduction of the English parish modified by local, ecclesiastical, and economic conditions.

(4) The theory of the "primordial cell," asserted that organized towns came from England to Massachusetts Bay and thence to Connecticut, that they were independent of legislative influence, and became, in a sense, political cells from whose unity developed Connecticut, and indirectly the subsequent federal state.

(5) The "Massachusetts charter theory" purported to trace the institutional origin of the town to a conscious imitation of the charter under which the colony was governed.[1]

The essay of Charles Francis Adams marked the last systematic effort to launch a new theory of town origins. It served, moreover, as an opportunity for a final symposium, and while there were those who were inclined to accept the results of Adams' research

[1] *Ibid.*, pp. 216–218,

as final, others were frankly skeptical.[1] As spokesman
for this group, Edward Channing again entered the lists,
and with a few well-chosen remarks did much to conclude the arguments of half a century.[2] In brief, the
Germanic influences had been pushed much further than
the facts permitted. The "primordial germ theory"
was untenable — both towns and state were of legal
origin. The charter influences so carefully sponsored by
Charles Francis Adams seemed obviously wrung from
reluctant records, and if any extraneous influence was
to be admitted, it was the English common-law parish
of 1600; [3] but it was inaccurate to speak of precedents
in the sense of prototypes — the towns were based on no
models, "they grew by the exercise of English common
sense combined with the circumstances of the place." [4]

The whole controversy was a small but vigorous eddy
in the back-waters of a European maelstrom. The "return to nature" that marked the romantic movement in
English literature, and the speculative hypotheses of a
pre-political state that were so attractive to governmental theorists of the eighteenth century, seemed to
require a more scientific investigation than unsupported
intellectual effort could give. It was in response to such
a demand that Sharon Turner's painstaking work on
*The History of the Anglo Saxons* (1805)[5] attempted to

---

[1] *Ibid.*, pp. 211–214. The remarks of Mellen Chamberlain at this point
(pp. 214–242) are among the ablest that the discussion produced.

[2] *Ibid.*, pp. 242–263.

[3] *Ibid.*, pp. 245–246, 250–251. Although in place of *survival* used in his
essay of a decade earlier (*Johns Hopkins University Studies in Historical
and Political Science*, II, no. 10, pp. 5–57), *representative* now seemed to
describe the relationship more accurately.

[4] *Ibid.*, p. 262.

[5] 2d ed., 2 vols., London, 1807.

put the early period of Britain on a documentary basis, and some years later, John Mitchell Kemble gave a more stable foundation to the field in his two volumes on *The Saxons in England* (1848).[1] It was this work that contained the first fateful chapter on the mark[2] describing it as a primitive Germanic polity of freemen from which English constitutional development was to be traced. Yet in spite of wide acceptance among English scholars (especially Maine, Stubbs and Freeman), the picture of this ancient unit as a cradle of modern democracy shortly received very rough treatment from another group of students. In 1883 Frederick Seebohm produced *The English Village Community* [3] and bluntly stated that while the early inhabitants of Britain might properly be termed "village communities" they were far from socially-minded, untrammelled democracies, but on the contrary quite plainly existed in a condition of complete serfdom under manorial lordship.[4] This was a severe shock. But when M. Fustel de Coulanges gave the world his *Recherches sur Quelques Problèmes d'Histoire* (1885) and characterized the early mark with its attractive precedents of freedom and self-government as a pure piece of historical abstraction, the whole theory received a blow from which it never recovered.[5] Many other writers — French, German, English and American — joined the "Germanist" reaction, and the theories of Turner, Kemble and Freeman insofar as constitutional

[1] Rev. ed., 2 vols., London, 1876.
[2] *Ibid.*, I, ch. 2.
[3] 4th ed., London, 1896.
[4] *Ibid.*, pp. vii–viii, preface; ch. 11, pp. 437–441.
[5] In his "De la Marche Germanie" in *Recherches sur Quelques Problèmes d'Histoire*, he concluded that "Ils ne peuvent faire commencer sur histoire avec quelque sûreté qu'au douzième siècle" (p. 356).

survivals from early Teutonic precedents were concerned suffered a definite and, it seems, a permanent rejection.[1] With this result it was no longer necessary to attack the Germanic theory of New England towns on the basis of insufficient sources or lack of continuity in institutional development. No one was eager to trace a democratic heritage to a condition of serfdom,[2] and the relation that the economists attempted to show between Roman and English villages aroused no response among New England proponents of survivals.

Of the remaining theories there is probably none that supplies a single predominant "influence," although most of them contain substantial elements of truth. The error was partly in undue emphasis — the endeavor to make one motive explain the whole or a preponderant part of what must always remain a most complex and obscure development. The influence of the colony charter in shaping the local political structure is probably the least important. There is certainly nothing in the

[1] W. J. Ashley has brought together a review of the controversy (*Surveys Historic and Economic* (London, 1900), pp. 39–60 and *passim*) as well as a critical analysis of many of the leading works produced. Summaries are also contained in the writings of H. M. Chadwick, particularly *The Origin of the English Nation* (Cambridge (Eng.), 1907), and his *Studies on Anglo-Saxon Institutions* (Cambridge (Eng.), 1905), chs. 6-7 and 9. The most recent survey of the movement is in H. J. Ford's *Representative Government* (N. Y., 1924), chs. 3-8. In 1880 Denman W. Ross came to the same conclusions in America that Coulanges had adopted ("The Mark and the Manor," *Studies in Medieval History* (Cambridge (Mass.), 1879); "Theory of Village Communities," *Studies in the Early History of Institutions* (Cambridge (Mass.), 1880).

[2] As Seebohm stated the problem (*The English Village Community*, p. ix, preface) it was simply an attempt to determine whether English economic history "began with the *freedom* or with the *serfdom* of the masses of the people." His own opinion was that it began in serfdom. For a definite criticism of Adams "The Germanic Origin of New England Towns" see E. A. Bryan's *The Mark in Europe and America* (Boston, 1893), ch. 7.

Dorchester provisions to indicate such a condition. There was, moreover, serious friction between colonists and company during the early formative period that would make emulation unlikely, and the theory of government expressed in the charter itself was clearly not designed with wide popular participation in mind.

Ecclesiastical influences were undoubtedly important — but more in matters of policy than framework. Very little is known of political organization between 1629 and 1635. The Dorchester record shows advanced development with almost no extant antecedents. It is certain that the guidance of local pastors was important in the early days, but to speak of the political services of the period as springing from the church organization is to say little more than that congregation and town meeting were at times composed of much the same people and extended over a similar territory.[1] The earliest records show a development in function and procedure that is distinctly political, and while it is impossible to deny the "representative" features of English local government (especially the common-law parish),[2] rapid adjustments

[1] No church or town records appear to have been kept in Salem until almost 1637. The foundation of the first church there is based upon contemporary reports, and it is from such sources that we have the account of the famous meeting of July 20, 1629 when Mr. Higginson and Mr. Skelton were chosen teacher and pastor respectively, by written ballots from the assembled people. Undoubtedly such an event took place. But a town meeting was not a gathering of the people for any purpose whatsoever, it was a meeting to decide certain *political* questions of interest to the community. Until this was done, there was no town meeting in Massachusetts. While church and town were probably at times a unit in both membership and area, they were different in function and almost always in personal jurisdiction. For full citations to the contemporary materials on this question see D. A. White's *New England Congregationalism* (Salem, 1861).

[2] It is impossible to disregard the similarities described by Beatrice and Sydney Webb in their *English Local Government from the Revolution to the*

to new conditions soon placed the town meeting on a plane unknown in the mother country, and left only a familiar nomenclature to mark the severance.

The analysis of Professor Channing still stands. "English common sense" may not be a scientific term, but it has nevertheless a very definite connotation. The "circumstances of the place" may likewise lack precision, but no one doubts the significance of economic, geographic, and social environments. Governmental organization is designed for a purpose, and men set up that mechanism which experience, aptitude, interests, and intelligence indicate as most likely to give effect to their aspirations. Those who have sat close to a modern municipal committee when changes in local government are under consideration see many and diverse pressures give shape to new proposals. It was doubtless so in those dim days before the records began.[1]

But while the discussions of historical origins did much to clarify one phase of town government, legal aspects of the same question remained a serious difficulty. Corporate existence was not in the early days

*Municipal Corporations Act. The Parish and the County* (London, 1906), ch. 1, "The Legal Framework of the Parish."

[1] A careful study has been recently made concerning the development and influence of the town proprietors of the New England colonies (R. H. Akagi, *The Town Proprietors of the New England Colonies,* Philadelphia, 1924), in which, after disposing of each theory of the past generation as inadequate, the author adds (p. 291): "The story of the New England proprietors shows no resemblance to any one of these hypotheses. On the other hand, it goes to show plainly that New England towns were founded as a result of a simple business arrangement to meet the exigencies of the colonists amid the new environment." But the matter is not settled. Within the past few months the Swiss cantons have been made to furnish models upon which the early town meeting was based (Alfred Worcester, "The Origin of the New England Town Meeting," *Waltham Hist. Soc. Pub.,* no. 2, 1925).

a matter of intention. Neither, accordingly, was it a matter of precision. The exact time that a "town" became a town was a problem containing many uncertainties. In the minds of early legislators, it seems that extensive municipal organization was quite possible under simple voluntary association.[1] Even if legal questions involving the power of the Massachusetts Bay Company to create local political units be resolved in favor of the colonists, there is little in the records to indicate that the General Court intended to exercise, formally, any such prerogative.

In the strictly historical sense, it is probably legally correct to define a municipality as the incorporation, *by the authority of the government*, of the inhabitants of a particular place, authorizing them in their corporate capacity to exercise certain specified powers of legislation and administration with respect to their local concerns.[2] But Massachusetts until 1684 was itself a corporation deriving authority from a crown charter. The only legal power of legislation that it possessed would seem to have come, therefore, from its ability to pass by-laws in the interest of better government; and it is significant that the few private corporations chartered during the period of the colony, were chartered during the English Civil War.[3] The exercise of local government functions is, however, the principal purpose, indeed, the distinguishing feature of a muni-

[1] A. M. Davis, "Corporations in the Days of the Colonies," *Col. Soc. of Mass. Pub.*, I, 191–195.

[2] J. F. Dillon, *Commentaries on the Law of Municipal Corporations* (5th ed., 5 vols., Boston, 1911), I, 59.

[3] J. S. Davis, "Essays in the Earlier History of American Corporations," *Harvard Economic Studies*, XVI, nos. 1-3, p. 20.

cipality;[1] and it is undeniable that the Massachusetts town, from the earliest period carried on the major powers that are associated with corporate capacity. The difficulty arose when inevitable development stretched the colonial charters far beyond their original purposes. In law they remained nothing more than medieval grants. In fact, they became free constitutions regulating the lives of increasing thousands of British subjects.[2] There is little to mark the legal beginnings of these early communities. Some settlements have nothing more definite in the court records to indicate their establishment than the order by which they received their English names, or by which their existence was first acknowledged by specific reference.[3] Others depend on mention in a tax list,[4] on a casual statement relating to the land that subsequently became the town,[5] or possibly the enactment under which the area was for the first time given corporate privileges.[6] Some communities, appar-

[1] Dillon, *Commentaries*, I, 59.

[2] C. H. McIlwain, *The American Revolution, a Constitutional Interpretation* (New York, 1923), pp. 180–181.

[3] There are many examples: "It is ordered, that Aggawam shalbe called Ipswitch" (*I Mass. Col. Rec.* 123), or "Saugust is called Lin" (*ibid.*, p. 211), etc. More casual reference is frequent: "All this to be att the common charge those of Mattapan & Salem onely exempted" (*ibid.*, p. 73), or "John Bennett is ffined Xs for being drunke att Marblehead" (*ibid.*, p. 106).

[4] Roxbury and Medford are first mentioned in this manner, September 28, 1630 (*ibid.*, p. 77).

[5] Wessagusus was settled in 1622. It was taxed first in September, 1630 (*ibid.*, p. 77). It continues to be mentioned (*ibid.*, pp. 89, 93, 121, 139), and on September 2, 1635, permission is granted to "21 ffamilyes to sitt downe at Wessaguscus" (*ibid.*, p. 149). The name of the plantation was subsequently changed to "Waymouthe" (*ibid.*, p. 156).

[6] "Winnacunnet," the record reads (I *Mass. Col. Rec.* 259), "is alowed to bee a towne, & hath power to choose a cunstable & other officers, & make orders for the well ordering of their towne, & to send a deputy to the Court, & Christo: Hussey, Willi: Palmer, & Richard Swaine to end all businesses

ently, were never formally established, and others not now recognized, have never become legally extinct.[1] It is significant that Boston as early as 1650, petitioned the General Court for an act of incorporation,[2] but not until an amendment to the constitution of the commonwealth in 1820, providing definitely for city government, was Boston through a special act incorporated — or more accurately, perhaps, *continued* as a municipal corporation, with a change of organization only, for it had always been recognized "even before it was declared by statute, that towns, as well as counties, territorial parishes and school districts, by virtue of their existence as *quasi* corporations, were capable of holding property and making contracts for the purposes for which they were established." [3] But it was not until the second charter, and more completely under the Commonwealth, that words were uniformly prescribed to invest towns, districts, and other corporate units with legal privileges of municipal organization.[4]

vnder 20 shs for this yeare; the laying out of land to bee by those expressed in the former order." This community later became the town of Hampton (*ibid.*, p. 271).

[1] Wright, *Report on the Custody and Condition of the Public Records*, pp. 25–26, 36.

[2] "In answer to a petition presented to this Court, in the name & in the behalf of the towne of Boston, that *that* they might become a corporation, it is agreed vpon by the Court that theire desire should be graunted, if the articles or terms, priuiledges & imunities thereof were so presented as rationally should appeare . . . . fit for the Court to graunte" (III *Mass. Col. Rec.* 207). See also IV *Mass. Col. Rec.* (pt. 1), 9; (pt. 2), 26–27, 56, 99, as well as Justin Winsor's (ed.) *The Memorial History of Boston* (4 vols., Boston, 1880), I, 219.

[3] Overseers of the Poor *v.* David Sears (1839), 39 *Mass.* 122–135; Hill *v.* Boston (1877), 122 *Mass.* 349.

[4] *Infra*, p. 103. Also J. B. Felt, "Statistics of Population in Massachusetts," *Amer. Stat. Assn. Coll.*, I (pt. 1), 28. Plymouth at a very early period (Feb. 12, 1638/9) adopted a definite form for establishing a town-

From the earliest times, however, the settled communities of Massachusetts Bay were towns in the colloquial sense, and to the Englishman of the seventeenth century, the term seems to have been descriptive of the diverse settlement that these communities exemplified.[1] Even before the company moved from Old England to New England, the concept of a town in the new world seemed to be understood. In the regulations concerning land allotments to adventurers in the common stock of the company (May 19, 1629), there is mentioned "the plott of ground whereon the towne is entended to bee built" and "to build his howse within the foresaid plot of ground sett out for the towne to bee built on," but it is clearly in the seventeenth-century sense that the term is used.[2] After the company came to America the word

ship (I *Ply. Col. Rec.* 113), but this, of course, gave no more legal sanctity to the community than the methods employed in the Massachusetts Bay Colony. The earliest reported cases in print are to be found in Josiah Quincy's *Reports of Cases Argued and Adjudged in the Superior Court of Judicature of the Province of Massachusetts Bay* (1761–1772) (Boston, 1865), and there are but two cases of interest in this matter: first, Province of Massachusetts Bay v. Paxton (1762) (*ibid.*, p. 548) and second, Wrentham Proprietors v. Metcalf (1763) (*ibid.*, p. 36). For an excellent account of corporate activities in the colonies see H. W. Rogers, "Municipal Corporations" (1701–1901) in *Two Centuries Growth of American Law* (1701–1901) (N. Y., 1901), pp. 203–260.

[1] "For you generally call that a Town in *America*," wrote John Palmer in 1690, "where a number of People have Seated themselves together, yet 'tis very well known, 'tis so in *Name* only, not in Fact: I take that Body of People to be a Town, properly so called, who by some Act of Law, have been *Incorporated*, and in that sense there is no such thing as a Town in the *Massathusets*, neither was there a Power to make such before his Excellency's Arrival [i.e. Sir Edmund Andros], for *One Corporation cannot make another*" (John Palmer, "An Impartial Account of the State of New England" (1690), *Andros Tracts* (Prince Soc. Pub.), 3 vols. (Boston, 1868–1874), I, 48).

[2] I *Mass. Col. Rec.* 43. It is of interest to note that Chief Justice Vaughn spoke of "some townships, vill, hamlet, or a county who are not corporate" (cited Hill v. Boston (1877), 122 *Mass.* 347), and Richard Verstegan in

plantation was used as apparently synonymous with town, and the first tax list was levied " out of the seuerall plantations." [1] The first mention of towns collectively occurs in the proceedings of the Court of Assistants for March 22, 1630/31:

> Further, it is ordered, that euery towne within this pattent shall . . . . take espetiall care that euery person within their towne (except magistrates & ministers,) as well servants as others, [be] furnished with good & sufficient armes.[2]

The third levy for public charges provided that the assessment be made "out of the seueral plantations, according to the last rate of townes." [3] And although from the time that the first order was passed describing the general powers of towns, the word "plantation" falls into disuse, the tax lists continue to use the term until April, 1637, when the expedition for the Pequot war was fitted out on the basis of towns.[4] Thereafter it was the designation in general use for fully established communities. Chief Justice Gray summarized the judicial view:

> At the first settlement of the Colony, towns consisted of

A Restitution of Decayed Intelligence: In antiquities (Antwerp, 1605), p. 295, gave his explanation of the condition:

"Moreover when necessitie, by reason of warres and troobles, caused whole thorps to bee with such *tnnes* [tunes, i.e., hedges] enuyroned about; those enclosed places did thereby take the names of *tunes* / afterward pronounced *townes* / and so gave cause that all *Stedes*, now *Cities*, all *Thorps*, now *villages*, all *Burghs*, now *Burrows*, and all places els, that conteyned but some number of tenements in a neernes together, got the names of *townes:* as vulgarly wee yet vnto this day call them."

[1] I *Mass. Col. Rec.* 77 (September 28, 1630).

[2] *Ibid.*, p. 84. "Town" was used, however, when Watertown was named (*ibid.*, p. 75), and the word appears still earlier in the records of the Plymouth colony (XI *Ply. Col. Rec.* 4, January 3, 1627/8).

[3] I *Mass. Col. Rec.* 138.

[4] *Ibid.*, p. 192.

clusters of inhabitants dwelling near each other, which, by
the effect of legislative acts, designating them by names, and
conferring upon them the powers of managing their own
prudential affairs, electing representatives and town officers,
making bye-laws, and disposing, subject to the paramount
control of the legislature, of unoccupied lands within their
territory, became in effect municipal or *quasi* corporations,
without any formal act of incorporation.[1]

[1] Hill *v.* Boston (1877), 122 *Mass.* 349. There was a more important
distinction between town and plantation, especially as the colony developed.
A plantation was evidently considered to be much more under the authority
of the General Court (MacLear, "Early New England Towns," pp. 14–16).
The establishment of "Nantascot" as a plantation for a fishing trade
(I *Mass. Col. Rec.* 326), with restrictions on the disposal of land, the character of the inhabitants admitted, the setting out of the meadows, the
provisions for "stage rome," etc., is an example. But the change from plantation to town was done by order of the General Court, the name frequently
changing with the status. The case of Winnacunnet (*ibid.*, pp. 259, 271,
*op. cit.* pp. 70–71, note 6) is a clear example. The Supreme Judicial Court
has said (Commonwealth *v.* the City of Roxbury (1857), 9 *Grey* (Mass.) 485):
"The terms 'plantation,' 'town,' and 'township' seem to be used almost indiscriminately to indicate a cluster or body of persons inhabiting near each
other; and when they became designated by name, certain powers were
conferred upon them by general orders and laws, such as to manage their
own prudential concerns, to elect deputies and the like, which in effect made
them municipal corporations; and no formal acts of incorporation were
granted till long afterwards."

# IV

## THE TOWN OF THE EIGHTEENTH CENTURY

THE two decades succeeding 1630 was the formative period of town government in Massachusetts. From the Body of Liberties through the legislation of the Colony, Province and early Commonwealth there is, with few exceptions, little more than a development of institutions that had their beginnings in the youthful years. The colonial laws of the edition of 1672 with supplements through the end of legislation under the charter (May 20, 1686) serve as a summary of town practice to near the close of the seventeenth century.[1] The principal regulations remained in force. The famous order of March, 1635/6 appeared substantially as enacted in the early days. Where the first version, however, read, "the ffreemen . . . onely have power to dispose of their owne lands . . . & make such orders as may concerne the well ordering of their owne townes," the word "onely" was dropped and the law read, "That the Freemen of every Town, with such others as are allowed . . . shall have power . . ." and the later edition contained the provision that town orders "be not of a Criminal, but of a Prudential nature." Town suffrage with the privilege of holding local offices was still based on the order of 1647.[2] In addition to freemen it belonged to all "English-men, that are settled inhabitants and

[1] Whitmore, *Colonial Laws, passim.*
[2] II *Mass. Col. Rec.* 197.

House-holders in any Town, of the age of *twenty-four years*, and of honest and good Conversations, being Rated at *eighty pounds* Estate in a single Country Rate, and that have taken the Oath of Fidelity to this Government." [1]

Legislation of a local character had continued to accumulate. Some thirty-three orders, penalties and permissive regulations directed to the township, and over sixty others pertaining to the enlarging or facilitating of the duties of the selectmen, were listed on the statute books.[2] These officers were to be chosen at least annually and were not to exceed nine in number. They continued to be embarrassed with such diverse functions as to set up cages for Sabbath-breakers, to require idle persons to work, to appoint individuals to search out unlicensed houses of entertainment, and to settle newcomers in proper and diligent employment.[3] Minor officers had become (both in Plymouth and the Massachusetts Bay Colony) increasingly numerous. Gaugers, viewers of pipestaves, surveyors of goods damaged on board ships, cullers of brick, measurers of salt,[4] and packers of meat and fish bore witness to growing commercial needs;[5] while under the title of *Presidents & Forms of things frequently Used*, were a dozen oaths binding subordinate local officials to a proper discharge of their duties.

But the government under the Colony came to a for-

[1] Whitmore, *Colonial Laws*, pp. 147, 148.

[2] *Ibid.*, "A Summary of the LAWS foregoing Alphabetically Digested," pp. 194–195; also pp. 388, 391.

[3] *Ibid.*, pp. 250, 294, 235, 337.

[4] *Ibid.*, pp. 16, 122, 295, 321, 134–135.

[5] Brigham, *Compact with the Charter and Laws*, pp. 95, 162; Whitmore, *Colonial Laws*, pp. 162–170.

mal end in October, 1684.[1] The *quo warranto* (issued in
June, 1683) under which the charter was subsequently
vacated (although a *scire facias* was necessary to complete the process), listed some fourteen infractions of the
original grant, the first of which was that of being a
"body corporate and politique" and thereby exercising
the "sole government of all that country." [2] The Province government began almost eight years later — May,
1692. As is well known, the interim was brief but turbulent. Without a charter Massachusetts was relegated to
the status of a crown colony; but the death of Charles II
delayed final disposition of its political affairs, and the
government continued much as usual until the arrival of
President Joseph Dudley.[3] Even then the life of the
people was altered very little. In a speech to the assembly on the opening day of the new order, the governor gave assurance that the necessary alterations "in the
Rule and Form of administration . . . need be but a
few," and in his proclamation at the close of the session
recognized the existing political organization of the
towns.[4]

It is true, moreover, that during his term of office,
there was little inclination to interfere in municipal matters. At a meeting of the president and council held in
Boston, June 8, 1686, land tenures, town boundaries, organization and taxing privileges were confirmed, with
the single proviso that all sums voted in town meeting

[1] "The Dudley Records," *Mass. Hist. Soc. Proc.*, 2d series, XIII, 224, 226.
[2] Thomas Hutchinson (ed.), *The Hutchinson Papers* (Prince Soc. Pub.)
(2 vols., Boston, 1865), I, 114: "Exemplification of the Judgment for vacating
the charter of the Massachusetts Bay in New England," *Mass. Hist. Soc.
Coll.*, 4th series, II, 246–278.
[3] For a copy of his commission see *Col. Soc. of Mass. Coll.*, II, 37–43.
[4] "The Dudley Records," pp. 227–229.

(as well as assessments and collections) should be subject to the approval of two justices of the peace or of one member of the council residing within the county.[1] Subsequent regulations were apparently made in an effort to maintain the old order rather than to weaken it, and except for the fact that the towns chose no deputies during the period, their political procedure was much as in the days of the charter.[2]

But the appointment of President Dudley had been regarded as purely temporary, and on Sunday, December 19, 1686, a new "Captain General, and Governour in Chief" in the person of Sir Edmund Andros, arrived at Boston.[3] While on the following day he was cordially received and was even escorted by a large number of distinguished citizens to the Town House,[4] his arrival was the beginning of increased disturbance. The new governor was allowed little discretion in forming his political organization. With the aid of an advisory council he was to make laws, levy taxes, dispense justice, and command the local militia. Yet he had no authority to call a popular assembly or to foster the traditional institutions of the colonies,[5] and it was soon evident that many of his principal difficulties were to center about the Massachusetts town.

Among his first acts was an order that

Selectmen, Constables, Overseers of the poor and all other Town officers for manageing the Prudentiall Affaires thereof

[1] "The Dudley Records," pp. 246-247.
[2] C. M. Andrews, *The Fathers of New England* (New Haven, 1919), p. 170.
[3] "Commission of Sir Edmund Andros," *Mass. Hist. Soc. Coll.*, 3d series, VII, 139.
[4] W. H. Whitmore (ed.), "Memoire of Sir Edmund Andros," *Andros Tracts* (Prince Soc. Pub., 3 vols., Boston, 1868-1874), I, xxvii.
[5] "Commission of Sir Edmund Andros," pp. 140-144.

be Continued and elected and are to act in all Town Affaires in their Severall bounds as formerly.[1]

But unfortunately further legislation did not bear out the promises contained in this measure. A tax was levied that compared to sums previously charged in the colony was a heavy burden — "a penny in the pound on all Estates personal or real, twenty pence *per* head as Poll Money, a penny in the pound for goods imported, besides an Excise on Wine, Rum and other Liquors." [2] The towns remonstrated. Many even petitioned to be exempt from payment, and some went so far as to refuse to collect the new levies.[3]

The question of land titles became acute. Andros interpreted the instructions in his commission to signify that he was to take control of all ungranted real property in the country, and to dispose of it in such manner as the King might see fit to prescribe.[4] This was subsequently made to mean that new patents should be taken out by every land owner at the expense of a heavy fee for the service, if he wished to enjoy a secure title to any

---

[1] "Andros Records," *Amer. Antiq. Soc. Proc.*, new series, XIII, 244 (January 3, 1686).

[2] John Palmer, "The Revolution in New England Justified" (1691); *Andros Tracts* (Prince Soc. Pub., Boston, 1868), I, 81.

[3] See the "Petition of Bristol to be excused from the tax recently ordered," *Mass. Hist. Soc. Coll.* (Usurpation Papers), 3d series, V, 171–172; Palmer, "The Revolution in New England Justified," pp. 81–85.

[4] Barry, *History of Massachusetts*, I (Colonial Period), 493. His instructions were certainly clear on the point: "And we do likewise give and grant unto you, full power and authority, by and with the advice and consent of our said Council, to agree with the planters and inhabitants of our said Territory and Dominion, concerning such lands, tenements and hereditaments, as now are, or hereafter shal be in our power to dispose of; and them to grant unto any person or persons for such terms, and under such moderate quit-rents, services and acknowledgements, thereupon to be reserved unto us, as shal be appointed by us" (*Mass. Hist. Soc. Coll.*, 3d series, VII, 147).

real property that might be in dispute. It appears, moreover, that the Governor even said that there was "no such thing amongst you as a Town," [1] and what was the deepest offense of all, caused to be enacted that henceforth it would be unlawful for the inhabitants of any town to assemble in town meeting except on the third Monday of May in each year — the time appointed for the choice of town officers.[2]

It is hardly necessary to say that "the Inhabitants of the Countrey were startled at this Law." It looked very much as if its main purpose was to restrain the discussion of well-known grievances, and curtailment in this direction inevitably aroused the bitterest opposition.[3] The accession of William of Orange (November, 1688) found an exasperated people eager for such an opportunity as the occasion offered, and, as is well known, the government was overthrown and Andros imprisoned. A hastily formed "Council for the Safety of the People and Conservation of the Peace" recommended that town meetings be held to choose not exceeding two persons from each town to convene in Boston, and in May (1689), sixty-six representatives

---

[1] John Palmer, "An Impartial Account of the State of New England" (1690), *Andros Tracts*, I, 48.

[2] *The Public Records of the Colony of Connecticut* (J. H. Trumbull, ed., 3 vols., Hartford, 1859), III, 427–429. Fragments of the legislation of the period are contained in this work. This act itself is of interest as embodying several minor modifications in local government. The selectmen are to be any even number, not to exceed eight, and are made a continuous body — *i.e.*, one-half are elected annually, the term being, therefore, two years long. A commissioner was to be chosen annually to levy the "several Rates, Duties and Imposts" (*ibid.*, p. 428). The selectmen are further ordered to meet once a month, and the constables, chosen at the annual meeting, are to be presented at the succeeding Court of Sessions, "there to take the oath usually administered for the faithful discharge of that office" (*ibid.*, p. 429).

[3] Palmer, "The Revolution in New England Justified," p. 80.

from forty-four towns and villages met as requested. Dissatisfied with so small a number, the Council for Safety declared a fuller representation necessary, and following two additional meetings, it was decided to assume the old charter until "an Orderly Setlement" arrived from England,[1] and before the middle of the summer, nearly every trace of the unhappy régime had vanished.

Yet the charter subsequently granted under date of October 7, 1691[2] was a very different document from the one of 1629 — a distinct decline from the freedom of the colonial days. It did, indeed, confirm the title to all "Lands, Tenements and Hereditaments . . . which any person or persons or Bodyes Politique or Corporate Townes Villages Colledges or Schools," might hold within the colony; and it granted a General Court to be held annually on the last Wednesday in May and at such other times as the Governor might determine, each town to elect two representatives. There was, however, no guarantee of local self-government — it was not, apparently contemplated — and the entire supervision of towns was placed under the authority of the Province.[3]

The first recorded act of the new government was "An Act for Continuing the Local Laws, to Stand in Force till November THE 10TH, 1692," and while this was subsequently disallowed by the Privy Council,[4] in

[1] Albert Matthews, "Notes on the Massachusetts Royal Commissions, 1681–1775," *Col. Soc. of Mass. Pub.*, XVII, 19, 20, 25; Barry, *History of Massachusetts*, I, 506.

[2] Massachusetts, General Court, *The Acts and Resolves, Public and Private of the Province of the Massachusetts Bay* (1692–1780) (21 vols., Boston, 1869–1922), "The Charter of the Province of the Massachusetts Bay," I, 1–20. Hereafter cited *Acts and Resolves*.

[3] *Ibid.*, pp. 9–10, 11, 16.

[4] Not, apparently, because of any fundamental objections to the principle, but because it was "judged necessary that in any new Law to be

November a general charter of town government was enacted containing elaborate provisions for regulating local communities. It confirmed the ancient town boundaries, substantiated, with few exceptions, the traditional forms of government, and gave detailed orders concerning many municipal functions. It provided that town meetings be held annually in the month of March; that warrants be issued by the selectmen, and that the meeting be warned by the constables or such others as the selectmen or "townsmen" might appoint. The election of local officers was to be by the majority of the qualified inhabitants assembled; and those to be chosen were fully enumerated — three, five, seven or nine selectmen, overseers of the poor (where the selectmen did not act), a clerk, "a commissioner for assessments," constables, surveyors of highways, tithingmen, fence-viewers, clerks of the market, sealers of leather, "and other ordinary town officers." [1]

It was basically much the same as its more famous predecessor of 1635/36, but while recognizing the earlier provisions, it added still others. Under the Province (as under the later years of the Colony) "the freeholders and other inhabitants of each town, rateable at twenty pounds estate" were qualified to vote in town meetings. The selectmen were fully instructed concerning the assessment of town and county charges, as well as in regard to the treatment of idle persons, the care of the poor, the

enacted for the said purpose the Laws to be continued be therein expressed & particularly specified" (I *Acts and Resolves*, 100, note).

[1] *Ibid.*, pp. 64–65. For detailed duties see p. 139 (fence-viewers, haywards, and field-drivers); p. 406 (assessors); pp. 409, 653 (collectors); p. 730 (hog-reeves); p. 155 (tithingmen); pp. 157, 384 (treasurers); p. 655 (surveyors and measurers of boards), etc.

admission of inhabitants and the disposal of intruders.[1] Perhaps the most important addition was the clause requiring that all town orders and by-laws, made either by the town, or by the selectmen under instructions, must be approved by the court of quarter sessions — a group of justices of the peace appointed by the Governor and Council (an arrangement new to the Province) — before becoming valid,[2] and that all town officers from whom an oath was required by law, be sworn before the same body, or before a single justice.

Supplementary legislation bore out the promises of the early period and emphasized a policy of close supervision and even compulsion in town affairs. The uncertain corporate status was brought partly to a conclusion by a law enabling towns, villages, and proprietors in common and undivided lands to sue and be sued.[3] Penalties were provided for refusing to employ a schoolmaster,[4] for neglecting to elect selectmen or assessors, for injury caused by defective ways, and for the failure of constables to collect a tax. A justice of the peace was given authority to call town meetings when the selectmen unreasonably refused. They were further empowered to fine the selectmen for neglecting to provide the town with a sufficient stock of arms and ammunition, or, if necessary, to appoint others for the same service, and were, in addition, to act in conjunction with them in assigning sites to slaughter houses in certain towns, in

---

[1] I *Acts and Resolves*, 65–68.

[2] *Ibid.*, p. 66. The General Court repealed this clause June, 1695, but the act in which the repeal was embodied was unfortunately disallowed (November 24, 1698), and caused annoyance for many years (*ibid.*, pp. 217–218, 248–249).

[3] *Ibid.*, pp. 182–183.

[4] *Ibid.*, p. 63.

appointing watchmen, and either with the selectmen or the overseers of the poor in setting the indigent to work and in binding out apprentices.[1] In December, 1715 an "Act for the Better Regulation of Town and Proprietary Meetings" was passed.[2] The preamble recited that because of "the disorderly carriage of some persons in said meetings, the affair and business thereof is very much retarded and obstructed." It was required, therefore, that moderators be chosen with power to impose fines for speaking without permission; that ten or more freeholders might compel the insertion of desired articles in the warrant, and that "no matter or thing whatsoever shall be voted or determined but what is inserted in the warrant for calling said meeting." [3] In January, 1742/3 [4] further supplementary legislation was enacted relative to the suffrage — all voters to be personally present at town meeting and of an estate rateable at £20, the precise methods of determining such status being fully prescribed.

[1] I *Acts and Resolves*, 407, 137, 411, 68, 132, 59, 381, 538, 654.

[2] The proprietor's meetings were largely an eighteenth century development. The proprietaries of the previous century had no legal independent status as distinct from the town. In most towns the grantees of the land included practically all of the inhabitants, and the problem of giving separate protection to proprietary rights did not arise. The town meetings were adequate to dispose of the land and the town records to protect titles. But growth of the population quite naturally altered this simple relation. Towards the close of the century the General Court was forced to protect proprietary rights, and proprietor's meetings were, accordingly, formally legalized. (XI *Ply. Col. Rec.*, Laws [1623–1686], 257; I *Acts and Resolves*, 704.) Their procedure was very similar to the town meeting (II *Acts and Resolves*, 30). The principal business was, of course, the division and regulation of the common and undivided lands. For a full account see R. H. Akagi's *The Town Proprietors of the New England Colonies* (Philadelphia, 1924), pp. 51, 55–57, 63*ff.*, etc. For a list of proprietor's records, see Wright's *Report on the Custody and Condition of the Public Records*, pp. 6–8.

[3] II *Acts and Resolves*, 30.

[4] III *Acts and Resolves*, 47–48.

The first tax list under the new charter contained eighty-three towns: Suffolk County, thirteen; Essex, seventeen; Plymouth, six; Barnstable, seven; Middlesex, seventeen; Hampshire, seven; York, four; Bristol, eight; Nantucket, one; and Martha's Vineyard, three.[1] Tiverton (Bristol County) was included — the first town incorporated under the new régime.[2] If to this list is added Dunstable, Deerfield and Woodstock (described in this period as "frontier towns"),[3] and Brook-

[1] I *Acts and Resolves*, 177–180 (September 14, 1694). The history of the counties in Massachusetts is comparatively unimportant in relation to the towns. The Colony was not divided into counties until 1643 (II *Mass. Col. Rec.* 38), at which time four "shires" were created — Essex, Middlesex, Suffolk, and Norfolk. Prior to that time, military divisions appear to have been known as "regiments" — "The proposition of choosing deputies for a yeare, & transacting and preparing all things for the General Court amongst the three regiments," etc. (I *Mass. Col. Rec.* 340). In its original condition, Norfolk County consisted of six towns — Salisbury, Haverhill, Hampton, Exeter, Dover and Strawberry Bank. But the latter four towns were "taken off" when New Hampshire separated from Massachusetts in 1680, the remaining towns were added to Essex and "old Norfolk" ceased to exist. (V *Mass. Col. Rec.* 264; Massachusetts, Secretary of the Commonwealth, *Abstract of the Census of Massachusetts, 1860* [G. W. Chase, ed., Boston, 1863], p. 230.) Various additional counties were incorporated as occasion demanded: Hampshire, 1662 (IV *Mass. Col. Rec.* [pt. 2] 52); Barnstable, Bristol and Plymouth, 1685 (Brigham, *Compact with the Charter and Laws*, p. 295); Nantucket and Dukes, 1695 (I *Acts and Resolves*, 216); Worcester, 1731 (II *Acts and Resolves*, 584); Berkshire, 1761 (IV *Acts and Resolves*, 432); Norfolk (new), 1793 (Massachusetts, General Court, *The General Laws of Massachusetts* [1781–1822], 2 vols. [Boston, 1823], ch. 72 [1792], p. 423, hereafter cited *General Laws*); Hampden, 1812 (*ibid.*, II, ch. 137 [1811], p. 306); Franklin, 1811 (*ibid.*, II, ch. 61 [1811], p. 289). See also the article on "County Government in Massachusetts" in the *Bulletins for the Constitutional Convention* (1917–1918), prepared under the direction of the General Court (2 vols., Boston, 1918), I, no. 8.

[2] I *Acts and Resolves*, 174.

[3] As early as 1645 inhabitants of "Concord, Sudberry and Dedham" (II *Mass. Col. Rec.* 122) were placed under certain restrictions because of their remoteness. In 1669 the term "frontier touns" is used (IV *Mass. Col. Rec.* [pt. 2] 439). It was a common practice during the Indian wars, and the early years of the Province (I *Acts and Resolves*, 194, 293, 402, etc.).

field and Worcester, which had been abandoned, there would have been at that time eighty-eight towns existing in Massachusetts.[1] By 1715 some twenty-three new communities were incorporated. Forty-five were added from 1715 to 1742, and five more by 1757. From that year until 1768, thirty-eight were added, and by 1780 the number was increased by forty more.[2] The great unevenness is due largely to the colonial wars that tended to make new settlements a perilous venture. The years succeeding the Peace of Utrecht (1713) were the first of comparative quiet that the colony had enjoyed since the outbreak of King Philip's War in 1675,[3] and under the turbulent conditions of border warfare, it was at times quite all that could be expected if the older settlements were maintained. So serious, indeed, did the situation become, that the General Court passed rigid legislation to prevent the desertion of frontier towns under penalty of forfeiture of estates held there, or in lieu of this, a heavy fine.[4]

But settlements were extended in a very different way from the old colonial method. The period brought

For a full account see F. J. Turner's "The First Official Frontier of the Massachusetts Bay" (*Col. Soc. of Mass. Pub.*, XVII, 250–271).

[1] W. H. Whitmore, "On the Origin of the Names of Towns in Massachusetts," *Mass. Hist. Soc. Proc.*, XII, 395.

[2] See I, II, III, IV, V *Acts and Resolves*, Index — Towns: Acts incorporating. Because some of the earlier communities were incorporated by order or resolution, it is necessary to supplement these volumes with others in the series, especially IX (1708–1719), X (1720–1725), XIII (1741–1747). The best list covering this period chronologically is compiled by J. B. Felt in his "Statistics of Towns in Massachusetts" (*Amer. Stat. Assn. Coll.*, I, 31–57). The confusion of towns, districts, plantations, and at times "reincorporations" makes accurate figures difficult.

[3] S. E. Morison, "A Generation of Expansion and Inflation in Massachusetts History, 1713–1741," *Col. Soc. of Mass. Pub.*, XIX, 271–272.

[4] I *Acts and Resolves*, 194, 402.

commercial and industrial expansion[1] and with it the element of speculation became for the first time of paramount importance in Massachusetts land policies. Few of the original grantees occupied the territory assigned to them. Land allotments in the nature of military awards for service in the various wars of the period became common. Such were the famous Narragansett Townships — a bonus for service in King Philip's War — for which the General Court made numerous grants.[2] In addition were the equally prominent Canada Townships, even more generously allowed in recognition of public service in the Canadian expedition of 1690. Petitions of claimants were steadily filed,[3] and townships six miles square were unstintingly voted, the grantees being only obliged to "bring forward the Settlement . . . in as Regular and defensible a manner, as the Situation and Circumstances of the Places will admit of." More specifically they were required to construct certain houses of a prescribed size, to establish an orthodox minister, and to build a meeting-house — all within a period of five years.[4] The need of border defense, moreover, determined the policy of "Frontier Townships," resulting in additional tiers of towns in the western and northern sections;[5] and there were nine townships and an additional tract auctioned off in 1762 — for over sixteen thousand pounds, each to be occupied within five years by sixty settlers with prescribed dwellings, and seven acres of land well cleared — "brought to English Grass

[1] Morison, "A Generation of Expansion and Inflation in Massachusetts," p. 272.
[2] XI *Acts and Resolves*, 325, 378, 769, 772, 796, etc.
[3] XII *Acts and Resolves*, 140, 141, 144, etc.
[4] *Ibid.*, p. 142.
[5] *Ibid.*, pp. 225, 232, 234, 306–307.

or Plowed," with the customary minister established in each community.[1] The process was compelled by economic or defensive policies that quite upset the cautious procedure of the previous century.[2]

The establishment or recognition of districts, plantations, precincts, parishes, villages and peculiars that so frequently marked the various stages to complete corporate status that the term town signified, was a regular procedure in provincial administration. The political features that distinguished these numerous areas are not, however, always easy to determine. As has been pointed out, even in the days of the Colony there were many instances of groups of individuals occupying loosely defined territories who received a partial corporate status, but that were nevertheless restricted in function and were not allowed representation in the General Court.[3] This practice was continued throughout the provincial period and has, indeed, come down to our day;[4] but the province government provided a variety of terms, some unknown to either colonial or contemporary law, which served to describe with more or less distinctness the political units found useful to a rapidly developing community.

[1] XVII *Acts and Resolves*, 148–149, 242–244.

[2] For excellent accounts of the movement, see L. K. Mathews' *The Expansion of New England* (Boston, 1909), pp. 82–85, and Akagi's *Town Proprietors of the New England Colonies, passim.*

[3] The colonial term for such a unit was "plantation." See *supra*, p. 74, note 1.

[4] Aside from occasional fire, water and improvement districts, Massachusetts makes no attempt to organize units less than a town today. Its many villages have a distinct social continuity but no separate political status. This, however, is not true in other New England states where minor political units of a quasi-corporate character are frequent. See F. G. Bates' "Village Government in New England" (*Amer. Pol. Sc. Rev.*, VI, no. 3, 367–385).

First, there was, of course, the town, representing complete municipal status involving all privileges of local autonomy known to the law, as well as the right of full representation in the General Court.

Second, there was the district, apparently identical with the town so far as local government was concerned, but without the privilege of sending a separate delegate to the General Court. Thomas Hutchinson tells that when a bill was passed by both houses to make the district of Danvers a town, there were objections from certain members of the council for:

By the king's instructions to the governor, he was strictly charged to consent to no act for making a new town, unless, by a clause in it, there should be a restraint of this power of sending representatives; and Danvers, a few years before, when it had been separated from the town of Salem, was made a district and not a town, because districts had not this power.[1]

Third in the hierarchy was the plantation, a still more restricted political division that seems to have been used

[1] *The History of Massachusetts*, 3 vols. (Boston and London, 1764–1828), III, 53. The act erecting Danvers into a separate district reads (III *Acts and Resolves*, 599): the "inhabitants . . . . shall do the duties that are required and enjo[y] [i]ned on other towns, and enjoy all the powers, privile[d]ges and immunities that towns in this province by law enjoy, except that of seperately chusing and sending one or more representatives to represent them at the general assembly." But an act of June, 1757, subsequently incorporated Danvers with all the powers, privileges and immunities that the "inhabitants of the towns within this province are or by law ought to be vested or endowed with." For the protest in England to this practice see IV *Acts and Resolves*, 5 (note). Likewise when Palmer was erected from a plantation to a district (1752), it was "invested with all the powers privile[d]ge[s] and immuni[ni]ties that the inhabitants of towns within this province are or by law ought to be vested with: *saving* only in the choice of a representative: which, it is represented, said inhabitants are not at present desireous of" (III *Acts and Resolves*, 598). The purpose of establishing such a unit was generally remoteness from a church or school. There are many examples.

primarily to provide taxing machinery for groups outside of regularly incorporated areas. Full regulations were subsequently passed to provide for their fiscal activities.[1]

Fourth in this medley came the parish or precinct — apparently (at least in the later provincial period) interchangeable terms. In the early days of the colony, both ecclesiastical and civil boundaries were alike denominated by the word town, and throughout the records, parishes were not mentioned as ecclesiastical subdivisions. But during the early provincial period the nomenclature changed, and town, precinct, parish and district were used with much indiscrimination for both ecclesiastical and civil purposes. About the time of the Revolution, however, precinct and parish took on a more strictly ecclesiastical meaning and were clearly distinguished by the court as "corporations established solely for the purpose of maintaining public worship," with their powers strictly limited to that object. "They may raise money," the court continued, "for building and keeping in repair their meetinghouse, and supporting their minister, but for no other purpose. A town is a civil and political corporation established for municipal purposes. They may both subsist together in the same territory, and be composed of the same persons."[2]

And lastly there were those obscure units known throughout the records as "peculiars." This term seems to have been common to other New England states and

---

[1] V *Acts and Resolves*, 254–256 (March 6, 1773). For a summary of such powers and duties see Samuel Freeman's *The Town Officer* (8th ed., Boston, 1815), pp. 254–257.

[2] Milford *v.* Godfrey (1822), I *Pick.* (Mass.), 91. The matter is well discussed in Edward Buck's *Massachusetts Ecclesiastical Law* (Boston, 1866), ch. 1.

signified a piece of land not included in any plantation or civil corporate unit. In English ecclesiastical law, a peculiar was a parish or church independent of the ordinary and subject only to the metropolitan, and this use may have accounted for the appearance of the term in America.[1] Like the plantation, it seems to have been largely used to assure the taxation for state and county purposes of isolated individuals or small groups that were not under a local jurisdiction. In his *Travels Through the Northern Parts of the United States* (1807–1808)[2] E. A. Kendall speaks of "Precincts or peculiars ... ordered to be rated at or in certain towns, and in such cases are rated and governed by the town." An act of the General Assembly of Connecticut (1737) outlining the duties of "listers" includes "all peculiars, or lands not as yet laid within the bounds of any town,"[3] and similar provision in a Vermont statute describes them in almost identical terms.[4] So far as their political privileges were concerned they seem to have been exceedingly slight — in Massachusetts they were mentioned in the

[1] See *Judicial and Statutory Definitions of Words and Phrases* (edited by editorial staff of National Reporter System, 8 vols., St. Paul, 1904), VI, 5256, and *Bouvier's Law Dictionary* (R. F. Rawle, ed., 3 vols., 3d rev., 8th ed., Kansas City and St. Paul, 1914), I, 712.

[2] 3 vols., N. Y., 1809, p. 17.

[3] Connecticut, General Assembly, *The Public Records of the Colony of Connecticut* (1636–1776) (C. J. Hoadly, ed., 15 vols., Hartford, 1850–1890), VIII (1874), 133. A few years before (1720) the General Assembly had enacted (*ibid.*, VI, 210): "That for the future, the town of Coventry send their list to this Assembly as other towns in this government do, that they may bear their proportion of the publick charge of the Colony; and that Mr. John Read, who dwells between Fairfield and Danbury, be likewise annually listed, as a peculiar to Danbury, for his polls and whole estate and farm or manour at Lonetime there."

[4] William Slade, Jr. (compiler), *Vermont State Papers* (Middlebury, 1823), p. 297.

regulation of common lands, and were authorized to choose fence viewers and field drivers.[1]

The natural order of political development was from the plantation, through the district to the town, but there were many variations in the process. At times a grant (frequently six or eight miles square) would be made to a group of prospective inhabitants "providing sixty families settle thereon" within a limited time, and a committee would be appointed by the Council to manage the settlement "until it shall become a town";[2] or upon petition of the inhabitants of part of an established community to be given an independent status, the area would be erected at once into a township.[3] Often an additional "precinct" was set off to facilitate "the worship of God and Support of a learned & Orthodox ministry among themselves,"[4] but in all other respects was to be considered as part of the older settlement.[5] The General Court might refuse the request for a separate status as in the case of Swansea,[6] as it could "see [no] reason as yet to Divide Swanzey into two Distinct

---

[1] I *Acts and Resolves*, 65, 138, 333.

[2] XXI *Acts and Resolves*, 712, 717 (Tiverton).

[3] *Ibid.*, pp. 697, 701 (Framingham), 694, 823 (Kittery), 794 (Swansea).

[4] *Ibid.*, p. 677 (Plymouth).

[5] *Ibid.*, pp. 680 (West Springfield), 741 (Roxbury), 747, 762 (Sudbury). Many of these changes are shown more completely through an examination of their legislative history, but the journals of the period are not always easily accessible. The Massachusetts Historical Society has published the journals of the House of Representatives in nine volumes for the years 1715–1731 (Boston, 1919–1928). They are carefully indexed and an examination will yield many references to settlement, representation, divisions, regulations, taxes, boundaries, etc., especially in the later volumes. For the years 1730 to 1776 the file of the Division of Archives of the Commonwealth is practically complete, and a guide to other depositories is found in W. C. Ford's "Bibliography of the Massachusetts House Journals, 1715–1776" (*Col. Soc. of Mass. Coll.*, IV, 201–289).

[6] XXI *Acts and Resolves*, 796.

Towns," or after numerous hearings grant the petition and, as in the days of the colony, assign a name to the community: "*Ordered* that the Village or District now called Manamoit be erected into a Township & the Town named Chatham."[1] But among the first acts of the Provincial Congress that met in Watertown in July, 1775, was an order that every district in the colony should henceforth be a town "to all intents [*and purposes*] whatsoever."[2]

Town government in the eighteenth century shows no fundamental change from the procedure of the charter period. The reports are more complete, warrants begin to appear in the records, bringing with them an air of precision and stability, and becoming increasingly elaborate as the century progresses.[3] They are issued under

[1] *Ibid.*, pp. 795, 806.

[2] V *Acts and Resolves*, 420.

[3] *Braintree Town Records*, p. 55:

"Braintrey, ye 26 November 1703.

The Inhabitants of Braintrey aforesaid being Regulerly assembled by warrant (under the selectmens hands) to the constable Richard Thayer
they then voted Captain John Wilson Esq Moderator for the day.

The warrant was as followeth: —

To Richard Thayer, Constable of Braintree.

Whereas there has been some dissatisfaction and disturbance in the Town respecting mr. Fisks maintenance, there being some of our neighbours who think that that vote which settles 90 Pound [per] annum upon him was not so legal & orderly made & to prevent any further Trouble in the Town thereabout we think it needful that ye Town should meet — these are therefore to require you in her majesties name to warn all ye Freeholders & other Inhabitants of this Town qualified as ye Law directs to voate in Town affaires to meet at ye meeting house on fryday the 26 of this instant november at Ten of ye clock in the forenoon to consider of this matter & to agree upon a sum for mr. Fisks maintenance for this present year the greatest part of which allready past and to settle a salary for him for the futar if ye Town shall so agree when they come together, given under our hands this 11th day of november. 1703.

Samuel Penniman ⎫
Theophilus Curtis ⎬ Selectmen"
Dependance French ⎭

the hands of the selectmen or of the town clerk by order
of the selectmen, and are usually addressed to the constables.[1] The warning is to the "freeholders and other
inhabitance"[2] or merely to the "Inhabetence of said
Town"[3] or perhaps to the "Inhabitants and propria-
tors"[4] — definite announcement of unrestricted attendance and participation. It is frequently issued in "his
Majesty's name," but at times no authority is cited, and
in later years when the difficulties with England became
acute, the phrase is formally altered to suit the new conditions.[5] The place designated for the meeting is the "Publick Meeting house"[6] or simply "the Town House,"[7] but
at times circumstances required other arrangements and
private dwellings were even used when the occasion demanded it.[8]

Apparently these eighteenth century gatherings themselves were not (like their modern prototypes) always
according to expectations. The General Court set aside
a town meeting in Freetown because "some persons who
paid no rates, and some in their nonage" were allowed
to vote.[9] In Watertown, when the moderator called for

---

[1] Town of Dudley, *Town Records of Dudley* (1732–1794) (2 vols., Paw-
tucket [Mass.], 1893), p. 10; *Watertown Town Records*, III, *passim*.

[2] *Ibid.*, III, 145.

[3] *Dudley Town Records*, 10.

[4] *Dedham Town Records*, V, 328; Town of Lancaster, *The Early Records
of the Town of Lancaster* (1643–1725) (H. S. Norse, ed., Lancaster [Mass.],
1884), p. 208.

[5] "October 12, 1776. The style of notice is changed. The freeholders,
etc., are notified and warned, in the name of the Government of the people
of this State, to meet," etc. (M. de W. Freeland [ed.], *The Records of Oxford,
Massachusetts* (1630–1894) (Albany [N. Y.], 1894), p. 367.

[6] *Watertown Town Records*, III, 109.

[7] Report of the Record Commissioners, *Boston Town Records* (1700–
1728), III (1882), 158.

[8] *Dudley Town Records*, 10, 44.

[9] XXI *Acts and Resolves*, 529–530.

a division "the negative refused to move up the gallery" to be counted,[1] and in Great Barrington, a majority of those present would no longer continue with the business under consideration.[2] It seems, indeed, that legislators of the eighteenth century were kept reasonably busy validating the irregular practices of town meetings, but in spite of such technical difficulties, "consent of the governed" was a very real element in local legislation. The records of Boston (although the largest town in the colony, and therefore, perhaps, more formal than in less important communities) offer the clearest examples of well-regulated procedure.

The March meeting (that is, the "annual meeting") was called in the morning at Faneuil Hall. It was opened by prayer, the warrant calling the meeting read, and frequently "Sundry laws" were communicated to the people. A moderator was chosen, followed by a clerk, after which the town proceeded to the choice of seven selectmen and the numerous minor officers. If, however, the meeting was for the purpose of choosing representatives to the General Court, this duty was frequently undertaken at the opening of the session. When a vote was ordered, the inhabitants were "directed to withdraw" whereupon they returned to place their ballots in the hands of the selectmen who legally received only "such as are unfolded." The meeting adjourned at noon to meet later in the day — usually three o'clock — at which time instructions might be voted to the town representatives and action taken on articles in the warrant.[3]

---

[1] *Ibid.*, p. 822.
[2] *Ibid.*, p. 464.
[3] *Boston Town Records* (1770–1777), 110–114, 128, 139, 150, 166. See also *Braintree Town Records*, 174, 468, 469, 475; *Dudley Town Records*,

A contemporary writer carries assurance that such in a general way were the formalities throughout the colony:

The selectmen, by their own authority, or upon the application of a certain number of townsmen, issue a warrant for the calling of a town-meeting. The warrant mentions the business to be engaged in, and no other can be legally executed. The inhabitants are warned to attend; and they that are present, though not a quarter or tenth of the whole, have a right to proceed. They choose a president by the name of Moderator, who regulates the proceedings of the meeting. Each individual has an equal liberty of delivering his opinion, and is not liable to be silenced or brow beaten by a richer or greater townsman than himself. Every freeman or freeholder, as the business regards either the freeholders in particular or the freemen at large, gives his vote or not, and for or against as he pleases; and each vote weighs equally; whether that of the highest or lowest inhabitant. At these town meetings the people are used to debate and conclude upon instructions to their representatives respecting matters before, or likely to come before the general court — freely to express their sentiments regarding public transactions — to agree upon the choice of a minister, and the salary they shall give him; upon building or repairing the meeting-house, and upon a variety of other interesting matters, which concern the exercise of their civil or sacred privileges.[1]

The part that the Massachusetts towns played in the Revolutionary War is well known.[2] The records set forth almost every political principle that would tend to relieve outraged local sentiment. When the General Court

156, 157, 159–161; Town of Brookline, *Muddy River and Brookline Town Records* (1634–1838) (By a committee of the Town, Brookline, 1875), pp. 244–246.

[1] William Gordon, *The History of the Rise, Progress, and Establishment, of the Independence of the United States of America* (3 vols., New York, 1789), I, 262–263.

[2] H. A. Cushing, "Political Activity of Massachusetts Towns During the Revolution," *Amer. Hist. Soc. Ann. Rep.* (1895), pp. 105–113.

voted (May 1, 1776) that on and after June 1 all political authority was to be performed in the name of "the government and people of the Mass[e][a]chusetts Bay, in New England," [1] June meetings in many of the towns voted with enthusiasm to sustain a declaration of independence. A town meeting in Taunton announced that if the American congress should declare independence of Great Britain, the inhabitants "with their lives and fortunes, do solemnly engage to support them in the same." Scituate, Methuen, Hanover, Tyringham, Alfred, Norwich, Palmer, and Acton, as well as many other communities gave similar assurance of allegiance, often justifying their position by a studied statement of grievances. In forming the committees of correspondence and safety, in voting bounties for volunteer service in the army, and in providing arms and ammunition they became the core of military activities.[2] Nor was their significance lost upon the mother country. "The town meeting at Boston," wrote a proponent of the king, "is the hot-bed of sedition. It is there that all their dangerous insurrections are engendered; it is there that the flame of discord and rebellion was first lighted up and disseminated over the Provinces." [3]

The long list of evidence presented by Lord North to the House of Commons in March, 1774, was composed of one hundred and nine "exhibits" in condemnation of

[1] V Acts and Resolves, 485; H. B. Dawson, Declaration of Independence by the Colony of Massachusetts Bay (Letter to Hon. Luther Bradish, Jan. 7, 1862, New York Hist. Soc., 1865[?]).

[2] Ebenezer Force, American Archives (6 vols., Washington [D. C.], 1837–1846), 4th series, VI, 698–707; J. A. Quincy, Municipal History of the Town and City of Boston (Boston, 1852), p. 18.

[3] "The Sam Adams Regiments in the Town of Boston," Atlantic Monthly, XII, 601 (note).

political conditions in Massachusetts,[1] and in spite of petitions from "several Natives of North *America*" (citizens of Boston)[2] against the rigors of the Boston Port Bill the measure passed the Commons on March 25, was announced as approved by the Lords on the thirtieth and the next day received the royal assent.[3] Events moved quickly. On March 28 a report was received from the committee of the whole asking permission to bring in a bill for "the better regulating the Government of the Province of the *Massachusetts Bay in North America.*" It was presented at the session of April 15. Action was delayed until May 2, when a second petition from America failed to move either Lords or Commons to leniency, and the lower house gave the famous act its affirmation — sixty-four to one hundred and thirty-nine. It was approved by the Lords, and received the royal assent on May 20.[4]

If the British government had heretofore shown a lack of interest in local politics, it evinced a detailed knowledge in the Massachusetts Government Act. After providing that the letters patent issued by William and Mary should be of no effect after August 1, 1774, it proceeded to detailed grievances and penalties. It outlined, briefly, the existing legislation of the General Court pertaining to local government in the towns, and asserted a gross misuse of its provisions. Accusations were made that contrary to both the purpose and the letter of the

[1] Great Britain, House of Commons, *The Journals of the House of Commons* (Nov. 1772-Sept. 1774), XXXIV, 541–543.

[2] *Ibid.*, p. 595.

[3] *Ibid.*, pp. 612, 615.

[4] *Journals of the House of Commons*, XXXIV, 601, 649, 697, 776; Great Britain, House of Lords, *Journal of the House of Lords*, XXXIV (1774–1776), 182–184, 192, 209.

law, undue advantage had been taken of the power to call town meetings, and the people had been misled into treating of matters of the most general concern, and of perpetuating their actions in dangerous and unwarranted resolutions. To remedy this condition it was enacted that on and after August 1, 1774, no town meeting was to be called by any lawful authority without written permission from the Governor specifying the business to be undertaken, and even the annual meeting was confined to the election of town officers, unless permission to consider other matters was first obtained.[1]

While the Massachusetts Government Act was received with greater alarm than the Boston Port Bill — for it affected not merely a municipality but an entire province — in practice the legislation appeared to have

[1] 14, *George 3*, ch. 45: "And whereas, by several Acts of the General Court, which have been from Time to Time enacted and passed within the said Province, For Freeholders and Inhabitants of the several Townships, Districts, and Precincts, qualified, as is therein expressed, are authorized to assemble together, annually, or occasionally, upon Notice given, in such Manner as the said Acts direct, for the Choice of Select Men, Constables, and other Officers, and for the making and agreeing upon such necessary Rules, Orders, and Bye-laws, for the directing, managing, and ordering, the prudential Affairs of such Townships, Districts, and Precincts, and for other Purposes: And whereas a great abuse has been made of the Power of calling such Meetings, and the Inhabitants have, contrary to the Design of their Institution, been misled to treat upon Matters of the most general Concern, and to pass many dangerous and unwarrantable Resolves: For Remedy whereof, be it enacted, That from and after the said first Day of *August* one thousand seven hundred and seventy-four, no Meeting shall be called by the Select Men, or at the Request of any number of Freeholders of any Township, District, or Precinct, without the leave of the Governor, or in his Absence, of the Lieutenant-governor, in Writing, expressing the special Business of the said Meeting, first had and obtained, except the annul Meeting in the Months of *March* or *May*, for Choice of Select Men, Constables, and other Officers . . . . and that no other Matter shall be treated of at such Meetings . . . . except the Business expressed in the leave given by the Governor, or, in his Absence, by the Lieutenant-governor."

little effect, and the towns continued to play a most active part in the revolutionary government.[1] The practices of local government seem to have been carried on in much the same manner as always, and aside from vehement entries concerning the conduct of the mother country, the dropping of his Majesty's name from the warrant, and the enlarged space given to martial actions in coöperation with the General Court and Continental Congress, the records show no essential differences from those of more normal times. It was not until the adoption of the constitution of the Commonwealth (1780) that complete opportunity was given to dispose officially of the vexing heresies of British legislation, and the event was made the occasion for casting in hard legal phrases long-accepted but recently denied principles of local autonomy.

Reference to the "people" was profuse.[2] The traditional forms of local control and the political integrity of the community were given final emphasis — indeed, in the struggle over ratification some of the objecting towns apparently regarded themselves as distinct bodies politic, and passed resolutions to the effect that they would accept the constitution without their favorite amendments provided two-thirds of the people so voted.[3] The town meeting was no longer held in jeopardy nor was it denied expression in matters of "general concern":

The people have a right, in an orderly and peaceable

---

[1] David Ramsey, *The History of the American Revolution* (2 vols., Philadelphia, 1789), I, 106. In Boston the annual town meeting was adjourned from time to time, and meetings held under this method until March, 1775 (Nathaniel Dearborn, *Boston Notions* [Boston, 1848], p. 148).

[2] *General Laws*, Constitution of Massachusetts, I, 12–40.

[3] S. E. Morison, "The Struggle Over the Adoption of the Constitution of Massachusetts, 1780," *Mass. Hist. Soc. Proc.*, L, 397.

manner, to assemble to consult upon the common good; give instructions to their representatives; and to request of the legislative body, by the way of addresses, petitions, or remonstrances, redress of the wrongs done them, and of the grievances they suffer.[1]

March 23, 1786 the legislature passed its first general act "for regulating Towns, setting forth their Power, and for the Choice of Town-Officers, and for repealing all laws heretofore made for that purpose." It replaced the town act of 1692 as the latter had replaced the older regulations of the colony, but collectively these documents form a series of local charters that deserve high rank in the political records of American institutional history.

The enactment of 1786 [2] commenced by confirming all existing town boundaries and providing that they be renewed once every five years. The method of "perambulation" was described in detail. The annual town meeting was to be held in March or April; to be notified by the constables of the town — "or such others as the Selectmen shall appoint." The meeting is directed to choose a moderator, a clerk, "three, five, seven or nine able and discreet persons of good conversation . . . to be selectmen or townsmen," three or more assessors, two or more fence viewers, a treasurer, surveyors of highways, surveyors of lumber, wardens, tithingmen, "and other usual town-officers," and the persons chosen were to be summoned by the constable to appear before the clerk to take the oath prescribed by law.[3]

[1] *General Laws*, I, 16.

[2] *Ibid.*, ch. 75, pp. 250–255.

[3] It seems that even at this time there was difficulty securing men to serve in town offices. A fine of thirty shillings was imposed for those failing to appear to take the oath of office. Nor could anyone be compelled to

Provisions for calling the town meeting were carefully prescribed — many of them a repetition of the first regulations of the Province. The warrant was to issue through the selectmen to the constables "or such other person as shall be appointed for the purpose," but the precise manner of summoning was to be agreed upon by the town. When ten or more freeholders signified that they desired a certain matter inserted in the warrant, the selectmen were required to insert it, and no question might receive legal action unless previously mentioned in the warrant. Should the selectmen unreasonably refuse to call a meeting, ten or more freeholders might apply to a justice of the peace within the county, who was authorized by the act to issue an appropriate warrant directed to the constables or, in the absence of such officers, to one of the freeholders signing the petition.[1]

At every town meeting it was required that a moderator be first chosen, who should "be thereby empowered to manage and regulate the business of the meeting." Should a vote be questioned by seven members "the moderator shall make the vote certain, by polling the voters, or such other way, as the meeting shall desire." No one was to speak without leave or act disorderly, under penalty of a fine; and should such a person persist in misbehavior he might be "put into the stocks, cage, or some other place of confinement, and there be detained for the space of three hours, unless the town-

serve for two years consecutively; nor, in the case of the constable or collector, within seven years of his former service (*General Laws*, I, 251). A writer of a few years later states: "Many, and in some places, nearly all town offices, are considered of very small importance, and it is with difficulty that any suitable person can be persuaded to accept of them" (Abijah Bigelow, *The Voters' Guide*, Leominster [Mass.], 1807, p. 86).

[1] *General Laws*, I, 252–253.

meeting shall sooner adjourn or dissolve." Towns were definitely empowered to grant and assess money for necessary charges; to make by-laws "for the directing, managing and ordering the prudential affairs"[1] and after a long hundred and fifty years of doubt the inhabitants were formally declared to be "a body politic and corporate" and as such capable of suing and being sued, while all places formerly known as districts were either definitely converted into towns,[2] or declared entitled to all privileges under the act.

[1] It is provided of course, that such laws be in no way repugnant to the "general laws of the Government" and that thev shall receive the approbation of the court of general sessions of the peace in the county (*General Laws*, I, 254).

[2] *Ibid.*, pp. 254, 255.

# V

## THE OLD TOWN AND THE NEW
## SOCIAL ORDER

IT was under the framework provided by the act of 1786 that the local governments of the Commonwealth continued political life.[1] Excluding the province of Maine, they numbered close to three hundred communities, with a population steadily approaching the four hundred thousand mark.[2] Thirty years after the

[1] *General Laws*, I, ch. 75. Hereafter the laws will be cited as follows: *The Revised Statutes of the Commonwealth of Massachusetts* (Boston, 1836), as *Revised Statutes; The General Statutes of the Commonwealth of Massachusetts* (1860), 2d ed., Boston, 1873, as *General Statutes; The Public Statutes of the Commonwealth of Massachusetts* (1881), Boston, 1882, as *Public Statutes; The Revised Laws of the Commonwealth of Massachusetts* (1901), Boston, 1902, as *Revised Laws; The General Laws of the Commonwealth of Massachusetts* (1919), 2 vols., Boston, 1920, as *Genl. Laws.* The session laws of 1780–1838 as *Laws of* —; of 1838–1915, *Acts of* —; 1915–1919, *General Acts of* — or *Special Acts of* — ; 1919 to date, *Acts of* —.

[2] The state census of 1765 mentioned 184 towns within the present limits of Massachusetts. Sixteen other towns or districts were incorporated before the close of the year. This made a total of 200 communities exclusive of Maine whose three counties (York, Cumberland, and Lincoln) are listed with 20 (*Abstract of the Census of Massachusetts* [1860], pp. 251, 259, 260). Felt lists the total number of districts, towns and plantations in 1784 as 372, including 89 in the province of Maine, making 283 in Massachusetts proper ("Statistics of Population in Massachusetts," *Amer. Stat. Assn. Coll.*, I (pt. 2), 166). Chickering estimates "incorporated towns and districts" (exclusive of Maine) in 1790, as 265 (Jesse Chickering, *A Statistical View of the Population of Massachusetts* [1765–1840], Boston, 1846, p. 40). This coincides very closely with the returns made under the first federal census of 1790 (United States, Bureau of the Census, *Heads of Families at the First Census of the United States* [1790], *Washington*, 1908; *Massachusetts*, pp. 9–11). Population statistics (exclusive of Maine) are given as follows: the census of 1765 gives close to 244, 149 (*op. cit.*, 251); Felt cites 350,000 in 1784 (*op. cit.*, 170); Chickering quotes 378, 787 for 1790 (*op. cit.*, 34), and

adoption of the constitution, there were still no cities in the State.[1] As late as 1820, Boston and Salem were the only towns exceeding twelve thousand inhabitants, while eighty-nine per cent of the people were distributed throughout the remaining communities, very few of which exceeded three thousand population.[2] For the years 1790 to 1800, the State gain was only a little over eleven per cent, and while the succeeding decade maintained an equal growth, the ten years preceding 1820 failed to keep up the record and showed a somewhat lesser increase.[3] At the same time, John Bacon listed three hundred and six towns in the Commonwealth with an aggregate population of slightly over half a million [4] — close to sixty-five per cent increase in communities and fifty per cent in population over a little more than half a century — on the whole, a well-balanced development avoiding undue congestion and requiring few political alterations. Local government could still be described in language that would have been quite applicable a hundred years before.[5]

the first decennial census of the Commonwealth (*Abstract of the Census of the Commonwealth of Massachusetts* [1855], Boston, 1857, p. 195) cites 352,000 for the year 1775.

[1] In a recent opinion the court said (Opinion of the Justices to the Senate (1918), 229 *Mass.* 609): "The fundamental and real distinction between the town and the city organization is that in the former all the qualified inhabitants meet together to deliberate and vote as individuals, each in his own right, while in the latter all municipal functions are performed by deputies. The one is direct, the other is representative."

[2] H. G. Wadlin, "The Growth of Cities in Massachusetts," *Amer. Stat. Assn. Coll.*, new series, II, no. 13, pp. 159, 161.

[3] *Abstract of the Census of Massachusetts* (1860), p. 289.

[4] John Bacon, *The Town Officers Guide* (Haverhill [Mass.], 1825), pp. 375–385.

[5] Jared Sparks, "Observations by Jared Sparks on the Government of Towns in Massachusetts," *Johns Hopkins University Studies in Historical and Political Science*, XVI, 579–611.

At no time, moreover, had the town been more prominent.[1] The famous Chapter Five in de Tocqueville's *Democracy in America* compelled attention to an institution that had, except during trying experiences with English sovereigns, been received as a matter of course since its inception two centuries before. It was the middle of the Jackson era when a large part of the people were deeply impressed with a new democracy, and sought feverishly to realize practical applications of its doctrines. Everywhere there were tendencies to rivet attention to politics. Public high schools increased within the Commonwealth from three established between 1821 and 1830 to forty between 1851 and 1855, while political science and United States history were given a prominence in school curricula heretofore unprecedented.[2] Competition among authors of texts in government — previously an untouched field — became increasingly active, and publishers possessed enough confidence in the popularity of their books to reissue them frequently.[3] "Town officers' guides" and local gazetteers were numerous — several running through many editions. Even the local histories of the State, until this

[1] Until this time town government in Massachusetts had received only the most cursory attention from students of history and politics. Even as late as 1832 Jared Sparks wrote that "no books treat of this matter" and Alexis de Tocqueville in a letter dated December 2, 1831, stated: "Le seul ouvrage dans lequel j'ai pu puiser jusqu'à présent quelques lumineres sur la marche pratique de votre système communal, est intitulé *Town-officer*. [Undoubtedly Bacon's *Town Officer's Guide, op. cit.*] Il m'avait été indiqué par M. Quincy, le-President de l'université de Cambridge" (H. B. Adams, "Jared Sparks and Alexis de Tocqueville," *Johns Hopkins University Studies in Historical and Political Science*, XVI, 570, 572).

[2] A. J. Inglis, *The Rise of the High School in Massachusetts* (New York, 1911), pp. 46, 57, 64.

[3] Edgar Dawson, "Beginnings of Political Education," *Historical Outlook*, IX, 440.

time generally confined to the older towns, more than doubled in the years between 1830 and 1845, and the increase continued undiminished until the Civil War.[1]

The town meeting was, moreover, at its highest point of development. The class that represented extreme popularism had only begun to supplant the veterans of the colonial and early federal periods.[2] The vital, daily interests of the people were still bound by the geographic area of the community, and happiness, as well as economic success, were to be had, if at all, through the conscientious regulation of town life. It was, indeed, within the town meeting that the "roots of society were reached," and their records reflect vindictiveness, petulance and ignorance as faithfully as sympathy, temperance and wisdom. For here was no "church of saints" or "metropolis of patriots" but an open democracy where every human feeling found expression.[3]

But very different decades were ahead. As has been

[1] A careful examination of Jeremiah Colburn's *Bibliography of the Local History of Massachusetts* (Boston, 1871) substantiates this statement. Before 1830 there are listed about twenty-one local histories, independent of fragments, "discourses," "reviews," "sketches," and the publications of the learned societies. About half of these are cited as less than one hundred pages in length. Of eighteen towns represented, two-thirds of them were settled before 1660. But in the fifteen years between 1830 and 1845, Colburn has recorded some thirty histories representing about forty-three towns and villages. Between 1845 and 1855, twenty-one new records were added — fifteen of them over two hundred and fifty pages in length. From 1855 to 1870 the increase is maintained with a total of twenty-nine local histories published, with two listed as in manuscript form. A conservative estimate from this compilation would indicate that local histories in Massachusetts increased close to three hundred per cent between 1830 and 1869 — the date of the last town history recorded by Colburn.

[2] C. F. Adams, *Three Episodes of Massachusetts History* (2 vols., Boston, 1892), II, 967–968.

[3] R. W. Emerson, "Historical Discourse, at Concord, on the second centennial anniversary of the incorporation of the town" (September 12, 1835), *Works* (12 vols., Centenary Edition, 1903–1904), XI, 46–47.

indicated, it had taken Massachusetts a century and a half to approach (exclusive of Maine) four hundred thousand inhabitants,[1] and it was 1820 before the half million mark was passed. The increase had been both steady and moderate, and always predominantly from the Celtic and Teutonic strains that had furnished so much of the original stock.[2] But the years between 1850 and 1860 witnessed the arrival of some two million and a half immigrants to the United States. Over the same period the foreign-born population of Massachusetts increased from one hundred and sixty-four thousand to over two hundred and sixty thousand, and the tide swept up in decennial bounds until the closing of the century found close to eight hundred and fifty thousand inhabitants of foreign birth within her borders.[3] Such a condition was to require adjustments. The local political activities of New England soon experienced that "gradual withdrawal of tender consciences" — the slow harbinger of what Emerson described as the "restless, prying, conscientious criticism"[4] which, while giving

[1] United States, Bureau of the Census, *A Century of Population Growth* (1790–1900) (Washington, 1909), p. 5.

[2] Chickering, *A Statistical View of the Population of Massachusetts*, pp. 8, 40, 71. The figures are as follows:

Increase in 10 Years

| Year | Census | Increase | Per Cent | Incorporated Towns and Districts | Increase |
|------|--------|----------|----------|----------------------------------|----------|
| 1790 | 378,787 | ...... | ....... | 265 | .. |
| 1800 | 422,845 | 44,058 | 11.63133 | 279 | 14 |
| 1810 | 472,040 | 49,195 | 11.63428 | 287 | 8 |
| 1820 | 523,287 | 51,247 | 10.85649 | 301 | 14 |
| 1830 | 610,408 | 87,121 | 16.64879 | 304 | 3 |
| 1840 | 737,700 | 127,292 | 20.85359 | 309 | 5 |

[3] *A Century of Population Growth*, p. 128.

[4] R. W. Emerson, "New England Reformers," *Works*, III, 255–256.

color to the middle period, made the "forties" the outstanding "quack" decade in American history.

From the Colony to the Commonwealth the people were predominantly agricultural, but from the days of the embargo they had gradually grown away from rural activities and had commenced a steady concentration in the manufacturing centers of the east. Lowell did not exist in 1825. In 1840 it had more than twenty thousand people. Over the same period Fall River increased 328 per cent, Chelsea, 272, New Bedford, 206, Springfield, 180, Cambridge, 155, Worcester, 153, and Millbury, 134 per cent.[1] In 1810, four cotton factories were reported in Middlesex County, seventeen in Worcester, thirteen in Bristol, ten in Norfolk, and none in Berkshire — which with ten others made a total of fifty-four in the State. But twenty-seven years later, thirty-four cotton mills were cited in the county of Middlesex, seventy-four in Worcester, fifty-seven in Bristol, twenty in Hampden, thirty-two in Norfolk, and thirty-one in Berkshire — a total (including some thirty-four additional ones) of two hundred and eighty-two, marking an increase exceeding fivefold. Woolen mills numbered one hundred and ninety-two. Worcester County led with sixty-six.[2]

"Massachusetts," wrote Baron Charles Dupin to Napoleon III, "makes by *millions* the boots and shoes necessary for the new population which is developed with so much rapidity in the immense basin of the Mississippi." He called attention to the total value of the annual

[1] Chickering, *A Statistical View of the Population of Massachusetts*, pp. 44–46.

[2] J. P. Bigelow (ed.), *Statistical Tables: exhibiting the condition and products of certain branches of industry in Massachusetts, for the year ending April 1, 1837* (Boston, 1838), pp. 169, 170, 172.

products of the State for 1837 — close to $91,000,000. Thirteen years later it was well over $161,000,000 — about $150 for each inhabitant.[1] In fisheries and ship building; in the manufacture of soap, candles, shovels, spades, ploughs and iron castings statistical sheets indicate marked activities and steady growth within the Commonwealth.[2] A total of eighty-eight manufacturing and commercial towns in a score of years from 1820, achieved an aggregate increase in population exceeding seventy-nine per cent, while two hundred and thirteen agricultural towns indicated a similar gain of only eight and a half per cent.[3] On the first of June, 1855, there were some 333,000 males in the State over fifteen years of age. Of these, over thirty-six per cent were mechanics; about eighteen per cent laborers; and but seventeen per cent, farmers.[4] There was, moreover, a great falling off in the incorporation of new communities at the very time that the influx of population was beginning to be felt. Between 1765 and 1790, sixty-five new towns were established. But from 1800 to 1810 there were eight; from 1810 to 1820, fourteen; from 1820 to 1830, three; from 1830 to 1840, five; and for fifty years the new municipalities had been due almost wholly to the division of old towns previously incorporated.[5]

[1] *The Baron Dupin's Report to the Emperor of the French upon the Progress in the Arts and Sciences in Massachusetts* (preface and supplement by E. H. Derby) (Boston, 1865), pp. 46–47.

[2] Bigelow (ed.), *Statistical Tables*, pp. 169–202.

[3] Chickering, *A Statistical View of the Population of Massachusetts*, p. 49.

[4] Theodore Parker, *The Material Condition of the People* (Boston, 1860), p. 6.

[5] Chickering, *A Statistical View of the Population of Massachusetts*, pp. 41–44. The figures check very closely with the material published in *Historical Data Relating to Counties, Cities and Towns in Massachusetts* (Massachusetts, Secretary of the Commonwealth, Division of Public Records, Boston, 1920).

It was a strange condition from the days of 1765 when the largest town in the Province was Boston with less than sixteen thousand population and its nearest rivals, Dartmouth, Marblehead and Salem, each under five thousand; and the days of 1840 with Boston a city close to one hundred thousand, with its competitors numbering sixteen towns and cities each containing more than five thousand inhabitants, and almost one-third of these with more than ten thousand.[1] The strain was being felt — the Procrustean beds of town meetings were with increasing difficulty meeting the requirements of their rapidly growing occupants. In an admirable paragraph, Charles Francis Adams has summarized the situation as it existed in that kaleidoscopic decade preceding 1840:

In the town, as in the nation, the process of absorption and amalgamation was now to be gone through with. The inrush of foreign elements had been too rapid. It tended to upset everything. Nor did it soon stop. Up to this time the agriculturists — the farm hands — had been mainly Americans. The Irish now began to take the place of these men in the fields; while the new generation of Americans either found employment in the shops and mechanical pursuits, or became shoe makers. The more adventurous and enterprizing went to the cities, or sought their fortunes in the West. But the result of it all was a complete change in the character of the town. It was a change also for the worse. The old order of things was doubtless slow, conservative, traditional; but it was economical, simple and business-like. The new order of things was in all respects the reverse. The leaders in it prided themselves on their enterprise, their lack of reverence for tradition, their confidence in themselves; but

[1] Chickering, *Statistical View of the Population of Massachusetts*, p. 15*ff*.; Felt, "Statistics of Population in Massachusetts," p. 148*ff*.

they were noisy, unmethodical, in reality incompetent, and much too often intemperate.[1]

The town of Boston was the first to discard the traditional forms of local government. It was a step taken with reluctance.[2] The events of the American Revolution had done much to foster an attachment to the old order; and the word "town" was associated in the popular mind with patriotic forums and political liberty. But the inadequacy of the time-honored method was becoming increasingly manifest. Its evolution had resulted in a complex system of administration little adapted to effective or even harmonious action in the presence of nineteenth century conditions. There was little or no direct control over town officers. The finances were under the supervision of a committee composed of the selectmen, overseers of the poor, and board of health, and the taxes they proposed were often voted at a town meeting in which the members of the boards themselves constituted a majority of those present.[3] The occasions, moreover, were far from the spontaneous gatherings of the old days. Prospective excitement then as now was the principal stimulus to a large attendance. Often enough the selectmen, town officers and a score or two of inhabitants impelled by official duty or private interest made up the gathering. "In assemblies thus composed," wrote Josiah Quincy, "by-laws were passed; taxes, to the amount of one hundred or one hundred and

1 Adams, *Three Episodes of Massachusetts History*, II, 949.

2 For previous attempts to incorporate Boston see *Col. Soc. of Mass. Pub.*, X, 352–356, and for protests against the incorporation, *ibid.*, pp. 345–352.

3 Josiah Quincy, *A Municipal History of the Town and City of Boston* (Boston, 1852), p. 29.

fifty thousand dollars voted, on statements often general in their nature, and on reports, as it respects the majority of voters present, taken upon trust, and which no one had carefully considered except perhaps the chairman." [1]

In May, 1784, a committee of thirteen distinguished citizens was appointed by the town to consider the expediency of applying to the General Court for an "Act to Form the Town of Boston into an Incorporated City," [2] and on June 4, two plans were reported; but at an adjourned meeting (June 17) after a warm debate both proposals were rejected by a large majority. In spite of this setback, another attempt was made in November of the following year, but the committee reporting on that occasion — probably because of the impracticability of making any change — found no defects "in the present Constitution of The Town," [3] and no further action was taken until December, 1791. At that time a committee was appointed to remedy an unsatisfactory police system and to deal with this condition, a change in the form of local government was recommended. The report that was submitted suggested the division of the town into nine wards, each ward to elect two men, who, with the selectmen, were to constitute a town council, this body to appoint annually all executive officers except those enumerated in the proposed act. But at an adjourned meeting this report also was rejected,[4] to be followed in 1804 by the refusal of a fourth report.[5] The

[1] *Ibid.*, p. 28.
[2] Report of the Record Commissioners, *Boston Town Records* (1784–1796), XXXI (1903), 25.
[3] *Ibid.*, pp. 42, 92.
[4] *Ibid.*, pp. 274–276.
[5] *Ibid.* (1796–1813), pp. 159–160.

next year, however, changes in administration through
the failure of valuable officials to obtain reëlection gave
fresh emphasis to the perils of the old system, and a town
meeting was called to hear the recommendations of a
fifth committee. While in outline the report and accom-
panying bill were very similar to previous efforts, it was
rejected by only thirty-one votes in a total of close to
two thousand.[1]

In 1821, with a population of over forty thousand of
whom some seven thousand were qualified voters, it was
clear that a change was imminent. A year previous an
amendment had been added to the constitution of the
Commonwealth removing the objection that the General Court had no legal authority to incorporate cities —
a question that had been zealously pressed at every attempt to alter the town form of government. In October,
1821, a committee of thirteen was appointed to report
"a complete system relating to the administration of the
town and county, which shall remedy the present evils." [2]
In December this committee recommended some mild
alterations,[3] but the report was referred back to an enlarged committee,[4] and on the last day in the month a
town meeting was held in Faneuil Hall, at which proposals for extensive changes were brought forward. The
debate lasted for three days. It was extensive and bit-
ter. The principal speaker in opposition concluded:

[1] *Ibid.* (1814–1822), pp. 34–44, 48.

[2] Quincy, *Municipal History of Boston*, pp. 28–30.

[3] The plan proposed was in principle a modest application of the limited
town meeting of today — a body of assistants to be chosen annually in the
wards in a ratio of one to nine hundred inhabitants, which would have
made a body of forty-one members. These, with the selectmen, were to
form a town council (Quincy, *Municipal History of Boston*, p. 31, note).

[4] *Boston Town Records* (1814–1822), p. 254.

The intended form of government is very similar to that of 1804, which the town almost unanimously rejected, and I am in hopes that there will be a motion now made to dissolve this meeting, the sooner the better, for I look upon this town corporation like the HARTFORD CONVENTION pregnant with evils?![1]

When the question, Shall there be a City-Government? was put, close to five thousand votes were cast, and the motion carried by a majority of eight hundred.[2] An act of municipal incorporation was accordingly passed by the General Court and upon acceptance by a meeting of the inhabitants Boston was committed to a new municipal life.[3]

The year 1840 found two other towns unable to cope with local political conditions. Early in the century, Salem had undergone agitation for a change, but nothing definite was done until a town meeting in January, 1836 was called to consider a city charter. A committee returned a favorable report, and in April of that year, the necessary legislation was approved for a representative form of government.[4] Lowell followed almost at once. The town had existed only from March, 1826, but its growth had been phenomenal. Upon incorporation, there were but twenty-five hundred inhabitants. Ten

[1] *A Full and Authentic Report of the Debates in Faneuil Hall, Dec. 31, Jan. 1, & 12, 1821–2. On Changing the Form of Government of the Town of Boston* (Boston, 1822), "Mr. Clough's Address," p. 47.

[2] *Boston Town Records (1814–1822)*, pp. 256, 263. Perhaps the most valuable single account of the change is found in Quincy's *Municipal History of Boston*. A list of the principal documents is printed in *Index to City Documents (1834–1909)* (Boston, 1910). See under "Class VI: Documents of the Town of Boston." Quincy, however, prints a synopsis of most of the plans proposed, and an excellent political background for the period.

[3] *Boston Town Records* (1814–1822), p. 265; *Laws of 1821*, ch. 110.

[4] H. M. Batchelder and C. S. Osgood, *Historical Sketch of Salem* (Salem [Essex Institute], 1879), p. 54.

years later, industrial needs had raised the population to over eighteen thousand.[1] The usual committee was appointed to consider a change, and subsequently submitted a report — the old story of "want of executive power and the loose and irresponsible manner in which money is granted and expended for municipal purposes."[2] The result was an act of the General Court for the incorporation of Lowell, accepted by the voters in April, 1836.

In 1840, the aggregate population of the three cities was almost one hundred and thirty thousand — close to eighteen per cent of the Commonwealth. Fifteen years later when the first State decennial census was taken, there were fourteen cities and one town, each containing more than ten thousand inhabitants. Between the years 1850 and 1855, while eighty-six towns in the Commonwealth lost inhabitants,[3] the largest proportional increase was in the industrial districts of Middlesex — almost twenty-five per cent in five years.[4] In 1875, there were nineteen cities, containing over fifty per cent of the population. Ten years later, there were twenty-three, with sixty per cent of the people within their borders. And another element had entered — the aggregate foreign born in the cities was over thirty-two per cent, with some municipalities exceeding the forty per cent mark.[5]

[1] F. W. Coburn, *History of Lowell and Its People* (3 vols., New York, 1920), I, 158, 162.

[2] *Ibid.*, "Report of the Committee," pp. 217–218.

[3] Due in a large manner to setting off new towns from old incorporated areas, but even this indicated a congested condition.

[4] *Abstract of the Census* (1855), pp. 216–221.

[5] Wadlin, "The Growth of Cities in Massachusetts," pp. 159–168. "It will be difficult to name a day in the future," quotes the census of

The countless needs made necessary the direct intervention of the central government to an increased degree. The building of turnpikes between the larger towns, the steamboat, railroad, telegraph, penny postage, telephone, electric railway and the bicycle made possible and necessary a political regulation undreamed of before their advent.[1] The *Revised Statutes of the Commonwealth* (1835) give more than twice the space to the powers and duties of towns that the first charter under the new government had required and devote four additional chapters to supplementary legislation.[2]

It had become necessary to define more closely the method of perambulation; to enumerate the specific purposes for which towns might grant money; to regulate the making of by-laws; to add several sections to the conduct of the town meeting and the duties of the moderator, and to insert further detailed provisions relative to the election, qualifications, and functions of town officers. The *General Statutes* (1860) added six additional pages with seven supplementary chapters,[3] and in the *Public Statutes of 1881* [4] the index occupied about half as much space as the original charter of 1785. A casual examination of the *Revised Laws* (1901),[5] as well as the

---

1855 (*Abstract of the Census* [1855], p. 236), when the number of American citizens, in the distinctive sense that this term is commonly used, will again constitute a majority of those who shall inhabit the present limits of Boston. It is also here worthy of remark, that while native voters have increased only 14.72 per cent. since 1850, the foreign voters have increased threefold, or no less than 194.64 per cent."

[1] R. H. Whitten, *Public Administration in Massachusetts* (New York, 1898), p. 14.

[2] *Revised Statutes*, chs. 15–19.

[3] *General Statutes*, chs. 19–25.

[4] *Public Statutes*, chs. 27–36.

[5] *Revised Laws*, chs. 25–34.

*General Laws* (1919),[1] show marked increase in extent and complexity, and is a sober reminder that the simple days when a single chapter, or even a moderate series of chapters will suffice to give a fair idea of the powers and duties of municipalities in Massachusetts, have long since passed.

Every phase of society has felt the effects of new social and political pressures. Poor relief was among the first problems. Between 1792 and 1820 the expense incident to the care of State paupers increased fivefold, although over the same period, the population failed to double.[2] The later middle period showed even a worse condition. In the decade following 1837 the paupers within the Commonwealth increased nearly one hundred per cent, and the towns not only failed to meet the situation, but were prone to take advantage of legal loopholes at the expense of the State.[3] Under such conditions, a legislative committee reported as early as 1821 in favor of a system of town and district almshouses with the suggestion that the whole subject of the poor in the Commonwealth be placed under the regular control of the Legislature.[4] Centralization was subsequently begun by creating a commission to appoint one or more persons to visit all almshouses where state paupers were maintained to report legal infractions — particularly the imposition of the towns upon the State in their joint accounts — and a few years later the State Board of Charities was

[1] *Genl. Laws,* chs. 39–49.

[2] Whitten, *Public Administration in Massachusetts,* pp. 43–44.

[3] Massachusetts, Board of Charities, *First Annual Report* (1865), "The Gradual Growth of the State Pauper System," p. 242 and *passim.*

[4] Massachusetts General Court, Committee on Pauper Laws, *Report of the Committee to whom was referred the consideration of the Pauper laws of this Commonwealth* (1821) (Boston [?], 1821), p. 11.

created "to investigate and supervise the whole system of the public charitable and correctional institutions." [1]

Boston had been the first town to establish a board of health (Feb. 13, 1799). By 1828, Salem, Marblehead, Plymouth, Charlestown, Lynn, and Cambridge had done likewise. But attention was called to a perilous condition when in 1849, the Asiatic cholera invaded the State, and over seven hundred persons died in Boston alone.[2] A sanitary survey was accordingly undertaken and the commission charged with the investigation reported that an amount of sickness which in former times would have created grave concern was treated as an ordinary event, and aroused no special attention whatsoever. Recognizing the tendency of the people to "social concentration," it cited the terrible features of British congestion of the period, and emphasized that the picture was reproduced at times with more frightful details in Massachusetts. To meet the situation, it recommended not only a general board of health, but in addition, a local board in every town "to be charged with the particular execution of the laws." It was twenty years before action was taken. In 1861 the Boston Sanitary Association was still requesting "more of the paternal care, watchfulness and protection of the legislature than they now receive," [3] and it was not until 1869 that a state board of health (with no compulsory powers) was established.[4]

The present state police organization originated in an

---

[1] *Acts of 1863*, ch. 240.

[2] Massachusetts General Court, Sanitary Commission, *Report of a General Plan for the Promotion of Public and Personal Health* (1850) (Boston, 1850), pp. 52, 78, 81, 153, 157, 115.

[3] Massachusetts General Court, *House Document 112* (1861), p. 1.

[4] Succeeding years of the century saw, however, the passage of numerous acts that added greatly to its authority. See W. C. Richardson's *Summary*

attempt to prevent the sale of intoxicating liquors. A prohibition law was passed in 1852. Its enforcement was difficult. In places, indeed, it seemed to be impossible, and supporters of the law favored more stringent measures. In 1863, a joint special committee on the question of metropolitan police emphasized a bad situation — "large classes, having the rights of citizens but not the welfare of government at heart, always run into large cities as the common sewers of the State, and are ready to make use of just such machinery as the present system affords to them."[1] But Boston protested against centralization. A committee of its citizens recalled that general laws administered in local communities by officers of their own selection had always been regarded as an essential principle of their free institutions, and was very definite that the police powers be left to the control of the towns and cities. It spoke in addition the traditional plea of the "right of self-government," and denounced the movement as an "imputation upon the loyalty to law and order of a community which has been always justly distinguished, at home and abroad, for the excellence of its municipal government."

A compromise measure was passed in 1865 creating a "Constable of the Commonwealth" who, with his deputies, was to use his "utmost endeavors to repress and prevent crime, by the suppression of liquor shops, gambling places and houses of ill-fame,"[3] and while in 1875

of *Seven Years' Work of the State Board of Health* (Boston, 1876), pp. 45–58, where many such acts are fully cited.

[1] Massachusetts General Court, *Senate Document 129* (1863), p. 3.

[2] *Ibid., Senate Document 163* (1863), pp. 1–2.

[3] *Acts of 1865*, ch. 249, p. 631.

the prohibition law was repealed, the police system was again reorganized, to assume the form of a State detective force, each member to have the powers of constables, police or watchmen. At the end of the first year the personnel of this new body numbered only fifteen men, but its activity had gone deep into local affairs. It inspected nearly all the large manufacturing establishments in the State — close to thirteen hundred of them. It gave particular attention to the examination of steam boilers, fire extinguishing facilities, and safety devices as well as to the observance of child-labor regulations. It made over five hundred arrests, condemned some thirty-five thousand gallons of liquor and recovered a large amount of stolen property.[1] When, in 1878, the State was infested with bands of tramps, the new department was given the special duty of enforcing the vagrancy laws,[2] and to the close of the century, increased activities gave it vigorous continuation — a recognition that the new conditions demanded a firm control that was not to be nullified by apathetic or inefficient local police.[3]

The school law of 1789 was the most rigid and detailed of any that had been enacted,[4] and laid the basis for a number of encroaching statutes. In 1826 each town was for the first time required to choose a school committee — consisting of not less than five persons, to have the general superintendence of all public schools in the com-

[1] Whitten, *Public Administration in Massachusetts*, pp. 80–86; Massachusetts General Court, Senate Document 11 (1876), *Report of the Chief Detective of the Commonwealth of Massachusetts* (1876), pp. 3, 13, 5, 8, 11.

[2] *Ibid.*, Public Document 37 (1877), *Report of the Chief of State Detective Force* (1877), pp. 17–30.

[3] Whitten, *Public Administration in Massachusetts*, p. 96.

[4] *Laws of 1788*, ch. 19; Whitten, *Public Administration in Massachusetts*, p. 22.

munity. One or more of the committee was to visit the schools at least once a month — "without giving a previous notice thereof to the instructor" — and was to make an annual report to the secretary of the Commonwealth.[1] In 1834, a state school fund was established from all money derived from land sales in Maine and from claims against the federal government, "for the aid and encouragement of the common schools," to be apportioned as the General Court should direct,[2] and three years later the state board of education came into existence.[3]

The entire movement was carried on with steady and unremitting emphasis. In 1838 there came a state bank commission; in 1853, a board of agriculture; in 1855, an insurance commission; ten years later a tax commission, and the following year, a commission on fish and game. In 1869, a railroad commission and bureau of labor statistics were created; in 1870 a corporation commission, and 1887 witnessed the first of those registration boards (dentistry, pharmacy, optometry, nursing, embalming, etc.) that were to perform such important functions in professional services.[4]

The legislation of the nineteenth century was carried forcefully into the twentieth and many pages of the *General Laws* bear testimony to expanding supervision. The overseers of the poor are required to keep complete records of their activities in a form prescribed by the

[1] *Laws of 1826* (Jan. sess.), chs. 170, 299, 300, 302.
[2] *Laws of 1834–1836*, chs. 69, 241
[3] *Laws of 1837*, chs. 141, 277.
[4] Massachusetts General Court, Commission on Economy and Efficiency, *Functions, Organization and Administration of the Departments in the Executive Branch of the State Government* (1914) (Boston, 1914), pp. 14–30.

department of public welfare, and to make annual and decennial reports of such matters as may be prescribed by the department.[1] Should the overseers (except in Boston) neglect to take proper care of pauper children, the department of public welfare is directed to perform the service, and such children are thereupon supported by the town, subject to the visitation of State officers, until the overseers give proper attention to their duties. In addition, some one hundred and thirty town and city almshouses are inspected annually — some several times a year — and it is significant that such institutions are steadily decreasing, due in part at least, to intelligent outdoor relief under the supervision of the State.[2]

The department of public health, in case of contagious or infectious diseases, exercises coördinate powers with the board of health in every town, and may require such boards (as well as various officers and physicians throughout the State) to give notice to the department of any disease that it may declare dangerous to the public health. In addition, it may prescribe certain sanitary measures for hotels and public buildings; consult and advise town officers relative to water and sewer problems and practically give its approval to all petitions to the General Court asking authority to introduce a system of water supply, drainage, or sewage disposal in local communities.[3]

The state police exercise throughout the Commonwealth the powers of constables and police officers,[4] ex-

[1] For each day's neglect, the town may forfeit one dollar, and several hundred dollars is collected each year from this source.
[2] *Genl. Laws*, ch. 117, secs. 32–37.
[3] *Ibid.*, ch. 111, secs. 7, 8, 17, 33–62.
[4] *Ibid.*, ch. 147, sec. 2.

cept as to the service of civil process, and furnish practically all the protection that rural communities enjoy. The force is composed of two hundred uniformed officers and men under the command of the governor, and they may advise, supplement, and, in extreme cases, even displace the local peace officer. Financial methods have been unified to include a close regulation of indebtedness, provision for the installation of a uniform accounting system, and central audits, while in the course of guidance in fiscal matters,[1] tactful state officers serve informally as consultants in almost every phase of town government, and local officials have come to depend on their counsel in many matters of community policy.[2]

The commissioner of education has supervision over the issuance of teachers' certificates in all high schools aided by the Commonwealth — some thirty-six of them. He suggests improvements in the public school system to the General Court; prescribes forms and receives and arranges reports from local school committees, and supervises the administration of a multitude of local regulations required by law. All superintendents of school unions (seventy-four in number, embracing two hundred and twenty-eight towns) are subject to the approval of the commissioner of education. Each town and city in the state receives state aid for teaching vocational subjects, and the effectiveness of this work is determined by periodic inspections from the commissioner's office. Un-

---

[1] *Genl. Laws*, ch. 44, secs. 1–13.

[2] A special commission recently recommended to the General Court (*Final Report of the Special Commission Established to Investigate Municipal Expenditures and Undertakings and the Appropriations of Money under Municipal Authority* [Boston, 1929], pp. 14–18) that a state bureau of municipal information for service to city and town officials be created.

der certain conditions the qualifications of teachers are subject to his approval, and special classes for handicapped children as well as all work in Americanization are under his direct supervision.[1]

In addition to these more elementary functions, others have felt the centripetal influences of state supervision and control. The regulation of public utilities, civil service requirements, central approval of by-laws, the care of local records, the conduct of elections, the maintenance of highways, and the responsibilities of metropolitan areas, have in many instances left the local communities of the Commonwealth small room for discretion.[2] It is often said in New England today: "The State runs the town for us now." And it can hardly be denied that from the administrative standpoint, at least, such must be the case in many essential services of the modern municipality — especially among that numerous group of communities colloquially known as "small towns."

[1] *Genl. Laws,* ch. 71, secs. 1, 5, 12.

[2] Whitten, *Public Administration in Massachusetts,* chs. VII-XI. Many of these are, however, voluntary restrictions, undertaken through acceptance of permissive statutes.

# VI

## TOWN MEETING GOVERNMENT TODAY

THE historical survey of the preceding chapters is not to be left without a contemporary capstone. In spite of a deep interest in the local constitutional history of the Commonwealth, practically all research has been of an antiquarian character, and analysis of the town meeting based very largely on faint and infrequent records of the past. But each year during the months of February, March and April[1] town meetings convene in the communities of Massachusetts with much of the fervor that marked their earlier vigor, and serve in some measure as "living tables of the law" to enliven aged documents from distant times.

The precise day of such meetings is usually provided in the town by-laws, but where there are no by-laws (and many small communities depend entirely upon state statutes for local regulations), it is determined by vote of the town or, if a special meeting, at such time as the selectmen may order.[2] Adjournment may be had from

---

[1] This is true (*Genl. Laws*, ch. 39, sec. 9) except for three town manager communities and the town of Walpole where the third Wednesday in January is prescribed by special act (Massachusetts, Secretary of State, Pub. Doc. 43 [1926], *Primaries and Elections*, pp. xxvi [Middleboro], xxviii [Walpole], xxx [Mansfield and Norwood]. See also acts cited *infra*, ch. viii).

[2] *Genl. Laws*, ch. 39, sec. 9. By-laws are now defined as such orders "not repugnant to law, as they [the towns] may judge most conducive to their welfare" (*ibid.*, ch. 40, sec. 21). Aside from the general privilege of making by-laws "For directing and managing their prudential affairs, preserving peace and good order, and maintaining their internal police" (*ibid.*,

time to time — over a few days or even several weeks — and special meetings are held throughout the year to attend to matters that may arise. Large communities, indeed, hold from one to half a dozen adjourned sessions, and even with this expedient, it is unusual for a single meeting to suffice for the year's business, four or five being not uncommon. Each meeting (whether annual or special) is called pursuant to the familiar warrant, issued normally, over the signatures of the selectmen or a majority of them[1] and directed to the constables of the town. Its provisions announce the place, day and hour of meeting, the business to be undertaken, and usually the directions for the service and return of the notice.

The warrant remains a vital part of town meeting government — indeed, there is no single document that gives a more complete idea of its procedure.[2] It is often

sec. 21 [1]), the statute specifically confers others (ibid., sec. 21 [2–13]), and additional purposes are authorized in other chapters. A penalty for infringement may be attached not exceeding twenty dollars for each offense, to be collected before a district court (ibid., ch. 218, sec. 26) or before a trial justice (ibid., ch. 219, sec. 25). They must be reasonable (Commonwealth v. Wilkins [1857], 121 Mass. 357; Commonwealth v. McCafferty [1888], 145 Mass. 385; Commonwealth v. Parks [1892], 155 Mass. 533; Commonwealth v. Hubley [1898], 172 Mass. 59), they must be acted upon only under an article appropriately inserted in the warrant (Loring v. Westwood [1921], 238 Mass. 10), and before taking effect receive the approval of the attorney general and be given publicity according to law (Genl. Laws, ch. 40, sec. 32).

¹ Reynolds v. Salem (1843), 6 Met. (Mass.) 340.

² This must, of course, be supplemented by others. Annual town reports are particularly useful for town warrants, selectmen's reports, and town meeting records, and town by-laws (issued locally at various times) contain sections on town meeting procedure. To these must be added chapters of the General Laws pertaining to powers, duties, officers and procedure (important sections of which are conveniently extracted in Municipal Bulletin No. 10, Department of Corporations and Taxation, December, 1927), as well as chapters 50–56 on electoral matters (likewise printed separately in four parts by the Secretary of the Commonwealth, Boston, 1921). These are conveniently supplemented by Massachusetts Cumulative Statutes (1921–1926)

published in the town report as well as in the local newspapers, and may appear in addition as an expansive broadside or even as a small pamphlet. In rural communities it assumes a highly informal character. Prepared blank warrants are supplied commercially and the town clerk has only to make the necessary entrances in the appropriate spaces. Ordinary letterhead paper may even be used and the sheets posted in juxtaposition or pasted end to end in a long narrow scroll to be promulgated from the walls of the town hall, village store or local post office.

The salutation is to *one* of the constables of the town or to *either* of the constables, or more definitely "To Howard F. Damon, Constable of the Town of Ashby," followed by directions in the name of the Commonwealth to notify the inhabitants that are qualified to vote in elections and in town affairs to meet as the warrant prescribes. The place is ordinarily announced as the town hall, or some suitable building within the community, and the day is set as "Tuesday, the eighth day of March next."[1] While elections are usually announced in the morning hours (the polls remaining open as may seem necessary throughout the afternoon)[2] busi-

(Charlottesville [Va.], 1926), and *Annual Supplement* (1927) (*ibid.*, 1927). Judicial features are traced through the usual legal indices particularly the *Massachusetts Digest* (11 vols., Boston and St. Paul, 1906–1928).

[1] *Ashby Town Report* (1926), p. 63. All town reports are thus cited in abbreviated form.

[2] In the election of town officers where official ballots are used, the law provides that the polls may be opened as early as 5:45 a.m., and that they shall be opened by noon. They are required to be kept open at least four hours (*Genl. Laws*, ch. 54, sec. 64). In voting by precincts in town elections (*ibid.*, ch. 39, sec. 20) the warrant must prescribe when the polls *may* close. In no case shall they be open after 8:00 p.m. (*ibid.*, ch. 54, sec. 64). Otherwise a town (unless restraining statutes have been accepted) may to a large extent regulate its own voting (*ibid.*, ch. 39, sec. 22).

ness meetings, especially in the larger communities, are frequently held in the evening. In smaller places, however, the forenoon and afternoon are commonly used, and occasionally both business and election are carried on simultaneously; but whatever the procedure, it is rare that a rural town will give more than a day (or sometimes only a forenoon) to the whole process.

The preliminary provisions in the warrant vary very largely according to the electoral procedure that is in use, and it is here that towns have departed most widely from old methods. If the community is small the call for the meeting as well as the first few articles will be simple:

### ANNUAL TOWN MEETING
### WARRANT, 1927

#### Commonwealth of Massachusetts

Barnstable, ss.
To Harvey T. Moore, Constable of the Town of Eastham, in said County,                                    Greeting:

In the name of the Commonwealth of Massachusetts, you are directed to notify and warn the inhabitants of said Town, qualified to vote in elections and Town affairs, to meet in the Town Hall of said Eastham, on Monday, February 7, 1927, at 10 o'clock in the forenoon, then and there to act upon the following articles, viz.:

Article 1. To choose a moderator to preside at said meeting.

Article 2. To hear the reports of the Selectmen and all reports and committees and act thereon.

Article 3. To choose all necessary Town Officers for the ensuing year.[1]

---

[1] *Eastham Town Report* (1926), p. 105.

But the exigencies of modern politics do not often permit such elementary methods, and many communities have found it necessary to adopt what are known in Massachusetts as "official ballots" for use in town elections. These were first provided in the statutes of 1888 and meant then as they mean now, "a ballot prepared for any primary, caucus or election by public authority and at public expense,"[1] as opposed to the informally prepared ballots familiar to the old town meetings. When provision for the use of such ballots is made, the nomination and election of all *town* officers to be chosen thereon must be (so far as applicable) in accordance with the chapters of the *General Laws* that pertain to the election of *state* officers.[2] Some two hundred and seventy-three towns have accepted the provisions of this statute,[3] and their warrants become, therefore, more explicit, enumerating the officers to be chosen and the hours of voting, as well as any questions to be passed upon by the electors at the polls.[4]

## WARRANT
## FOR ANNUAL TOWN MEETING

Commonwealth of Massachusetts,

Worcester: ss.

To either of the constables in the Town of Millville, in County of Worcester

GREETINGS:

In the name of the Commonwealth of Massachusetts you are hereby directed to notify and warn the inhabitants of

[1] *Genl. Laws*, ch. 50, sec. 1; Sweeney v. Selectmen of Natick (1909), 202 *Mass* 540.

[2] *Genl. Laws*, ch. 41, sec. 6; *ibid.*, chs. 50–56.

[3] Pub. Doc. 43 (1926), p. v.

[4] *Genl. Laws*, ch. 54, sec. 64.

the Town of Millville, qualified to vote in election of town affairs to meet at Forester's Hall, Millville, on Monday, February fourth, Nineteen Hundred and Twenty-four, at 9 o'clock in the forenoon, then and there to bring in their votes on one ballot to the election of officers for the following offices, to wit:

A Moderator for one year.
A Town Clerk for one year.
Three Selectmen for one year.
A Tax Collector for one year.
A Highway Surveyor for one year.
Three Overseers of the Poor for one year.
One Assessor of Taxes for three years.
A Treasurer for one year.
A School Committeeman for three years.
A Tree Warden for one year.
Two members of Board of Health — one for an unexpired
  term of two years and one for a term of three years.
Five Constables for one year.
Two Trustees of Public Library for three years.

Also on the same ballot to vote Yes or No in answer to the question: "Shall licenses be granted· for the sale of certain Non-intoxicating Beverages in this Town"?

The polls will begin at 9 o'clock in the forenoon and may close at 4 o'clock in the afternoon.

Also to act on the following articles, viz.:

Art. 1. To hear the reports of the several town officers and committees and to act thereon . . . etc.[1]

There is, however, another expedient that has added an additional feature to the electoral process. It has been found convenient to have the annual town meeting fall into two parts — one for the choice of town officers and another for the transaction of business. Where precinct voting is not involved (that is, where the com-

[1] *Millville Town Report* (1924), p. 8.

munity is still a single district for electoral purposes) the procedure for such a separation may be arranged in open meeting, in which case the warrant need contain no express provisions for the necessary adjournment. After the balloting for town officers has been completed, a motion is made to close the polls at a certain hour with the proviso that when the moderator has declared the results of the election, the meeting will adjourn to a definite time and place.[1] At times, however, a separate warrant may be issued for each part, one providing for the election and one for the subsequent business meeting,[2] or the order may be reversed — that is, the business be transacted first, and adjournment taken to choose all necessary officers.[3] It is customary, however, for the town by-laws to provide a suitable procedure,[4] and when this is the case, the warrant may read:

In accordance with the By-laws, the meeting will then [*i.e.*, after balloting] be adjourned until Saturday, March 10, next, at one thirty o'clock P.M. to consider the following articles: . . .[5]

But where precinct voting is involved additional provisions are necessary.[6] The warrant then announces not

---

[1] *Ibid.*, pp. 10, 13, 16; *Avon Town Report* (1926), p. 67.

[2] *Maynard Town Report* (1926), pp. 39, 45.

[3] *Hanson Town Report* (1926), p. 45; *Provincetown Town Report* (1926), pp. 14–15.

[4] *Genl. Laws*, ch. 39, sec. 22.

[5] *Milton Town Report* (1923), p. 37; *ibid.*, "Revised By-Laws," ch. 2, sec. 3.

[6] The general laws recognize two types of precinct voting: *first*, for state elections only — which may be arranged by the town instructing its selectmen to determine suitable voting precincts, and to submit their recommendations to the town for approval (*Genl. Laws*, ch. 54, sec. 6). When this is done the town may take a *second* step and establish precinct voting to include town elections, by a vote held at least fourteen days before the annual town meeting (*ibid.*, ch. 39, sec. 20). There are some fifty-four towns that have

only the precincts themselves as well as the polling place in each precinct; but also the hours during which the polls will remain open together with provisions for the adjourned meeting. The opening articles become, therefore, somewhat more elaborate:

## TOWN WARRANT

Commonwealth of Massachusetts.                    Middlesex, ss.

To either of the Constables of the Town of Lexington, in said County, Greeting:

*In the name of the Commonwealth of Massachusetts, you are directed to notify the inhabitants of the Town of Lexington, qualified to vote in elections and in town affairs to meet in their respective places in said town, (Precinct One, Emerson Hall: Precinct Two, Town Hall) on*
MONDAY, THE FIRST DAY OF MARCH, A.D. 1926, at Six o'clock A.M., then and there to act on the following articles:

Art. 1. To choose by ballot the following town officers: One Town Clerk for the term of one year: two Selectmen for the term of three years; one Town Treasurer for the term of one year: one Collector of Taxes for the term of one year: one Cemetery Commissioner for the term of three years: one member of the School Committee for the term of three years: two Constables for the term of one year: one Moderator for the term of one year: one Trustee of Public Trusts for the term of six years: two members of the Planning Board for the term of three years.

The polls will be open at 6 A.M. and will remain open until 5 P.M.

You are also to notify and warn the inhabitants aforesaid to meet in Town Hall in said town on Monday, the eighth

accepted the statutes providing for precinct voting in town elections (Pub. Doc. 43 [1926], v).

day of March, 1926 at 7:30 P.M. to act on the following articles:

Art. 2. To receive the report of any Board of Town Officers or of any Committee of the town, and to appoint other committees . . .[1]

There are, however, many variations in these types. Even in towns where official ballots are not used, the officers to be elected at the polls are frequently enumerated in the warrant — a procedure, incidentally, to be encouraged in the interest of clarity.[2] A town may as a practical matter, have precinct voting in town elections without accepting the general laws relative thereto, and arrangements within the precincts remain substantially a matter for its own regulation.[3] The order of the first three or four articles is frequently altered, although the statutes provide that a moderator (if he be elected in open meeting) shall be chosen first.[4] The election may come either before or after the business meeting — on the same day or at some subsequent time[5] — and while

---

[1] *Lexington Town Report* (1926), p. 14.

[2] *Montgomery Town Report* (1926), p. 3; *Prescott Town Report* (1926), p. 33; *Holland Town Report* (1926), p. 44.

[3] *Dennis Town Report* (1926), p. 3 (back). This, however, is irregular.

[4] *Genl. Laws*, ch. 39, sec. 14.

[5] The statutes make provision that in those towns accepting chapter 39, section 23 of the *General Laws* the choice of town officers shall take place either within seven days *before* or within seven days *after* the annual meeting for the transaction of business, and some towns have accepted the latter arrangement (*Hingham Town Report* [1926], pp. 12, 42; *Provincetown Town Report* [1926], pp. 8, 14; *Hanson Town Report* [1926], pp. 40–45; *Hanover Town Report* [1926], pp. 8, 18; *Marblehead Town Report* [1926], pp. 99, 111). It seems that such a procedure is based on the idea that boards and officers responsible for expending an appropriation should still be in office and accountable when the town meeting convenes. In towns accepting precinct voting only (*Genl. Laws*, ch. 39, sec. 20) the town meeting must come within thirty days of the annual election and not later than April 30. If neither of these provisions has been accepted the matter is a subject for local regulation.

the principal officers must be chosen by ballot, less important officials are often nominated and elected in open meeting with the informality of acclamation.

The methods that may be used in the choice of such minor officers will likewise affect the warrant. The statutes prescribe that every town at its annual meeting shall choose certain officials for definite terms, unless other provisions are made by law. The list embraces the principal officers (with the exception of the moderator) and concludes with the injunction that "All other town officers shall be appointed by the selectmen unless other provision is made by law or by vote of the town." When a community adopts official ballots, it must determine at the same meeting what officers (in addition to those that the law requires to be elected by ballot) shall be chosen thereon, and if not already arranged, the number and terms of such officials.[1] Some towns leave no regular officers to be chosen in open meeting. In such cases early articles may omit all reference to minor electoral matters and provide at once for receiving the reports of town officers,[2] — in any event, always an early provision. Other communities, however, elect minor officials from the floor and an article permits, accordingly, the choice of "all necessary Town Officers and Committees,"[3] or "such Town Officers as are required by law to be chosen in the months of February, March, and April, annually, not elected by written ballot at the Annual Election,"[4] or more definitely, "two or more surveyors of wood and bark, and surveyors

[1] *Genl. Laws*, ch. 41, secs. 1, 7.
[2] *Marblehead Town Report* (1926), p. 182.
[3] *Concord Town Report* (1926), warrant, p. 2 (end).
[4] *Danvers Town Report* (1926), p. 10.

of lumber and all other usual town officers and trustees, and also any committees of the town." [1]

In the larger towns, the moderator remains the only important officer who is still chosen in open meeting. Formerly (before 1902) he was selected at the beginning of each session, but the law now provides that he may be elected for the term of one year to preside at all town meetings held during that period. If a town accepts this provision, the warrant (in so far as it pertains to the business meeting) will thereafter make no mention of his choice, and his name will appear on the regular ballot to be nominated and elected as other town officers so chosen. If, however, an annual moderator is not previously elected, his choice will be the first business before the assembly, and article one will contain the familiar injunction, "To choose a Moderator to preside in said meeting." [2] This is often done, even though other principal town officers be elected by ballot on a different day. [3]

Such matters are, however, merely preliminary. They embrace only the "call" and the first few articles in the warrant. The provisions that follow are the real basis for the meeting. These are arranged in the familiar "articles" numbered consecutively and varying from one to at times a hundred and thirty or forty. They contain the greatest variety of local matters. The townsman may be asked to express his sentiment concerning a proposed tennis court on the common, or to purchase a snow-removal outfit, or to raise three hundred dollars for the

[1] *Framingham Town Report* (1926), p. 16.

[2] *Acts of 1902*, ch. 346. In such a case, however, the procedure must be by ballot and the voting list used (*Genl. Laws*, ch. 39, sec. 14).

[3] *Dennis Town Report* (1926), p. 3 (end).

suitable celebration of the Fourth of July. He may be requested to increase the salary of the chairman of the board of assessors, or to give his consent to having the town bell rung on suitable occasions, or to approve the purchase of new seats for the town hall. And recently he has been urged to instruct the selectmen to suppress the illegal sale of intoxicating liquor, to see if the town will conduct its business on standard time, and, with increasing frequency, to appoint a committee to consider a change in his form of town government.

Matters of finance occupy a large part of every annual warrant. There is often inserted an article authorizing the town treasurer with the approval of the selectmen to borrow money in anticipation of revenue.[1] Sometimes there is a general item to see if the town will vote to raise and appropriate "such sums of money as may be necessary to defray town expenses ... and act fully thereon"[2] or to fix the amount of compensation "to be paid Town Officers for the ensuing year and appropriate money therefor."[3] There is usually a group of articles providing definitely for general matters of town administration:

Article 7. To see what action the town will take in regard to defraying any part of the expenses of Memorial Day.

Article 8. To see if the town will appropriate the dog fund.

Article 9. To see if the town will raise and appropriate money for the Free Library.

Article 10. To see if the town will raise and appropriate money for public water.

---

[1] *Genl. Laws*, ch. 44, sec. 4; *Oakham Town Report* (1924), p. 8; *Hancock Town Report* (1926), p. 2.

[2] *Harwich Town Report* (1926), p. 39.

[3] *Topsfield Town Report* (1926), p. 10.

Article 11.  To see if the town will raise and appropriate
money for police service and how much.

Article 12.  To see if the town will raise and appropriate
money for sidewalks.

Article 13.  To see what amount the town will raise and
appropriate for repairing highways and bridges, sewers and
sidewalks, for the ensuing year . . . etc.[1]

The town may act under the recommendations of a finance
committee,[2] and insert more precise information describing in a general way the object of each proposed expen-
diture[3] or in larger communities more formal budgetary
headings may be used; as, general government, life and
property, board of health, highways and bridges, charities, schools, etc.,[4] and the recommendations of the committee follow each article that carries an appropriation,
and at times, other articles as well:

## SIDEWALKS
Article 40.  To see if the town will make provision for the
further construction of granolithic sidewalks, appropriate
money therefore, pass any vote or take any action thereto.

[1] *Ware Town Report* (1926), p. 43.

[2] Finance committees are now compulsory in all towns whose valuation
for the purposes of apportioning the state tax exceeds a million dollars
(*Acts of 1923*, ch. 388).

[3] *Colrain Town Report* (1926), p. 21:
Article IV.  To see if Town will vote to make the following appropria-
tions as recommended by the Finance Committee and raise by taxation the
required amount, or pass any vote or votes in relation thereto:
Sec. 1  Six thousand, five hundred and fifty dollars for highway
maintenance.
Sec. 2  One thousand dollars for Incidentals.
Sec. 3  Fourteen hundred dollars for Support of Poor.
Sec. 4  Six hundred and fifty dollars for Old Bills.
Sec. 5  Three hundred dollars for compensation of the Town Treas-
urer. . . ." etc.

[4] *Wellesley Town Report* (1926), pp. 9–11.

We move the sum of $8,000 be granted for further construction of granolithic sidewalks under the sidewalk act.[1]

Such recommendations may even be expanded and published in a pamphlet report to be given to the voter for his guidance in town meeting — a procedure that not only affects the arrangement of the warrant, but that tends to alter vitally the character of the meeting itself.

When the word *warned* is used in connection with a town meeting it implies that due notice of the warrant and its contents have been given to the inhabitants. The law simply provides that the document be directed to the constables or to some other persons, who shall proceed to give notice at least seven days before the proposed meeting in such manner as the by-laws of the town may prescribe; or, in the absence of by-laws, as the town may direct,[2] and where neither statute nor town regulation offers a suitable guide, the courts have accepted the procedure that is "according to the usual custom" as sufficient and reasonable notice.[3]

The last few paragraphs of the warrant, however, generally contain instructions to the serving officer. It is often required that attested copies be displayed in the

---

[1] Town of Framingham, Finance Committee, *Report* (1924), p. 22.

[2] *Genl. Laws*, ch. 39, sec. 10. In Great Barrington the warrant is directed to the Chief of Police (*Great Barrington Town Report* [1926], p. 125). While this is unusual, police officers in the Commonwealth have the same powers as constables except as to the service and execution of civil process (*ibid.*, ch. 41, sec. 98). The chief of police, moreover, is regularly employed at a salary, and to use his services is, therefore, to save the expense of a constable.

[3] Commonwealth *v.* Smith (1882), 132 *Mass.* 293. In this case the warrant (aside from other irregularities) was not directed to a constable nor to "some other persons appointed by the selectmen." Neither was it served by such persons, nor was there any return whatsoever (*ibid.*, 294). But inasmuch as only eight qualified voters were absent from the meeting, the court deemed the warning sufficient.

local post office or other public place seven days before the time of meeting, and in addition there may be directions that not less than one hundred copies be left in frequented localities for more general distribution.[1] Such places are more clearly designated as the town hall, the village store, the fire rooms, the meeting-house or "in each of the four villages,"[2] with a frequent provision for additional publicity in the local newspapers "as directed by the By-Laws of the Town."[3] The serving officer must, moreover, make due report of his activities in the case. His return is nearly always to the town clerk, although occasionally to alternate officers such as selectmen or precinct wardens.[4] The time is usually set at the hour and place of the proposed meeting, or perhaps "on or before said meeting,"[5] or, if before, a definite period of several days may be required,[6] but by-laws uniformly give guidance in this matter.[7]

There are, however, many small communities where there are no formal pronouncements to guide the serving officer, and any procedure that he may follow is based upon a long accepted practice, from time to time altered in detail as occasion may require. Under such circumstances the courts have found it necessary to regulate the various processes. They have held that due notice

---

[1] *Avon Town Report* (1926), p. 85.

[2] *Palmer Town Report* (1926), p. 102.

[3] *Andover Town Report* (1926), p. 12.

[4] *Ashby Town Report* (1926), p. 67 (selectmen or town clerk); *Marblehead Town Report* (1926), p. 194.

[5] *Endfield Town Report* (1926), p. 5.

[6] *Montague Town Report* (1926), p. 17.

[7] The warrants uniformly bear the signature of the selectmen or a majority of them (Reynolds *v.* New Salem [1843], 6 *Met.* [Mass.] 340). The return of the writ (as well as the attest) is signed by the returning officer, although at times the attest may be signed by the town clerk.

of the meeting is given through posting either the original warrant or an attested copy.[1] The proper place for posting is usually the town hall[2] or wherever the meeting is to be held,[3] or even at a number of prescribed public places,[4] not necessarily, it seems, the usual place,[5] but anywhere that the notice is likely to be seen. The return of the writ should be signed by the officer in his official capacity[6] and may in the absence of other requirements be dated any time after notice and before the meeting.[7] The simplest formality is accepted. The judicial view merely assumes that the purpose of the warrant is to give previous notice of the subjects to be acted upon at the proposed meeting, and if this is done, the methods employed are deemed sufficient.[8] The most informal warning is apt to be approved unless contrary to town regulation or so plainly unreasonable as to raise the presumption of fraud.[9] In the very nature of small municipalities, irregularities in their records and proceedings are inevitable, and excessive judicial strictness is prudently avoided, lest, as Chief Justice Parker once said, it "throw the whole body politic into confusion."[10]

The compilation of a warrant is largely the work of

[1] Norris v. Eaton (1834), 7 N. H. 284; Brown v. Witham (1862), 51 Me. 29.

[2] Briggs v. Murdock (1832), 13 Pick. (Mass.) 305.

[3] Commonwealth v. Sullivan (1896), 165 Mass. 183.

[4] Brown v. Witham (1862), 51 Me. 29; In re Smith (1904), 89 N. Y. Suppl. 1006.

[5] Stoddard v. Gilman (1850), 22 Vt. 568.

[6] Commonwealth v. Shaw (1843), 7 Met. (Mass.) 52.

[7] Bucksport v. Spofford (1835), 12 Me. 487.

[8] Wood v. Quincy (1853), 11 Cush. (Mass.) 491.

[9] Saxton v. Nimms and others (1817), 14 Mass. 315; Gilmore v. Holt (1826), 4 Pick. (Mass.) 261.

[10] Welles v. Battelle (1814), 11 Mass. 480.

the selectmen, and the precise time and place of the
meeting (except for provisions in the by-laws), as well as
the subject matter comprising the various articles are, in
most cases, the results of their initiative. In the larger
towns, however, the arrangement for publication is usually undertaken by the town counsel, while in smaller
communities the town clerk or the clerk to the selectmen
(frequently the same officer) takes much of the responsibility. In general, no action on the part of the town
meeting is valid unless the subject matter is contained in
the warrant,[1] and while the liberal phrasing of an article
is not thereby precluded,[2] each item must be specifically
stated, and such general language as "to transact any
other business said proprietors may think proper, when
met" is not admissible under a statutory requirement
that the warrant contain each article to be acted upon.[3]
But towns do insert such phrases as "To transact any
other business" that may legally be presented,[4] or even
"To act on any business that may properly come before
said meeting," [5] and under such authority they may pass
resolutions, instruct town officers, and take other actions
of a supplementary character.

The voter is not, however, entirely dependent upon
the selectmen either for the time of the meeting or for
the subjects to be considered, for the law gives him the
privilege of a liberal initiative. Should the selectmen

[1] Loring v. Westwood (1921), 238 Mass. 10.
[2] Sherman v. Torrey (1868), 99 Mass. 473; Sawyer v. Manchester (1882), 62 N. H. 135.
[3] Evans v. Osgood (1841), 18 Me. 213.
[4] Adams Town Report (1926), p. 183; Agawam Town Report (1926), p. 13; Dalton Town Report (1926), p. 13.
[5] Dana Town Report (1926), p. 4; North Andover Town Report (1926), p. 19.

"unreasonably refuse" to call a meeting, a justice of the peace upon the written application of either one hundred registered voters or ten per cent of the total number, may issue a warrant directed to the constables of the town if there are any, or otherwise to any of the persons making the application, requiring that the inhabitants qualified to vote on town affairs be summoned to assemble at the time, place, and for the purpose indicated in the warrant.[1] The selectmen must, moreover, insert in the warrant for the annual meeting all subjects requested in writing by ten per cent or more of the voters, and if for a special meeting, all subjects requested by one hundred voters or ten per cent of the total number. The use of this privilege varies, but nearly every warrant contains articles introduced by the citizens, and, in some, more than half are initiated in this way. In substance they deal largely with matters of public improvements — highways, sewers, and sidewalk questions, a new street light, hydrant or graveled road. Some towns, indeed, have found such requests so numerous as to make the warrant top-heavy with minor matters, and have attempted to remedy the difficulty by adopting a general article instructing the selectmen to take proper action when required. But it is ordinarily sufficient for a townsman who desires the insertion of an article to notify the

---

[1] *Genl. Laws*, ch. 39, sec. 12. This is rarely done. In 1915, however, the provision as embodied in *Acts of 1913*, ch. 835, sec. 396, was invoked in Revere. The selectmen were petitioned in writing to call a town meeting within twelve days (not later than July 14) to consider the repeal of a certain by-law. The selectmen set the day for the meeting some ten weeks later (September 8) and a justice of the peace thereupon called a meeting for July 21. The court upheld this action on the ground that a postponement of ten weeks was equivalent to a refusal to call the meeting within a reasonable time (Walsworth *v.* Casassa [1914], 219 *Mass.* 204–205).

selectmen to that effect, and the request is likely to be granted without further formality. Frequently the warrant describes the origin of each article by printing after it "Inserted at request of Unitarian Men's Club" or "at the request of Herbert Cleaves," [1] or "Petition of Gordon Currier, Town Treasurer," [2] or simply "Board of Selectmen" or "agreeable to the petition of the School Committee" [3] or, at times, merely the name or title of the originator as "Administration Building Committee" or "George H. O'Brien et al," or "American Legion." [4]

In the country towns — especially on "the Cape" and in the Berkshires — there is still much of the old-fashioned procedure. The voters gather, usually in the town hall, and the day is given to the business of the community. In the early hours before the meeting there is likely to be considerable agitation for favorite aspirants for local offices, and caucuses frequently provide lists of nominees. But independent candidates are always possible and frequently successful — an uncertainty that adds to the occasion. There are, moreover, small groups in every community that undertake to control the political situation, and these find the early hours useful in making their various positions as secure as possible.

Under such conditions, the meeting is called to order by the moderator, or, if the moderator is to be elected, by the clerk. The warrant may be read, together with the constable's return, but after hearing the call and the first few articles, it is usually moved to dispense with further reading. The election of town officers is then in

[1] *Harvard Town Report* (1926), pp. 93, 94.
[2] *North Andover Town Report* (1926), p. 11.
[3] *Saugus Town Report* (1926), pp. 14–15.
[4] *Scituate Town Report* (1926), insert.

order.[1] If official ballots are used, the procedure is largely controlled by statute — the prescribed ballots having been previously prepared by the town clerk, election officers are appointed and sworn, the polls declared open and the voting begins.[2] But there remain some forty-three towns in the Commonwealth that continue to choose their officials according to local rules, and here the procedure assumes a character that savors much of those less enlightened, but perhaps more effective methods.

The first business is the election of a moderator [3] — a procedure that is frequently unanimous, and the town accordingly moves to cast a single ballot for its nominee. It then continues to a choice of the remaining officers. A separate ballot may be cast for each position, in which case the election is conducted by individual votes much as in any informal assembly.[4] In smaller communities the ballot-box is placed in front of the room. Sometimes it is held by the moderator. At others, it is placed upon a table behind a guard rail or set on a small platform before the election officers. The ballots are made in a variety of informal ways. It frequently happens that the

[1] Town officers may be nominated by primary, caucus, or nomination paper, depending upon the method adopted and put into effect by the town (*Genl. Laws*, ch. 53, secs. 56, 71). The caucus and nomination paper greatly predominate. The caucus, however, varies very much in importance. In some towns it practically determines the election. In others, it is entirely absent or its influence is slight. But whatever its place in electoral matters, it seems to exert little or no influence on the policy of the business meeting. Local matters seldom offer permanent lines of cleavage.

[2] *Millville Town Report* (1926), p. 10.

[3] *Milford Town Report* (1926), p. 10 (Town Records).

[4] The voting list is used in the choice of all officers whose election is required by law to be by ballot; but in the choice of other officers, the meeting determines whether this method shall be followed (*Genl. Laws*, ch. 41, sec. 5).

candidates themselves prepare them.[1] They may be printed, typed, stamped with a rubber stamp, or written in long hand. Friends of aspiring office seekers may bring a supply to the meeting and pass them around at the appropriate time, or when the election for a particular office is called, hastily prepare additional copies and give them enthusiastic distribution. At all events, when the moderator announces the polls open the voter comes to the platform and puts his ballot in the box.[2] As he does so, the moderator calls his name, and the teller makes the appropriate check on the voting list. This procedure is continued until electoral matters are disposed of, whereupon the town turns to the remaining articles in the warrant.[3]

These are sometimes taken in consecutive order; more often, however, they are considered as the meeting directs. The reports of town officers and committees come early in the session. It is often moved to accept these as

[1] They usually consist of a small piece of paper with the candidate's name (and sometimes his office) written thereon.

[2] Almost a century ago the procedure was described as follows: "The mode adopted by the selectmen of Lynn, for reasons which appeared to them satisfactory was, to place a large box on the table behind them, for the reception of votes, beyond the reach of the voters, to take the ballot from the voter, and, after seeing the name checked, to deposit it in this box" (Gates *v.* Neal [1839], 23 *Pick.* [Mass.] 311). The statutory provision of colonial days still requires that no vote be received by the moderator unless presented "open and unfolded" so that he may know that only one ballot is presented (*Genl. Laws*, ch. 41, sec. 8).

[3] Many towns now prescribe that the names of all elected officials shall appear "on a single ballot." If this be the case, precinct voting may be used, and a subsequent meeting provided for the transaction of business (*Dennis Town Report* [1926], pp. 69–70). If precinct voting is not used, balloting may be carried on simultaneously with the business meeting, and the whole procedure completed in a single session (*Harvard Town Report* [1926], p. 80). Both methods, of course, are for towns where "official ballots" are not accepted.

printed in the town report, but questions are frequently raised or further explanations required. Special reports are always made under a separate article, and if important, may even be the object of an adjourned meeting. The choice of minor officials not elected on the principal ballot is usually the next business. Some towns omit them entirely, and even when chosen they are apt to be of comparatively slight importance — uncontested and frequently an opportunity for that intimate humor that only the small town can effectively apply.[1]

With such preliminaries completed, the more significant articles are reached. Popularly conceived as a patriotic forum where phrases redolent of extreme "Americanism" find eloquent utterance, the town meeting falls short of expectations. Its interests are, on the contrary, appallingly objective. Highways, schools and sewers would probably sum up the citizen's idea of an average session. The building of a new fire station, the paving of Main street, a zoning system, an improvement on the town common, a new bridge, lighting proposals, or a municipal building — these are questions that are certain to elicit his condemnation, tolerance, or hearty support. True to both English and American traditions he is far more prone to express a grievance than to propound a theory, and certainly fewer appeals to democratic philosophies are heard in town meeting than in the

[1] The story is told of a popular minister in a western Massachusetts town who was elected hogreeve by a unanimous vote of his parishioners. In a little speech of acceptance he assured his fellow townsmen that he had supposed himself to be serving in the capacity of a shepherd to his sheep, and it was with some surprise that he learned that he was keeper of quite a different kind of animal (H. B. Adams, "Norman Constables in America," *Johns Hopkins University Studies in Historical and Political Science*, I, no. viii, 35).

average city council, when, returning with a hastily assumed dignity from the informality of executive session, the members speak to "the record" — and the gallery. At times, it is true, trivial matters receive the most consideration — they are the ones that often affect most deeply the intimate daily contacts of the townsman. Personality and family prestige count heavily in debate, but everyone, nevertheless, has a chance. Fluency, vigor and resourcefulness may mark the discussion.[1] A sharp witticism or a thinly disguised personality often has decisive influence over the carefully planned argument, for the "funny man" is a power to be reckoned with in the town meeting. A smiling crowd is not a reasoning one, and humor very quickly engenders sympathies far beyond its provocation. But article after article is disposed of, and a firm, tactful, and at times aggressive moderator guides the procedure to adjournment.

In large communities, the voters gather in the most spacious hall available. They do not all attend. It would, in most cases, be physically impossible; but it is rare that people are formally turned away. At the opening session there may be as many as a thousand present,[2] and if the warrant holds promise of acute local issues, even a larger number may come. There are no assigned places. Some towns, however, provide that the seats be

---

[1] J. S. Garland, *New England Town Law* (Boston, 1906), p. 9.

[2] Towns may prescribe by by-law the number of legal voters necessary to constitute a quorum, except as to the parts of meetings devoted exclusively to the election of town officers (*Genl. Laws*, ch. 39, sec. 13). Numerous towns make such provision — either a certain per cent of the total registered vote, perhaps four per cent (*Manchester Town By-Laws* [1920], art. 1, sec. 3), or a designated number — twenty-five, fifty, or seventy-five (*Danvers Town By-Laws* [1915], art. 2, sec. 2; *Franklin Town By-Laws* [1914], p. 5; *Hamilton Town By-Laws* [1921], p. 5).

reserved for registered voters, or that visitors (if there are any) must remain in the galleries. It is usual, however, for those who are to speak to be seated near the front of the room. At times, indeed, the front row resembles a Treasury bench opposite or around which opposing parties sit according to their convictions. The meeting is called to order either by the moderator or the town clerk. A local pastor may offer prayer, and the clerk then proceeds to read the warrant. But as in the smaller towns, after hearing the call and perhaps the return, further reading is commonly dispensed with, and the first articles are taken under consideration. A motion may be made to give the moderator power to appoint all minor officers, or, on the contrary, a list of citizens may be nominated to such positions. In either case the moderator puts the question to vote, declares the result, and announces consideration of the next article.

Reports of town officers are then received. The article providing for this matter often remains open, however, during the entire session and business is considered under it when occasion arises. Where a finance committee exists, much of the subsequent procedure is often determined by its chairman. This official with his secretary may occupy the platform to the right of the moderator, while the town clerk sits before a table to the left. As the chairman of the finance committee obtains recognition from the presiding officer, he introduces article after article, followed by the recommendation of his committee as to the proper action to be taken.[1] But such pro-

[1] These recommendations, as has been indicated, are frequently printed separately or they may appear below each article on the warrant. As each voter enters the hall he is furnished with a warrant, the recommendations

cedure is extreme. In many cases he takes no active part. Indeed the recommendations may be read by the secretary of the committee, and the chairman participate more or less moderately as circumstances require. The speaking is practically confined to a few town officers, the leading citizens, and the consistent member who desires to talk on every question. Many articles are passed without comment. Some, on the contrary, excite the greatest interest, and the moderator has difficulty keeping the speakers on the subject. It is not unusual for a large town meeting to pass half a million dollars in appropriations as mere routine business, the action being listlessly ratified by a scattering vote; but when an apparently minor article charged with local interests and animosities is announced, the meeting eagerly takes sides and records itself with emphasis.

Procedural matters offer frequent difficulties. General election laws are not intended to apply to town meetings, unless expressly stated in the statute.[1] Such regulations pertaining to voting, canvassing and declaring the result are, moreover, of the most general character. They hardly extend further than to require the election of designated officers for certain terms, the use of voting lists and ballots in prescribed cases, and certain other minor requirements of procedure;[2] but town by-laws often contain more definite guides.[3] It may be required that a single election ballot be used,[4]

of the finance committee (if separately printed), and any printed reports of importance that will be introduced before the meeting.

[1] State v. Avery (1875), 42 Conn. 165; Page v. McClure (1906), 79 Vt. 83.

[2] Genl. Laws, ch. 41, secs. 1–11.

[3] Ibid., ch. 39, sec. 15.

[4] Plymouth Town By-Laws [1912], art. 1, sec. 4.

and the officers whose names are to appear thereon will usually be enumerated.[1] It is frequently provided that all articles be considered in consecutive order, unless otherwise decided by the town.[2] There are provisions that printed copies of the warrant be furnished at all meetings; that at the order of the moderator, no person whose name is not on the check list shall be admitted;[3] that on the demand of the presiding officer, motions shall be submitted in writing; and there is the frequent requirement that no warrant be dismissed until every article is disposed of. Reconsideration is restricted, the previous question occasionally provided,[4] and even a brief outline of motions supplied to serve as a basis of parliamentary conduct.[5] Such skeleton provisions are often given additional scope by a requirement that the duties of the moderator shall be "deter-

[1] *Mattapoisett Town By-Laws* (1903), art. 1, sec. 3.

[2] At times a two-thirds vote is required (*Dighton Town By-Laws* [1921], art. 1, sec. 3).

[3] *Belmont Town By-Laws* [1923], art. 2, secs. 1–2.

[4] *Manchester Town By-Laws* [1919], art. 1, sec. 11.

[5] *Danvers Town By-Laws* (1913), art. 2, sec. 5:

Sec. 5. When a question is before the meeting, the moderator shall entertain no motion that does not relate to the same, except a motion to adjourn, or some other motion that is privileged in its nature. And he shall entertain no motion relating to the same, except:

1. To lay on the table.
2. For the previous question.
3. To postpone to a time set.
4. To commit or re-commit.
5. To amend.
6. To postpone indefinitely.

These motions shall have precedence in the order in which they are arranged. The motion to adjourn whenever the effect of an adjournment would be to dissolve the meeting, and the motions to lay on the table and for the previous question, shall be debatable for not more than ten minutes; and no person shall speak thereon more than two minutes."

mined by the general rules of parliamentary law, so far as they may be adapted to town meetings," [1] or that the general provisions of the "parliamentary law of Massachusetts as recognized by the Massachusetts Legislature shall constitute the rules for the procedure of business . . . in all points to which they relate." [2] But the predominant provision — one that is met in a large part of town by-laws, reads:

Town meetings shall be governed according to the rules of parliamentary practice contained in Cushing's Manual, so far as they are applicable and not inconsistent with law, or with these by-laws. [3]

The voting is usually *viva-voce* and most of the questions are settled by "ayes" and "nays" or by a show of hands. A large vote in a business meeting is rarely over a few hundred — even in the large towns with a potential voting strength of five thousand or more — and counting is, as a rule, simple enough. [4] But a statutory provision requires that should a count be immediately questioned by seven or more voters, the moderator "shall verify it by polling the voters or by dividing the meeting unless the town has by a previous order or by

---

[1] *Billerica Town By-Laws* (1897), art. 1, sec. 15; *Franklin Town By-Laws* (1914), art. 1, sec. 10.

[2] *Lynnfield Town By-Laws* (1913), art. 1, sec. 3.

[3] *Nahant Town By-Laws* (1902), art. 2, sec. 4.

[4] The law provides that if the vote required by statute is two-thirds, the count shall be taken and the result recorded by the town clerk. But if the vote be unanimous, no count need be taken (*Genl. Laws*, ch. 39, sec. 15). The moderator is required to receive the vote of any person whose name is on the voting list, or who presents a proper certificate from the registrars (*ibid.*, sec. 18). In the larger meetings, however, he is more than likely to receive anyone who comes. Many attend who are not voters, and the moderator can do little more than admonish the assembly and then count the hands he sees.

by-law provided another method." [1] When this happens, the dissatisfied voter simply rises in his place and
says, "I doubt it." The moderator then ascertains if
there are six others. If so, there are frequently several
procedures open to him. After putting the question, he
may proceed systematically to count the uplifted hands.
If he still remains uncertain, he will appoint tellers,
assign a section of the hall to each, and the votes in each
section will be polled for and against the question. Each
teller when called upon by the moderator, will then
announce the result of his count.[2] In extreme cases,
ballots may be provided or at times the house may be
actually "divided"— an expedient, however, that seems
to be falling into disuse.[3]

But the success of town-meeting procedure is a matter
of personality rather than of more formal regulation —
particularly the personality of the moderator. It is this
officer who presides over the gathering, decides all questions of order, and makes declarations of the vote.[4] As
has been indicated, the by-laws at times offer a fragmentary guide, but rules of order in the strict sense play only
a minor part. On the one hand, the moderator is likely
to have but a scant knowledge of their provisions, and
on the other, the town meeting (aside from a few mem-

---

[1] *Genl. Laws,* ch. 39, sec. 15.

[2] *Framingham Town By-Laws* (1920), sec. 7 ; *Provincetown Town By-
Laws* (1913), art. 11, sec. 2.

[3] The method of "division" is well shown in the by-laws of Lexington
for 1898 (*Lexington Town By-Laws* [1898], art. 2, sec. 7). When a vote is
"doubted" the presiding officer "may proceed at once to poll the house by
causing those who are in favor of the question to pass directly in front of
the chair, and afterwards those who are opposed to it; and when the house
be thus divided, the Clerk shall duly record the number of votes for and
against the question respectively."

[4] *Genl. Laws,* ch. 39, sec. 15.

bers) is even less likely to be informed. To control, moreover, a thousand restless citizens untrained in the practices of deliberative assemblies, requires qualities far rarer than a technical knowledge of legislative procedure. Parliamentary tangles are common occurrences. They are usually resolved with the same facility and method that Alexander is reported to have used on the prophetic knot of King Gordius, and the court quite readily lends its support to such summary procedure. A popular assembly is not a representative body, and its problems must be met by methods suited to its structure.[1] It may be useful for Congress or a state legislature to wrangle hours over points of order, but a town meeting very easily becomes weary, and is quite capable of going home. A recent meeting was half emptied when the local fire bell rang in the midst of deliberations, and on another occasion when parliamentary difficulties were thrown in the way of adjournment, the gathering, in groups that grew increasingly large, walked slowly out of the hall, and left those interested to settle it. Like many another political institution, it has assumed a formality in organization and procedure that it actually possesses only to a limited degree. Documentary evidence tends to foster such a condition. Uniform practices are gleaned from formal records, and an orderly arrangement of the results often gives a false symmetry to the institution. Throughout history, popular assemblies have been much more than political bodies, they have been intimate reflections of the reactions of people

[1] The court has said (Wood *v.* Milton [1908], 197 *Mass.* 533): "The ample powers possessed by moderators, recognized from earliest times and growing out of the imperative needs of the office, are inconsistent with many incidents of ordinary parliamentary law."

to the problems of living together, and have proved in a way only a little more susceptible to strict and uniform regulation than any other gathering indiscriminately assembled for a common but temporary purpose.[1]

The selectmen are the chief administrative officers of the town. Formerly [2] they were three, five, seven or nine in number, but the commission appointed to complete the work of revising and codifying the laws relating to towns found no town having more than five. Feeling, moreover, that this was a sufficient number, it recommended the present requirement — three or five.[3] The predominant number is three, and the statutes require that they be chosen for one or three years. In some places the board is continuous — that is, one member is elected yearly for the longer term — while in others (and they are the more numerous) all members are elected annually for one year.[4] Their duties continue to be increasingly various — to such an extent, indeed, that the burden is becoming too heavy to permit the ablest men to undertake the work.

[1] Adams *v.* Townsend Schoolhouse Building Committee (1923), 245 *Mass.* 548–549. In Wood *v.* Milton (*op. cit.*, 532–533), the judicial view is well expressed: "Judicially the town meeting is not a representative body, but a pure democracy, where the citizens, as to matters within their jurisdiction, administer the affairs of the town in person. It exercises both legislative and executive function. The freest discussion prevails, yet in some respects its proceedings are inherently somewhat summary. The technical rules of parliamentary law, designed for the regulation of deliberative assemblies, are in some respects ill adapted for the transaction of the affairs of a town meeting. Hence, although in general the action of town meetings conforms to parliamentary procedure, it never has been held that they are governed by the strict rules of legislative practice."

[2] *Acts of 1913*, ch. 835, sec. 400.

[3] Massachusetts General Court, Senate no. 2 (1919), *Report of the Commission to Complete the Work of Revising and Codifying the Laws Relating to Towns*, p. 12.

[4] *Genl. Laws*, ch. 41, sec. 1.

The town by-laws usually assign them the general direction and management of local property and affairs, full authority to act as agents of the town, as well as power to regulate the local police. But these are as nothing compared to their statutory functions which have descended upon them through three centuries of legislation. In a general way the subjects that most frequently occupy their attention are finance, public improvements, licenses and permits, public protection, election affairs, appointments, social relief and town-meeting matters. Their weekly meetings (in small places they are less frequent) are principally concerned with establishing street lines, arranging public ways, caring for town property, and providing local improvements — especially the assessment of betterments under the State betterment act. In large places much effort is expended in granting licenses and permits for building and construction purposes, as well as for regulating hawkers, peddlers, lodging houses, gasoline stations, and amusements of various kinds. At times a letter from the governor may be received relative to a public emergency; attention may be called by some interested citizen to a local nuisance, or the selectmen may arrange a special "hearing" on this or any other question that may come before them, and all citizens affected are invited to attend. In electoral matters they are called upon to establish voting precincts, provide polling places, appoint election officials — to undertake, indeed, the general conduct of elections, and in smaller towns to serve, in addition, as registrars of voters.[1] The statutes provide some forty separate officers whose appointment is, under

[1] *Genl. Laws*, ch. 54, secs. 6–8, 12, 24, 105; ch. 51, sec. 16.

various circumstances, vested in them. They compose a bewildering array of inspectors, weighers, commissioners and measurers; assessors, collectors, police officers and purchasing agents; caretakers, superintendents, trustees, and boards.[1] The town meeting is dependent upon them. They prepare the warrant, conduct hearings on disputed articles, arrange special meetings, and take a prominent part in the proceedings themselves. They (with the moderator) are the "first men" of the community. Their influence is strong and often determining, and in spite of increased duties, they continue, for the most part, the vigorous perpetuation of their traditions.[2]

Every town has a clerk. In many respects he is the most important local officer — if not in dignity at least in general service. He probably holds his position for longer periods of time than any other — twenty to forty years being not uncommon, and occasionally the office remains in the same family for successive generations. The *General Laws* provide that he shall record all votes at town meetings, administer the oath of office to all town officers who apply to him to be sworn, inform the secretary of the Commonwealth of the results of local elections, notify the county court of the qualified con-

---

[1] *Ibid.*, index volume, p. 892.

[2] In towns where no provision is made for the election of assessors of taxes and overseers of the poor the selectmen are chosen to such offices (*Genl. Laws*, ch. 41, sec. 20). Recent legislation has permitted communities to use their services still further. Upon following a designated procedure the town may order the selectmen to assume the duties of sewer boards, water commissioners, park commissioners, boards of health, assessors, and overseers of the poor, and to appoint suitable officers to administer such services (*Acts of 1920*, ch. 591). The acceptance of such legislation would amount in practice to placing the town under commission government, but already overworked boards have a tendency to look a little dubious in the face of increased functions, and no town has as yet taken full advantage of the statute.

stables, and make and keep an index of the numerous instruments which the law requires shall be recorded in his office.[1] But this is a very small part of it. In addition to many statutes giving him a multitude of miscellaneous duties,[2] he is the person upon whom everyone feels quite at liberty to place additional burdens. All other town officers rely on him for a knowledge of the law. Details of all elections are intrusted to him. The by-laws and regulations of the numerous boards, commissions and departments are filed with him. A day spent in his office (usually in the town hall) is a revelation in minor services. Here enters the citizen in search of a dog license, a marriage permit, or a hunting and fishing license. Here are filed mortgages, bills of sale, physicians' registrations, and vital statistics. Here are the records of the town meeting, and the citizen who feels himself harshly treated in the turmoil of direct democracy resorts to the clerk's office to check the extent of his damage or gather data for further action. In the larger communities, it is a full-time occupation; in small places, only a few hours a week informally conducted at the town clerk's home. Remuneration may be slight — possibly only the statutory fees collected in the performance of his duties.[3] But he is, nevertheless, an officer of

---

[1] *Genl. Laws*, ch. 41, sec. 15.

[2] *Ibid.*, index volume, pp. 188–192.

[3] For the most part, town officers receive little remuneration. The selectmen may be paid as high as five hundred dollars a year. A moderator is given only a small sum — five or ten dollars for each meeting and a little less for special meetings, or at times a lump sum of twenty-five, fifty or a hundred dollars a year. A town clerk may receive a salary, part salary and part fees, or simply fees (*Genl. Laws*, ch. 46, sec. 26). Both treasurer and collector may likewise work on a commission basis. In small places there are often no salaries amounting to more than thirty dollars a year, but in larger communities remuneration for the leading officers compares favorably

great importance. Indeed, it is not too much to say that the whole structure of town meeting government is built around him.

The financial officers of the town are usually three in number — assessors, collector and treasurer — although in smaller places they are frequently combined in various ways. Assessors, if elected, are required by law to be three or five, chosen for a term of three years.[1] The selectmen may, however, if the proper statutory provisions are accepted, appoint suitable persons to the office, and in many instances, when so elected, or where no other provision is made, serve in this capacity themselves. There is nothing peculiar in their duties. They determine the property valuation of the town and make the proper apportionments of the tax among the inhabitants.[2] In the smaller places the collector is frequently the treasurer (both functions are on rare occasions given to the clerk)[3] but in many communities large and small, a collector is elected separately. Upon receiving the tax list and warrant from the assessors, he proceeds to gather the taxes by sending a notice to each person assessed,[4] and to pay the funds obtained to the treasurer. This officer has the general duties common to his position. He receives and cares for all money belonging to the town, pays out such funds according to the order of the town or its authorized officers, and forwards state and county taxes to the proper persons.[5] The statutes

with those of cities. The matter is very largely regulated by the town (*ibid.*, ch. 40, secs. 5 [30], 21 [13]).

[1] *Genl. Laws*, ch. 41, sec. 1.
[2] *Ibid.*, sec. 29.
[3] *Pelham Town Report* (1926), p. 1.
[4] *Genl. Laws*, ch. 60, secs. 2-3.
[5] *Ibid.*, ch. 41, sec. 52.

give him many miscellaneous duties. He is charged with notifying the director of accounts of all municipal indebtedness,[1] of keeping standards of weights and measures furnished by the Commonwealth in safe and accessible places, and is the custodian of all trust funds (unless other provisions are made) which he invests as directed by the various commissioners.[2]

Aside from additional local officers that are common in all forms of municipal government — town counsels, engineers, commissioners, trustees, committees and directors of various kinds — minor officials more or less peculiar to New England are almost as numerous as in the early periods. Their functions, however, have in most cases undergone serious alteration or restriction. The records are quite uniform in announcing the appointment or election of fence viewers, pound keepers, and field drivers of colonial days. The duties of fence viewers embrace not merely the correction of insufficient fences, but extend to the establishing of division lines when a boundary is in dispute. Each town may "appoint a pound keeper for each pound and one or more field drivers for the town." It is further directed that "Every field driver shall take up horses, mules, asses, neat cattle, sheep, goats or swine going at large in the public ways, or on common and unimproved land within his town and not under the care of a keeper." Beasts so taken shall be "forthwith impounded"[3] and the field driver shall be "entitled to ten cents each for sheep and goats and fifty cents each for other beasts so taken up by

[1] *Genl. Laws*, ch. 44, sec. 28.
[2] *Ibid.*, ch. 41, sec. 46.
[3] *Ibid.*, ch. 49, secs. 2, 14, 22, 24–26.

him," and the pound keeper shall receive four cents each for "animals impounded in his pound." Practically all towns elect such officers and in rural communities they are still useful.[1]

Weighers, measurers, and surveyors of commodities are still widely appointed:

The mayor or the selectmen, on the written request of any person engaged in buying, selling or transporting goods or commodities which require weighing, surveying or measuring, shall appoint weighers, measurers or surveyors of such goods or commodities, who shall be sworn before entering upon their duties, shall serve for one year, and may be removed at any time by the appointing authority.[2]

These officers are the official measurers of their respective commodities. A carload of lumber arrives for a local company — the surveyor of lumber certifies as to its quantity upon arrival. A car load is exported — the surveyor will likewise certify its amount to avoid dispute with the foreign buyer. In many cases they are employees of the concerns dealing in the goods to be measured, but at least one must not be so engaged. Constables are still universally chosen. They are directed to serve all warrants and other orders given to them by the selectmen, may serve within the town various writs or processes carrying limited damages or values,[3] and at certain times may act as special police

[1] See the *Report of the Special Commission on Obsolete Laws* (Massachusetts General Court, Senate no. 4 [1926]) where some of these officers are declared to be in whole or in part obsolete — especially pp. 8 (justices of the peace and trial justices), 9 (measurers of leather), and 34 (pound keepers and field drivers).

[2] *Ibid.*, ch. 41, sec. 85.

[3] *Ibid.*, ch. 41, secs. 92, 94. Legal firms in larger cities frequently have members sworn as constables in order to serve processes in which they are interested.

officers. In the larger towns they are frequently unimportant, and although still chosen, they usually fail to qualify for service at process in civil action. In practice, the local police are quite likely to look after the general peace matters of the community, and the sheriff to serve most of the civil writs. One of them, however, is designated by the selectmen to post the town warrant for which duty he receives a small fee. But in rural communities, they still remain the sole peace officers (save for state patrols), attend the ballot-boxes at election time and post all official notices.

Such, in brief outline, is the town meeting today. It is plain that in the larger urban areas it can no longer function under even a semblance of its early procedure. This is in no way to condemn the form of government as originally conceived; it is not even to disparage it as an effective instrument of popular control under many simple conditions that still exist. It is to be remembered that the vast majority of the municipalities throughout New England operate under the old methods of direct democracy, and except in the larger communities (those, perhaps, over six thousand population), there is little desire for a change, or even discontent with the old order. But it is apparent that numbers are of paramount importance in a town meeting; that there are certain questions confronting every municipality that require skilled, technical attention for solution; that political problems in congested areas demand a closer and more constant supervision than a primary assembly — potentially of several thousand voters but actually of several hundred and often of a few dozen — can possibly give. A committee appointed by the town of Framingham — the largest community in the Commonwealth to retain an unlimited town meeting — to investigate the expediency of adopting another form of local government, reported the defects of the old system as follows:

(1) It is impossible to obtain adequate deliberative action from so large a group as the annual town meeting provides.

(2) Because of the limited information at the disposal of the voter — a condition impossible to overcome — the average citizen is unfitted to vote effectively on a great majority of the complex questions submitted for his approval.

(3) A scattering vote of several hundred citizens, upon which a large amount of the town legislation is based, in no way indicates either the will of the people or even a fair decision of the minority.

(4) The long ballot — i.e., the attempt to elect so many officers that a careful selection on the part of the average voter is impossible — has been firmly established.

(5) The geographical condition in Framingham, with its development into scattered units each with problems peculiar to itself, seems to indicate, plainly, the need of representative government.

Nor does the committee find that the method of legislation and election are the only faults. The provisions for administration contain many of the evils that the modern science of government associates with inefficient city management.

(1) The framework has become in a real sense a "patchwork government" — a mass of boards and offices with overlapping functions and uncertain jurisdictions.

(2) Each department of the town is practically an independent unit — a small government of its own with no definite responsibility.

(3) There is no method for holding those who are directing the affairs of the government to a strict and immediate accountability.

(4) The officers are so numerous, their duties so scattered, and their authority so decentralized that the entire structure

appears to be entirely inadequate to fulfill the tasks that modern democracy requires.[1]

For many years, town government was a factor of tremendous social and political significance in Massachusetts. It had a picturesqueness that when emphasized in the democratic decades of the middle period, made a deep and lasting impression. Simple political principles applied to simple social problems will permit almost any kind of a government to work. For two hundred years, Massachusetts communities functioned under such conditions. For close to another century, the framework has been maintained in eighty-five per cent of them, and will undoubtedly remain in form, at least, for many years to come. The townsman evinces a deep-seated reluctance to relinquish an institution to which he has been so long accustomed, and which meets well enough his idea of local needs and aspirations. Yet there is an inexorable pressure, of which increased numbers, narrowed interests, precinct voting, official ballots, and scientific methods are undisputed evidence and not to be permanently glossed by emotional references to past greatness. It is not to be forgotten that many arguments of the past intended as eulogies, have won their immortality as epitaphs.[2]

[1] Town of Framingham, Town Meeting, *Report of Committee on Change of Town Government* (March, 1923), pp. 3-4.

[2] Charles Francis Adams wrote (*Three Episodes of Massachusetts History*, II, 967): "Just in the degree in which civic population increases . . . the town meeting becomes unwieldy and unreliable; until at last it has to be laid aside as something which the community has outgrown. It becomes a relic, though always an interesting one, of a simple and possibly better past. Moreover, the indications that the system is breaking down are always the same. The meetings become numerous, noisy and unable to dispose of business. Disputed questions cannot be decided; demagogues obtain control; the more intelligent cease to attend."

# VII

## THE LIMITED TOWN MEETING

WHATEVER may appear to be the advantages of direct democracy in smaller communities, larger places are finding the old town meeting impossible. In spite of patriotic admonitions, local expedients, and statutory aids, towns have been forced to seek relief in more or less definite departures from the old order. Representative government as exemplified in conventional city charters has (especially in recent years) made slight impression, for unlike Gribouille, hesitating communities have shown little inclination to jump into the water in order to avoid the rain. The result has been efforts at modification rather than abolition — attempts to devise a framework that will maintain the merits of the old methods while giving more effective expression to the necessities of the new.

The essentials of this compromise contain elements unique in American municipal methods. It is known as the limited or representative town meeting. The community is first divided into a various number of precincts — practice has established from four to nine. From each precinct an equal number of delegates (usually between thirty and forty) known as "town meeting members" are chosen by popular vote. Collectively — and in conjunction with certain designated officers as members *ex officiis* — they compose the town meeting which exercises practically all powers vested in the town as a corporate body. No other change is contemplated. Warrants are issued, elections conducted, appointive positions filled and town meetings assembled as formerly. Electors, indeed, may still speak at any meeting. In this respect they are almost as unrestricted as under the old form, but voting is reserved to the duly qualified town-meeting members who compose the new assembly.[1]

The idea is not entirely of recent origin. Proposals made by the early committees in Boston were similar insofar as the representative principle was concerned.[2] The first few plans submitted on those occasions provided for representation on the basis of two members from each ward. But the committee reporting in 1821 had proposed "a body of assistants" to be chosen annually on a ratio of one for every nine hundred inhabitants in each ward, which at that time would have meant a body of forty-one members. This report met with opposition. It was criticised because it "had not gone far enough in its alterations," and was accordingly returned to an enlarged committee for further study.[3]

[1] A recent advisory opinion (1918) of the Supreme Judicial Court (229 *Mass.* 601) placed certain restrictions on the acceptance of this form of government — *i.e.*, limiting its adoption under the constitution to towns of twelve thousand population or over, and refusing to sanction the establishment of representative government through a general law without the application of the town preceding action by the General Court. (See also Larcom *v.* Olin [1893], 160 *Mass.* 102.) But an amendment to the constitution in 1926 removed the restriction in part by authorizing the General Court to provide for limited town meetings in towns of more than six thousand inhabitants (*Acts of 1927*, p. 494: *Genl. Laws*, Constitution, Amendments, Art. 70).

[2] A. D. Chandler, *Limited Town Meetings with a General Legislative Bill therefore*, "An Address by Alfred D. Chandler, Esq., at Hyde Park, Mass., Monday, Jan. 18, 1914," pp. 6–7, 25.

[3] Quincy, *A Municipal History of Boston*, p. 31.

As has been seen, however, the recommendations of all early Boston committees were consistently rejected. The people seemed unable to agree on a new form of government and there was apparent a deep-seated reluctance to any change. It was thought, moreover, that legal requirements prohibited representative methods, for the state constitution demanded that the inhabitants of each town should meet together "on the first Monday in *April* annually, forever" for certain prescribed purposes of election at which "The Selectmen . . . shall preside."[1] In the constitutional convention that met in Massachusetts in 1820, Mr. Lemuel Shaw sponsored a movement to amend this section. The difficulty as he described it to the convention was that while the General Court could grant powers as occasion might require, it could not dispense with the mode of organization prescribed in the Constitution.[2] The voters, he explained, had both electoral and deliberative functions to perform, and several thousand people could not exercise the latter duty effectively through meeting in a single body. At the session of December 26, accordingly, a resolution providing that the legislature have the power to grant charters of incorporation to towns of more than twelve thousand inhabitants was read and passed, and the following provisions (the second amendment to the present Constitution) were subsequently accepted by the people:

The General Court shall have full power and authority to erect and constitute municipal or city governments, in any corporate town or towns in this Commonwealth, and

[1] *Acts and Laws* (1780–1781), Constitution, pt. 2, ch. 1, sec. 2, art. 2; ch. 2, sec. 1, art. 3.

[2] Massachusetts Constitutional Convention (1820–1821), *Journal of Debates and Proceedings* (Boston, 1821), p. 98.

to grant to the inhabitants thereof, such powers, privileges and immunities, not repugnant to the Constitution, as the General Court shall deem necessary or expedient, for the regulation and government thereof; and to prescribe the manner of calling and holding public meetings of the inhabitants, in Wards, or otherwise, for the election of officers under the Constitution, and the manner of returning the votes given at such meetings. Provided, that no such government shall be erected or constituted in any town not containing twelve thousand inhabitants; nor unless it be with the consent, and on the application, of a majority of the inhabitants of such town, present and voting thereon, pursuant to a vote at a meeting duly warned and holden for that purpose. And provided, also, that all by-laws, made by such municipal or city government, shall be subject, at all times, to be annulled by the General Court.[1]

In spite of this provision it was close to a century before there was an application of the principle advocated by the Boston committee of 1821, but in 1897, Alfred D. Chandler was recommending that it be used in Brookline. He proposed that the town be divided into five wards from each of which sixty men should be chosen to

[1] *Ibid.*, pp. 185, 276, 285; Massachusetts Constitutional Convention (1820–1821), *Amendments of the Constitution of Massachusetts, proposed by the Convention of Delegates. . . . With their Address to the People of this Commonwealth* (Boston, 1821), p. 8. In explanation of its work relative to the incorporation of towns to become cities, the convention said (p. 30): "It appeared to us, that it would be convenient, and proper, that towns, containing more than *twelve thousand inhabitants*, should, on application of their qualified voters, by petition to the Legislature, be incorporated, with *municipal, or city, powers, and privileges*. Without such powers and privileges, the inhabitants of such towns, must continue to vote, in one meeting, *however numerous they may become*. This is already found to be an inconvenience in *two towns*, for the removal of which provision ought to be made. Under the limitations, and restrictions, which we have provided, we can see no reason why the power to incorporate should not be vested in the legislature. And we, therefore recommend an alteration of the Constitution, so as to effect that purpose."

constitute the town meeting.[1] Massachusetts was not, however, destined to be the first to make the suggestion effective. In June, 1906, the city of Newport, Rhode Island, after over fifty years under a city charter, decided to give the plan a trial. Legislative power was placed in a "representative council" of one hundred and ninety-five members, thirty-nine to be chosen from each ward; and provision was made that, subject to such conditions as might be determined from time to time by this representative council, any tax payer or voter of the city might speak but not vote at its meetings.[2]

In 1915 Brookline had a population approaching thirty-four thousand.[3] Even during the last decade of the nineteenth century, the town meeting had experienced difficulties. The inhabitants were of a mixed type, and the electorate, accordingly, was from all classes. Proximity to Boston caused difficulty in attendance, and while several policemen with a check list at the door of the town hall helped to relieve this embarrassment, their appearance was formidable enough to reduce the legitimate attendance. One hundred and fifty to two hundred and

[1] C. W. Kellog, Jr., "The Brookline Town Meeting," *Brookline Historical Publication Society Publications*, 2d ser., no. 13, pp. 33–34.

[2] Rhode Island General Assembly, *Public Laws* (1906–1907), ch. 1392. A full discussion is given by F. E. Chadwick in his paper on "The Newport Charter" (*Amer. Pol. Sc. Assn. Proc.*, III, 58–66). See also Alfred D. Chandler's *Local Self-Government: Elective Town Meetings for Large Towns* (Brookline, 1908), pp. 1, 57, 63. It is significant that the same year (1906), the town of Westfield, Massachusetts, definitely refused a city form of government, although at that time the community was among the largest towns in the State — close to fourteen thousand inhabitants. The rejected charter was typical of those in use at the time, its fifty-eight sections occupying some nineteen pages in the statutes (*Acts of 1906*, ch. 409).

[3] Massachusetts, Secretary of the Commonwealth, *The Population of Massachusetts as Determined by the Fourteenth Census of the United States* (1920) (Boston, 1921), p. 23. Hereafter cited *Census* (1920).

fifty seemed to be about the usual number. Five or six hundred was large.[1] The town had tried most of the recognized methods designed to relieve overcrowded communities attempting to conduct their local affairs as they did in the days of the Colony and the Province. For many years there had been a finance committee of twenty citizens who examined the articles of the warrant and made recommendations in print to the town.[2] In 1890, in common with other communities, Brookline accepted the act providing for official ballots, the regulation of polling hours, methods of nomination, and conduct of town elections.[3] The same year there was a proposal to divide the town into voting precincts,[4] — it then contained a population of over twelve thousand[5] — but the question was indefinitely postponed,[6] to be accepted, however, in May, 1894[7] when the town was close to sixteen thousand.[8] In 1901 it was voted to accept chapter 201 of the acts of that year, "An Act Relative to Town

[1] A. D. Chandler, "Brookline, A Study in Town Government," *New England Magazine*, VIII (new series), 788: "The town hall is not far from the city line of Boston; across that line there are many saloons. It was at one time found that when large appropriations were under discussion, especially for labor, strangers from over the line, as well as local non-voters, would attend the town meetings, and would influence the vote."

[2] Kellog, "The Brookline Town Meeting," p. 33.

[3] *Acts of 1890*, ch. 386; *Ms. Letter*, Town Clerk to Secretary of the Commonwealth (Brookline, Feb. 16, 1890). All manuscript letters cited are from the files of the Secretary of the Commonwealth, State House, Boston, Mass.

[4] *Acts of 1890*, ch. 423, sec. 72.

[5] Massachusetts, Secretary of the Commonwealth, *The Population of Massachusetts as Determined by the Thirteenth Census of the United States* (1910) (Boston, 1911), p. 19. Hereafter cited *Census* (1910).

[6] *Ms. Letter*, Town Clerk to Secretary of the Commonwealth (Brookline, Dec. 28, 1893).

[7] *Acts of 1894*, ch. 132; *Ms. Letter*, Town Clerk to Secretary of the Commonwealth (Brookline, June 9, 1894).

[8] *Census* (1910), p. 19.

Meetings in the Town of Brookline." [1]  This was a frank
recognition that the primary assembly was becoming too
large to give satisfactory results without unusual safe-
guards being applied.  It provided for the use of the
check list at the door for every town meeting, or as an
alternative, a system of registering turnstiles. [2]  It required, further, that certain votes should, upon petition,
be submitted for ratification at a subsequent town meeting, and prescribed the process to be followed.  In 1914,
"An Act to Abolish the Enrolment of Members of Political Parties and to limit the Membership of Ward and
Town Committees" [3] was submitted to the voters of the
state at the annual state election, and Brookline accepted the proposal. [4]  It was an effort to regulate party
organization by improving the form of primary ballots,
simplifying electoral administration and restricting committee membership.  In 1910, the town had exceeded
twenty-seven thousand in population.  Five years later
it was over thirty-three thousand.  The legislature then
passed an act "to Provide for Precinct Voting, Limited
Town Meetings, Town Meeting Members, a Referendum and an Annual Moderator in the Town of Brookline," [5] and at the general election of November 2, 1915,
the new proposal was accepted by a very large majority. [6]
The step was taken with little disturbance.  The selectmen's report for the year makes casual reference to "a

[1] *Ms. Letter*, Town Clerk to Secretary of the Commonwealth (Brookline,
March 24, 1902).
[2] *Acts of 1901*, ch. 201.
[3] *Acts of 1914*, ch. 790.
[4] *Ms. Letter*, Town Clerk to Secretary of the Commonwealth (Brookline,
March 2, 1921).
[5] *Special Acts of 1915*, ch. 250.
[6] *Brookline Town Report* (1915), p. 74.

change in our form of government" and is careful to state that it "simply regulates the size of the town-meeting."[1]

The act was short — twelve sections occupying a brief six pages. Upon its acceptance, the selectmen were directed to divide the town into precincts — not less than eight nor more than twelve. From each precinct the registered voters were to choose by ballot twenty-seven "town meeting members" — their nominations to be made by petitions signed by not less than thirty voters from the precinct in which the candidate resided.[2] In addition, certain town officers were designated as "town meeting members at large," and these, with the elected members, were to form the "town meeting."

This group was to exercise all powers vested in the municipal corporation. Its procedural matters were regulated to the extent of requiring that a quorum be one-half of the total membership, that all meetings be held with open doors, and that, subject to such conditions as the members might see fit to prescribe, any registered voter might speak but not vote. The meeting, moreover, was forbidden to bind the town in any matter affecting its municipal existence or the form of its government without action (by ballot) from the voters of the town at large.

In addition, the act contained provisions for a referendum. Affirmative votes on special appropriations exceeding $25,000 did not go into effect until five days

---

[1] *Ibid.*, p. 99.

[2] But any town meeting member might become a candidate for re-election by giving written notice to the town clerk at least twenty days before such election; while any vacancies in the precinct delegation were to be filled for the unexpired term by the remaining members from the precinct (*Special Acts of 1915*, ch. 250, sec. 4).

from the dissolution of the meeting at which the vote was taken. If within that period a petition signed by twenty registered voters from each precinct was filed with the selectmen asking that the question be submitted to the voters of the town, within fourteen days the selectmen and moderator were to submit the question within the several precincts, and a majority of those voting was necessary to sustain the action.

In 1919, Watertown followed the example of her larger neighbor. The previous history of this town — as of most of the larger communities in the State — had been similar to that of Brookline. Attempts to adjust the political machinery to a growing population had resulted in the acceptance of various legislative acts. After an attempt in 1890 to make a more satisfactory adjustment of the voting precincts,[1] a town meeting in 1893 abolished the precincts entirely,[2] only to re-establish them in 1913.[3] In 1908 the town accepted "An Act Relative to Town Meetings in the Town of Watertown,"[4] providing, as in Brookline, for the use of turnstiles at all town meetings, and for a referendum (with a few exceptions) on any "vote passed at an original or adjourned town meeting to which three hundred and fifty or more voters shall have been admitted."[5]

[1] *Ms. Letter*, Town Clerk to Secretary of the Commonwealth (Watertown, Feb. 6, 1891); *Acts of 1890*, ch. 423, art. 72.

[2] *Ms. Letter*, Town Clerk to Secretary of the Commonwealth (Watertown, Jan. 11, 1895).

[3] *Ms. Letter*, Town Clerk to Secretary of the Commonwealth (Watertown, June 26, 1913).

[4] *Acts of 1908*, ch. 361; *Ms. Letter*, Town Clerk to Secretary of the Commonwealth (Watertown, Aug. 25, 1909). The vote is announced as seventy-three for and forty-five against. The town then had a population of over twelve thousand.

[5] *Acts of 1908*, ch. 361, secs. 1-2.

But the meetings continued to be numerous and poorly attended. In 1914 the warrant for the March meeting contained thirty-five articles. Three additional meetings were held during the year to consider an aggregate of thirty articles. At the first meeting some two hundred were present; at the second, one hundred and sixty-five; at the third, less than a hundred.[1] In 1915 conditions were similar.[2] The next year an article was inserted in the warrant by petition to see if the town would ask the General Court for the necessary legislation "to establish precinct voting and limited Town Meetings for the Town of Watertown." It was ordered that a committee of fifteen be appointed by the moderator to consider the question and,[3] in 1918, a preliminary report was made recommending a delay until legislation pending before the General Court was disposed of.[4] The report was accepted and the committee enlarged. Meetings continued throughout another year, and in 1919, a complete report was given. "The chief defect in our present form of government," the committee concluded, "is to be found in the legislative function as exercised in the Town Meeting." It called attention to the fact that with a potential voting strength of thirty-three hundred, only ten per cent, because of the smallness of the hall, could possibly exercise their suffrage rights — a condition favoring minority legislation, and a minority "which may be, and sometimes is, actuated by purely personal or sectional interest." Yet it felt, also, that steps should be

1 *Watertown Town Report* (1914), pp. 113–124, 156–158, 176–177, 193–194.
2 *Ibid.* (1915). Those present were: March 22 (708); April 14 (172); April 30 (30); June 28 (236); December 10 (178).
3 *Ibid.* (1916), pp. 122, 149.
4 *Ibid.*, p. 127.

taken to retain the active interest of as many citizens as possible in the affairs of the town, "consistent with having a workable legislative body." It suggested, therefore, the limited town meeting (as in Brookline) and attached a proposed bill to its report.[1] With minor changes the recommendations were accepted, and the selectmen were authorized to petition the General Court for the necessary legislation.[2] At the state election (Nov. 4, 1919), the question was placed on the ballot, and chapter 205 of the *Special Acts for 1919*, providing the desired change, was accepted.[3]

The next year Arlington and Winthrop [4] took steps to abandon the old town meeting. The former community had a population exceeding eighteen thousand.[5] It had made various attempts to relieve a congested situation.[6] Town meetings of various kinds were extremely frequent. In 1912, there were five meetings and three elections. A year later — six meetings and three elections. In 1914,

[1] "Report of the Committee to Consider a Change in the Form of Town Government," *Watertown Town Report* (1919), pp. 165–173.

[2] *Ibid.*, pp. 173, 175. There were 332 present at the meeting. The vote stood 211 in favor with 34 opposed. The question that the selectmen be given authority to petition the General Court had been inserted in the warrant for the annual meeting, March 3 (*Watertown Town Report* [1919], p. 115), but the question was made a matter for the special meeting of April 3 (*ibid.*, p. 146). See also *Acts of 1924*, ch. 358.

[3] *Watertown Town Report* (1919), p. 202.

[4] The act providing for limited town meetings was passed at the election of November 2, 1920 (*Winthrop Town Report* [1920], p. 128). See *Acts of 1920*, ch. 427; *Acts of 1921*, ch. 5. Documentary records of the change are meager; but inquiry indicates no unusual circumstances.

[5] *Census* (1920), p. 23.

[6] The establishment of a board of survey to superintend the laying out of streets and highways (*Acts of 1897*, ch. 249); the institution of a board of public works, consolidating the functions of surveyors of highways, water commissioners, and sewer commissioners (*Acts of 1904*, ch. 3); and the usual regulation of town meeting procedure through turnstiles and referenda (*Acts of 1906*, ch. 168).

there were four meetings. In 1917, there were three meetings, and four elections. The attendance was meager and interest lax.[1] In 1916 a question of a change in town government was seriously considered, and under an article in a warrant for March 6, a committee of five was appointed to report on the advisability of a change in town government.[2] But its subsequent recommendation tending to favor a town manager was referred back for further investigation.[3] At a special March meeting (1919) the committee reported that it did not think it advisable at that time to make any change.[4] In 1920, however, a new committee was appointed to investigate specifically the "Limited Town Meeting." Its report was favorable, and at a meeting held November 30, 1920 the committee was discharged, and the selectmen empowered to petition the General Court for the necessary legislation.[5]

Substantially in accordance with the recommendations of the committee, a bill was presented to the General Court and passed with minor alterations.[6] A special town meeting was called in January, and as there appeared to be no serious opposition to the change, the selectmen made early provision for dividing the town into voting precincts to accord with the proposed act.[7] At a meeting of the voters on January 24, 1921, the ap-

[1] "Report of the Committee to Investigate Forms of Town Government," *Arlington Town Report* (1919), pp. 27–28.

[2] *Ibid.* (1916), pp. 14–36.

[3] *Ibid.* (1917), p. 43.

[4] *Ibid.* (1919), p. 27.

[5] *Ibid.* (1920), pp. 17, 73–74. Two hundred and nineteen attended this meeting.

[6] "Selectmen's Report," *Arlington Town Report* (1920), p. 83.

[7] *Ibid.*, pp. 83–84; *Arlington Town Report* (1921), p. 11; *Acts of 1920* (extra session), ch. 642.

propriate legislation was accepted — one hundred and eighty-six to fourteen.

It has remained for eleven other towns to take similar action. Weymouth, at the annual town meeting of 1919, appointed a committee to investigate the expediency of a change in town government.[1] At a special meeting (November 12, 1920), the selectmen were instructed to petition the General Court for legislation to provide the town with a limited town meeting to follow the outlines of the Watertown act.[2] Proper legislation was prepared and accepted at the annual town election, March 14, 1921.[3] As early as 1914, the town of Methuen had started agitation for a change. The next year, a committee reported to continue "the Town form of Government carrying out the so-called commission form now in force in several of the Cities as far as practicable to Towns" and appended a proposed charter to its report.[4] But a limited town-meeting government was applied for and a subsequent statute embodying the plan accepted by the town at a special election in July, 1916.[5] In January of the following year, however, the selectmen petitioned the court for a city charter, and at the State election in 1917 "An Act to Incorporate the City of Methuen" was accepted by the voters.[6] But because

[1] *Weymouth Town Report* (1920), p. 35.

[2] *Ibid.* (1920), pp. 35–43, 79. The report of the committee is printed in full and gives a brief summary of the Norwood plan (the town manager), the Brookline plan, and mentions the possibility of the consolidation of functions provided in *Acts of 1920*, ch. 591. See *infra*, pp. 206 ff.

[3] *Weymouth Town Report* (1921), p. 32; *Acts of 1921*, ch. 61.

[4] *Methuen Town Report* (1914), pp. 154, 156–173.

[5] *Special Acts of 1916*, ch. 116. See Attorney General *v.* City of Methuen (1921), 236 *Mass.* 564.

[6] *Acts of 1917*, ch. 289; *Ms. Letter*, City Clerk to Secretary of the Commonwealth (Methuen, Jan. 17, 1918).

of irregularities in the procedure through which this change of government was made,[1] the community reverted to the town form. In February, 1921, however, the town voted to apply to the General Court for legislation providing precinct voting and the limited town meeting, and at a special meeting, April 16, 1921, a suitable act submitted to the voters was accepted.[2]

About the same time, Greenfield took action. At an adjourned town meeting (March 12) it was voted to apply to the legislature for a representative town meeting, and at a special meeting September 1, the enabling act was accepted.[3] West Springfield, in 1922, adopted the new form. For many years a change had been advocated.[4] A committee was appointed under vote of the town meeting of December 27, 1920 "to investigate a modified form of town government." After studying the legislative acts accepted by Brookline, Watertown and Arlington, a draft act was prepared "with such modifications as seemed desirable to meet the particular conditions in West Springfield."[5]

---

[1] The Methuen case is of interest. The difficulty in substance was that the selectmen instead of the town petitioned the legislature for a change of government. The decision of the court as briefed (Attorney General *v.* City of Methuen [1921], 236 *Mass.* 564), said: "The General Court under art. 2 of the Amendments to the Constitution has no jurisdiction to constitute a city government in a town unless and until its action to that end is sought by the inhabitants of the town who have signified their consent to such an application being made by vote at a meeting of the town called under a written warrant, setting out in fairly intelligible language the subject or subjects to be acted upon by the voters and signed by the selectmen or, in the event of their unreasonable refusal to sign, by a justice of the peace, and served by the constable or other designated person."

[2] *Methuen Town Report* (1921), p. 4.

[3] *Greenfield Town Report* (1921), pp. 121, 134, 145; *Acts of 1921*, ch. 440.

[4] "Selectmen's Report," *West Springfield Town Report* (1922), p. 58.

[5] Town of West Springfield, Town Meeting, *Report of Committee Ap-*

It was four years before the number of communities adopting the plan was increased, and then Belmont and Dedham were added.[1] The constitutional amendment of that year (1926), allowing the application of the plan to towns of more than six thousand inhabitants, permitted Dartmouth and Swampscott to join the list and in the same year Milton accepted similar legislation. In 1928 Saugus and Winchester followed, making a total of fifteen towns in the Commonwealth to accept legislation providing the new form.[2]

The provisions through which each of these communities adopted the modified town meeting are very similar. The Brookline charter determined both principle and structure. Section 1 in each instance (except the Milton act), provided for the division of the town into precincts. Brookline had required "not less than eight nor more than twelve," containing approximately an equal number of registered voters, but at least six hundred in each precinct.[3] The Watertown act provided from five to ten precincts, to "be plainly designated," to contain approximately an equal number of voters, but not less than three hundred nor more than one thousand.[4] The Arlington act required a minimum of five voting precincts, each containing at least six hundred voters, the districting to be done by members of the board of selectmen, the board of public works and the board of assessors.[5] In

pointed to Investigate a Modified Form of Town Government (West Springfield, 1921); Acts of 1922, ch. 311.

[1] Acts of 1926, chs. 302, 358.

[2] Acts of 1927, chs. 26 (Dartmouth), 27 (Milton), 300 (Swampscott); Acts of 1928, chs. 55 (Saugus), 167 (Winchester).

[3] Special Acts of 1915, ch. 250, sec. 1. Hereafter cited Brookline Act.

[4] Special Acts of 1919, ch. 205, sec. 1. Hereafter cited Watertown Act.

[5] Acts of 1920 (extra session), ch. 642, sec. 1. Hereafter cited Arlington Act.

Greenfield, six to twelve precincts were prescribed, to be arranged by the selectmen, assessors and the registrars — each to have not less than six hundred voters, and to contain approximately the same number.[1]

In determining the basis for town-meeting membership, there was less uniformity. The Brookline act had provided a definite number — twenty-seven — to be chosen from each precinct, a third to be elected for one, two, and three-year terms respectively; and after the first election each precinct was to choose, annually, nine members for a term of three years. But the Watertown act made provision for the election of six per cent of the male voters in the precinct. At the first election (as in the Brookline charter) one-third were to be elected for one, two, and three-year terms, respectively; but thereafter the voters in each precinct were to elect two per cent of their number for a three-year term.[2]

Two methods were thus suggested — equal representation from each precinct, and proportional representation based on the total number of voters in each precinct. Winthrop started with the Watertown provision;[3] but an act approved in January of the following year (1921), changed the basis to "the largest number which is divisible by three and which will not exceed three per cent of the voters in the precinct," and added that such number was to be determined on the basis of "registered voters in the precinct as of the first day of January prior to the annual town election."[4] Arlington,[5] Methuen[6] and

1 *Acts of 1921*, ch. 440, sec. 1. Hereafter cited *Greenfield Act*.
2 *Watertown Act*, sec. 2.
3 *Acts of 1920*, ch. 427, sec. 2. Hereafter cited *Winthrop Act*.
4 *Acts of 1921*, ch. 5, sec. 3.
5 *Arlington Act*, sec. 2.
6 *Acts of 1921*, ch. 241, sec. 2. Hereafter cited *Methuen Act*.

Greenfield,[1] went a step further than the provisions of the Winthrop amendment. The Arlington act read:

Sec. 2 . . . . the representative town meeting membership shall in each precinct consist of the largest number divisible by three which will admit of a representation of all precincts by an equal number of members and which will not cause the total elected town meeting membership to exceed two hundred and seventy.[2]

With the exception of West Springfield, which followed the Brookline practice by requiring a prescribed number — thirty from each precinct — this has been the principle upon which subsequent acts have based their representation. While it lacks the simplicity of the Brookline and Watertown methods, it has the double advantage of keeping the total membership almost stationary, and at the same time providing an equal number of representatives from each precinct regardless of the number of precincts or number of registered voters.

In addition to the elective town-meeting members, all of the acts (except that of Swampscott) provided for membership in the town meeting designated as "town meeting members at large." The initial provision in the Brookline charter admitted the following officers:

(1) the members from Brookline in the general court of the commonwealth of Massachusetts, (2) the moderator, (3) the town clerk, (4) the selectmen, (5) the town treasurer, the chairman of each of the following boards: — (6) of the

---

[1] *Greenfield Act*, sec. 2.

[2] *Arlington Act*, sec. 2. For example, under the act Arlington was divided into seven precincts. Two hundred and seventy (the maximum number of elective town meeting members) divided by seven gives a quotient of 38.57. The largest number divisible by three and that if multiplied by seven will not exceed two hundred and seventy is thirty-six. Each precinct elected, therefore, thirty-six town meeting members (*Arlington Town Report* [1921], pp. 32–44).

assessors, (7) of the school committee, (8) of the trustees of
the public library, (9) of the trustees of the Walnut Hills
cemetery, (10) of the water board, (11) of the park commissioners, (12) of the planning board, (13) of the committee
for planting trees, (14) of the gymnasium and baths committee, and (15) of the registrars of voters.[1]

Similar provisions modified to meet the local conditions
were contained in the Watertown act; and the members
of the finance committee, as a body, were included as
members.[2] After extensive enumeration embracing all
leading town officials, the Weymouth act added the
chairman of "any board of town officers hereafter constituted by law or by the acts of the town."[3] The
Methuen act reduced materially the number of members at large. Provision was made only for any member
of the General Court from the town, the moderator, the
town clerk, selectmen, chairman of the school committee, and "the chairman of the trustees of the Nevins'
Memorial."[4] The Greenfield act, however, contained a
long list allowing each board or commission to designate
a member or members (as the act provides) to act with
the town meeting. The more recent legislation pertaining to Belmont, Dedham, Dartmouth, Milton, Saugus
and Winchester confined the representation of important
town committees very largely to the chairman of each
group, and Swampscott made no provisions for members
*ex officiis* whatsoever.[5]

[1] *Brookline Act*, sec. 3.
[2] *Watertown Act*, sec. 3. When the act was amended in 1924 (*Acts of 1924*, ch. 358, sec. 1) an attempt was made without success to alter this provision. There was some fear that a finance committee of thirty-one members
might exert, as a body, too great an influence on the meeting.
[3] *Weymouth Act*, sec. 3.
[4] *Methuen Act*, sec. 3.
[5] The original draft of the act named some fifteen town officers as mem-

All of the acts provide that the town clerk shall give proper notification to the members of the time and place that the town meeting is to be held, the usual provision being that such notice be given by mail at least seven days before the meeting. Each contains numerous regulations pertaining to procedural matters. Eleven are uniform in the requirement that a majority of all the town-meeting members shall constitute a quorum but that a less number "may organize temporarily and may adjourn from time to time." The Brookline charter, however, provides that a quorum consist of "not less than one-half of all of the town meeting members." The Watertown act required a majority, but an amendment in 1924 [1] changed the number to thirty per cent, and the recent acts for the towns of Belmont and Winchester require one hundred members.[2] It is uniformly provided that all town meetings be held with open doors, that each meeting be the judge of the election and qualifications of its members, that adjourned meetings be given publicity according to a prescribed procedure — and perhaps most significant of all each act contains in substance the provision that:

Subject to such conditions as may be determined from time to time by its members . . . any registered voter of

bers *ex officiis*, but during the legislative hearings it was decided to eliminate them, largely, it seems, for three reasons: their membership would upset the equal representation from the various precincts; it might serve as a stimulus for larger departmental appropriations; and some town officials were not named among those selected. Under the act, however, any town officer might run for membership, and at the first election many did. The result was that some twenty-four members of the town's administrative services were duly chosen to the town meeting.

[1] *Acts of 1924*, ch. 358, sec. 1.
[2] *Acts of 1926*, ch. 302, sec. 3; *Acts of 1928*, ch. 167, sec. 3.

the town who is not a town meeting member may speak, but not vote, at such meeting.[1]

In each act the miscellaneous provisions are similar. In every case a moderator is provided to be nominated and elected, like other local officers, to preside at the meetings of the town. The method of nominating town-meeting members is presented in detail. In all acts, nomination papers are prescribed. The number of required signatures is provided in the several acts, and vary from as low as ten voters in a precinct in Weymouth, Watertown, Winthrop, West Springfield, Dedham, Milton, Swampscott, Saugus and Winchester, to fifteen in Arlington, twenty in Dartmouth, twenty-five in Methuen, Greenfield and Belmont, and thirty in Brookline. The petitions are to be filed with the town clerk — usually ten days before election, with the endorsement of the candidate thereon. Resignations pertaining to town-meeting memberships may be filed with the town clerk. Removal from the community or the precinct, or election to a position that entitles the holder to an *ex officio* seat causes the membership to lapse. In each case, vacancies are filled for the unexpired term by the remaining members of the precinct meeting at the call of the town clerk (usually upon petition of the precinct delegates) in accordance with a simple procedure outlined in each act.[2]

[1] The Newport charter (sec. a) had contained a similar clause, and provision was accordingly made that any taxpayer desiring to address the meeting should submit his request in writing to the chairman, stating the subject on which he desired to speak. Upon being subsequently recognized by the chair, he might speak for a period not exceeding ten minutes (*Rules of the Representative Council of the City of Newport* in *Manual of the City of Newport* [1919], pp. 47–48).

[2] Removal from a precinct, however, does not cause membership to lapse until the end of the elected term.

Every act, moreover, made provision for a referendum, and the Brookline plan again served as the basis.[1] Winthrop provided that the referendum embrace any vote making an appropriation of $25,000 or more, that the petition be signed by twenty-five voters from each precinct, and that "The questions so submitted shall be stated upon the ballot in the same language and form as when presented to the representative town meeting by the moderator, and as they appear upon the records of the said meeting."[2] Weymouth extended the delay of five days to any act except a vote to adjourn or an "emergency measure" requiring a "two-thirds vote of the town-meeting members present and voting thereon,"[3] and stipulated that the petition for a referendum be signed by "not less than one hundred voters of the town." Methuen required the signatures of fifty. Greenfield followed the Weymouth provisions. Arlington extended the five days' delay and subsequent referendum to any vote "under any article in the warrant, except a vote to adjourn," and required the signatures of one hundred registered voters of the town. The Watertown act contained a similar injunction but required the selectmen to call the special meeting for the referendum within five days instead of fourteen, and West Springfield limited the procedure of its assembly as well: "No article in the warrant shall at any representative town meeting be finally disposed of by a vote to lay upon the table, to indefinitely postpone, or to take no action thereunder."[4]

[1] *Brookline Act*, sec. 8.
[2] *Winthrop Act*, sec. 8.
[3] *Weymouth Act*, sec. 8.
[4] *West Springfield Act*, sec. 8. The more recent acts contain similar provisions varying only in details of procedure.

All of the acts provide that their provisions shall not abridge the right of the citizens to hold general meetings "according to any right secured to its voters or to the people by the constitution of this commonwealth." They further limit action of town-meeting members by prohibiting them from binding the community to any change affecting its municipal existence, or form of government "without action thereon by the qualified voters of the town at large, using the ballot and the check lists thereof."[1] But otherwise, all "lawful action" upon articles in the warrant, is defined as having the same effect as "heretofore under . . . town meetings." The acts conclude with a clause providing for submission of the act to the people, and, in the advent of its acceptance, the time at which it shall go into effect.

Fifteen towns in Massachusetts have attempted a new experiment in democracy. Each is comparatively large in population. Until Dedham joined the list there were none below fifteen thousand, with electorates for the most part well over five thousand. Dedham has close to fourteen thousand inhabitants. Milton and Saugus have nearly thirteen thousand and Winchester nearly twelve. Dartmouth and Swampscott have about nine thousand each — the first towns to take advantage of the new amendment to the Constitution. These communities are comparatively prosperous. Few cities of equal size can claim like Brookline a total valuation of close to $137,-000,000, a tax rate that even during the peak years of war never reached $22, present expenditures of almost $4,000,000 a year, and a debt that for fifty years (with

[1] *Brookline Act,* sec. 10.

slight exceptions) fluctuated between one and two million dollars. Each appears, moreover, generally satisfied with the new experiment, and can seek some assurance for its success in the interest manifested by other towns in the Commonwealth.

The unique features of the plan are the provisions for the active participation of the voter in the meetings, and the requirement for *ex-officiis* memberships for administrative officers. It is, however, an axiom of political science that statutes have little practical significance until they have been proved through application. In practice, do the voters attend the meetings as is their privilege? In nearly all cases they do. The attendance varies, of course, with the interest in the business that happens to be before the town. Even in the larger towns two hundred seems to be a generous number, five hundred is large, but on one occasion Weymouth reported as many as a thousand. Do the citizens, moreover, avail themselves of the unusual privilege of addressing their representatives? They do, although such participation is in general not frequent. But as Edward H. Baker of Brookline, a close student and able advocate of the system, rather effectively remarked, "the privilege is there." A political framework can, after all, do little more than offer the voter an occasion to make his influence felt, and the effectiveness of any such plan as a restraint on representative government may well be in the opportunity rather than in the use.

As to the town-meeting membership, there has been apparently little difficulty in securing candidates. About ten per cent (and sometimes a higher proportion) are women, and they seem to be quite as faithful in their duties as the men. Re-election is frequent — in some cases even customary. Duties are not arduous enough to offer a barrier to service, for in spite of the fact that articles in warrants continue to run from fifty to a hundred in number, special meetings are usually few, the total number during a year rarely exceeding four or five. The attendance of the delegates (who serve, incidentally, without remuneration) seems on the whole to be very good, but at times there has been difficulty in securing a quorum. As has been indicated, in all towns except Brookline, Watertown, Belmont, and Winchester, a majority of town-meeting members is required to do business. Brookline provided for fifty per cent of the total town-meeting membership, Watertown thirty per cent, and Belmont and Winchester for one hundred members. The principal difficulty in securing the required number seems to have been at special meetings; but instances of this kind have been infrequent, and where they have occurred unusual circumstances have often helped to explain the occasion.

Procedural difficulties have not, it seems, been serious. With far less formality than the ordinary legislature, much is left to the fairness and intelligence of an able moderator, and all of the towns utilize the services of some form of advisory committee, whose recommendations on the various articles of the warrant are usually held in high esteem. In spite of the somewhat elaborate provisions for the referendum in each act the device has been used infrequently. Greenfield exceeds all others — four times in five years, on two of which the proposition was rejected. Watertown has used the referendum twice — both times on questions of zoning, one of which was upheld and one reversed. Weymouth and Winthrop have used it once each — in the former case the decision of the town meeting was upheld, in the latter, reversed — while the remaining towns have made no use of the provision.[1]

The disadvantages of the limited town meeting that seem to most impress the Massachusetts townsman are the anticipated difficulty of securing properly qualified representatives, the uncertainty of obtaining a quorum at the meetings, the need of administrative reform for which the plan makes no provision, and the fear that on acute questions the attendance and participation of the average voter would lead to confusion. To the proponents of the plan these objections are dismissed as largely theoretical and as offering little difficulty in practice. In addition they point to opportunities for the assertion of increased public spirit, of less likelihood of unwholesome partisan influence, and of the assurance of the same type of competent officers that is felt to have characterized many town administrations under the old order. To form an estimate of its success is difficult. Its trial has been a matter of a few years — in some cases only a few months. Obviously it cannot be fairly judged out of the New England environment. The plan does leave the administrative problems of the community untouched. The medley of town officers, boards, and commissions with their conflicting jurisdictions and lack of adequate responsibility, remain without substantial alteration.[2]

[1] Town of Winchester, Town Meeting, *Report of the Town Meeting Committee* (1927) (Winchester, 1927). This is perhaps the best summary of the limited town meeting as a "going concern" that has yet been compiled.

[2] "Here in Watertown," reads a "Report of the Selectmen" (*Watertown Town Report* [1920], p. 15), at the close of the first year under a limited

The "long ballot" is not reduced — indeed, elective offices are increased through the large number of popularly chosen delegates. The town meeting is large — perhaps too large for deliberation and precise action, and must face the danger of accentuating local animosities that opportunities for party organization engender. Two to three hundred is the usual number, but as has been indicated, each meeting does much to facilitate its procedure by using an advisory or finance committee whose recommendations on articles in the warrant are only in rare instances overruled.

There seems, moreover, to have been little pronounced dissatisfaction, and with the exception of Watertown — where at a meeting in May, 1926 the question of a city government was seriously considered and rejected — little organized opposition has developed. Other New England States have given but slight attention to the plan. Newport, Rhode Island, has attempted to alter its early act in favor of a city manager charter, partly, at least, because of difficulty in securing qualified men to stand for election to the council. Some towns in Rhode Island are tending to apply the idea in a restricted way under the form of "limited financial councils" to minimize the danger of voting funds in an open and unlimited town meeting. But other communities have sought relief in administrative revisions utilizing the town manager under various guises, or have frankly adopted representative government.

town meeting, "there are some forty elected officers or members of boards or committees, each unit independent of the other and responsible directly and only to the town. It is not practicable to intelligently lay down policies, build a budget, spend money, or administer affairs with such a disjointed organization."

Whether the towns of Massachusetts that have given the new structure a serious trial will find the arrangement a permanent one is a matter for conjecture. The experience of Brookline would appear to offer hope that the plan would be sufficient for many years to come. There have been no attempts to alter the various charters since their inception, except for the purpose of reducing the quorum in Watertown, and for minor matters in Brookline and Winthrop,[1] and at the present time, there seem to be no amendments contemplated. Indeed, the most recent acts have shown few tendencies to change the plan even in the more detailed features. The original idea is still on trial, and able men are in sympathy with the work. The Commonwealth has given many examples of democracy in politics, and the consent of the governed has, perhaps, received more effective realization in political action through her town meetings, than under any other form of political control. The new legislation is drawn to protect this feature. It lays little claim to administrative improvements. It is a study in policy formation — one of the few recognitions in recent municipal reform that the efficiency expert cannot alone solve the problems of popular government. It is worthy of comment that politics is not only what is best, but

---

[1] The added legislation in Brookline (*Acts of 1921*, ch. 36), was largely a matter of assuring constitutionality because of procedural irregularities in 1915. The Watertown Act was changed in 1924 (*Acts of 1924*, ch. 358) to alter the quorum for a town meeting from a majority to thirty per cent, and to permit the town clerk to provide for filling vacancies in town meeting membership through election by the remaining members from the ward in which such vacancy occurs, without waiting for a petition from such members. The alterations in the Winthrop Act (*Acts of 1921*, ch. 5) did little more than make proper changes due to the increased suffrage under the 19th amendment, and, in addition, a few minor changes in procedure.

what is possible. The temper of New England communities has not proved favorable to representative government. The historical basis speaks definitely from the first few chapters of this book, and it is a fact of community life that can neither be ignored nor denied. Whatever its merits or defects, the limited town meeting has been found useful — a transitional phase, perhaps, but in many cases a necessary one.

# VIII

## IMPROVING THE ADMINISTRATION

A T present, there are three hundred and sixteen towns in Massachusetts, which, classified according to number and population, are as follows:

| Population | No. | Per Cent of Total Number | Population (total) | Per Cent of Population |
|---|---|---|---|---|
| Less than 500 [1] | 44 | 13.9 | 13,315 | 1.1 |
| 500 to 2,500 | 133 | 41.9 | 183,932 | 14.9 |
| 2,500 to 6,000 | 70 | 22.4 | 264,868 | 21.5 |
| 6,000 to 12,000 | 46 | 14.5 | 378,408 | 30.7 |
| 12,000 to 20,000 | 18 | 5.7 | 259,127 | 20.9 |
| 20,000 to 43,000 | 5 | 1.6 | 134,788 | 10.9 |
| | 316 | 100.0 | 1,234,438 | 100.0 |

The total population of these communities is close to a million and a quarter.[2] Of those exceeding six thousand inhabitants, fifteen have adopted the limited town meeting. Until the constitutional amendment of 1926 giving the smaller places the privilege of the new form, each town that made the change contained well over twelve thousand people, and one (Brookline) more than thirty-three thousand. It was the embarrassments caused by an

[1] Six of these are less than one hundred and fifty. Mt. Washington is the smallest — fifty-eight (*Census* [1925], p. 22).

[2] The total population of the State is 4,144,205. Within the thirty-nine cities there are 2,909,767 (70%). This leaves 1,234,438 (30%) within the towns — 405,971 (9.8% of the total population) of whom live in communities of less than 5,000 (*Census* [1925], pp. 4, 5, 16, 19),

unduly enlarged assembly that appeared the principal difficulty to be remedied, and the changes outlined in the preceding chapter were designed almost solely with this purpose in mind. But a group of more moderate sized communities (none at present exceeds fifteen thousand inhabitants) turned their attention to removing administrative defects through devices that city government appeared to find successful.[1]

As early as 1908, the town of Norwood began to experience embarrassments in financial administration. A cumulation of extensive civic improvements accompanied by assessment difficulties and an increasing tax rate, called attention to the need of a better revenue procedure and subsequently to more adequate supervision of expenditures. In 1913 the warrant for a town meeting contained an article,

> To see if the town will vote to appoint a committee to consider and report at a later town meeting upon the advisability of having an official known as a town manager or engineer, the scope of his duties and the necessary action required to secure and maintain such official or take any other action relative to said matter.[2]

A committee of seven was accordingly appointed,[3] and at an adjourned meeting presented a report. It was felt to be advisable for the town to concentrate as far as practicable the responsibility for monetary expenditures, and to secure this end, adequate authority in the person of a "Town Manager, Engineer or Superintendent of

---

[1] They were: Norwood (1915), 10,977; Middleboro (1920), 8,453; Stoughton (1920), 6,865; Mansfield (1920), 6,255; Orange (1929), 5,141 (*Census* [1925], pp. 17, 18).

[2] *Norwood Town Report* (1913), p. 32.

[3] *Ibid.*, p. 35.

Public Works" was thought to be required. It was be-
lieved, moreover, that the existing form of government
did not lend itself to such a project; and it was therefore
recommended that the committee be enlarged under the
title of the "New Charter Committee," to prepare a
plan providing not only for a manager, but also for the
creation of a scheme of government that would be in
harmony with his existence.[1]

The activities of the new committee led subsequently
to the adoption of an act known as the "Norwood
Plan" or more popularly, "the town manager form."[2]
The title was "An Act to change the time of holding
the annual meeting of the town of Norwood, to enlarge
the powers and duties of the selectmen, to abolish
certain offices, and to provide for the administration
of town affairs."[3] Section 1 declared that the annual
meeting should be held on the third Monday in January, beginning with the year 1915. Section 2 provided
for the election of five selectmen to be a continuous
body holding office (after the first election) for three
years each. They were directed to act as overseers of
the poor and surveyors of highways, and in addition
were to have all the duties and liabilities imposed by
law upon the former water commissioners, sewer commissioners, park commissioners, municipal light board
and tree warden — which offices were, thereupon,
abolished. The functions of town treasurer and collector of taxes were consolidated under a single officer
to be elected annually. The selectmen, subject to the

---

[1] "Report of the Committee," *ibid.*, p. 40.
[2] The plan was adopted October 6, 1914 (*Norwood Town Report* [1914],
p. 84).
[3] *Acts of 1914*, ch. 197. Hereafter cited *Norwood Act*.

confirmation of the tax commissioner of the Commonwealth, were directed to appoint three assessors, and, on their own initiative, a town clerk and accountant (consolidating the two offices then existing), a board of relief of three members (now known as the board of public welfare), and a "general manager" to be "the administrative head of all departments of the town government."

This officer was to be the keystone of the new structure. He was to be appointed by the selectmen to hold office at their pleasure. His education, training, and experience were to be such as should qualify him for his duties, and he was to be selected without regard to his political beliefs or his place of residence at the time of appointment. Specifically he was to organize such departments as the selectmen might order, or, in the absence of their direction, such as he deemed necessary for the efficient conduct of his office. He was to appoint upon merit and fitness, and to remove, after proper notice, superintendents, chiefs, and subordinate officers and employees in the town departments, as well as to fix (according to law) the salaries and wages of such officers. He was further to attend all regular meetings of the selectmen and to advise them fully as to the needs of the town; as well as to keep full and complete records of the activities of his office, and to furnish the selectmen with a written, detailed estimate of the appropriations required during the ensuing fiscal year for the proper conduct of all departments of the town under his control. Further consolidation was provided by placing certain matters formerly in the care of the trustees of the Morrill

¹ *Norwood Act,* secs. 5–8.

Memorial Library and of the school committee in the hands of the selectmen to be exercised by the general manager.[1]

A finance commission of three members was to be chosen by the qualified voters,[2] and several sections of the act were devoted to its duties. In brief, the commission was directed to submit to the selectmen each year an estimate of the probable expenditures of the town for the ensuing year, and also of amounts contemplated as collectible from all sources of revenue. The commission was to examine all articles in the town warrant requiring the appropriation of money, and to report thereon in writing to the town meeting, and was given, in addition, adequate powers to investigate excessive claims against the town.[3] The remainder of the act provided for the recall of any holder of an elective office, for restraints on certain town officers from making contracts with the town, and provisions for submitting the act to the voters at a special election, as well as establishing the time when, if accepted, it should go into effect.[4]

While numerous communities have given the plan serious consideration, only three (before 1929), had followed completely the example of Norwood. An article in the warrant for the town of Mansfield at a meeting in

[1] These included the repair of the building and the purchase of supplies (except books) (*Norwood Act*, secs. 13–14).

[2] *Ibid.*, sec. 16.

[3] *Ibid.*, secs. 18–21.

[4] *Ibid.*, secs. 27–37. A system providing for preferential voting (House Bill 1587) was at the same time introduced, but the committee reported "leave to withdraw" and the General Court concurred (*Bulletin of Committee Hearings and Record of Legislative Action* [1914], pp. 26, 206; *Journal of The House of Representatives* [1914], p. 561; *Journal of the Senate* [1914], p. 553).

September, 1918, proposed "To see if the town will investigate the Town Manager plan and appoint a committee to report at a future meeting."[1] The committee was appointed, and submitted a report at the March meeting of the following year recommending a plan of government similar to that of Norwood. A tentative plan was drafted, and upon its adoption[2] by the town action was started in the General Court. The desired legislation was obtained, and on July 12, 1920, the town accepted the act by a large majority thereby providing the community with a town manager.[3]

Middleboro underwent much the same process. A committee reported to the town in March, 1919, that a "consolidation of various departments and the redistribution of the work now performed" was vitally needed. It characterized the existing situation as "excessive division of responsibility" and recommended that the General Court be petitioned for suitable legislation. The report was accepted, and a committee of five was appointed to put the recommendations into effect.[4] March 1, 1920,[5] a plan was reported to the town, and at a special meeting on November 6 of the same year, an act embodying the principles contained therein was adopted.[6] Stoughton followed the example of her three neighbors. Agitation commenced seriously in 1916,[7] and

[1] *Mansfield Town Report* (1918), p. 28.
[2] *Ibid.* (1919), pp. 19, 29.
[3] *Ibid.* (1920); *Acts of 1920*, ch. 586. Hereafter cited *Mansfield Act.*
[4] *Middleboro Town Report* (1919), pp. 87, 88.
[5] *Ibid.* (1920), p. 29.
[6] *Ibid.* (1920), p. 140. *Acts of 1920*, ch. 592. Hereafter cited *Middleboro Act.*
[7] *Stoughton Town Report* (1916), pp. 18, 36.

culminated in the adoption of a manager charter at a special town meeting held June 11, 1921.[1]

As the acts providing for the limited town meeting followed closely the principles of the Brookline plan, those creating a town manager based their provisions very largely on the Norwood model. The Mansfield act, however, made no provision for a separate finance committee,[2] but required that the town manager submit to the selectmen a detailed report of anticipated expenditures, and that the selectmen act as a finance committee in making proper recommendations to the town relative to appropriations provided in the warrant. The town treasurer and collector of taxes was to be appointed by the manager. The selectmen were to appoint an official to serve as town clerk and accountant, three overseers, a chief of the fire department, five library trustees, a planning board of five members, two constables (and others as occasion might require), six sinking fund commissioners, and the town manager, whose duties were specifically enumerated.[3] In addition, the last section provided for a "Revocation of Acceptance." After the expiration of four years and within six from the acceptance of the act, provision was made for the voters of the town to revoke the act, in which event the legislation providing for the town manager became null and void, and thereafter all general laws respecting

---

[1] *Ms. Letter*, Assistant Town Clerk to Secretary of the Commonwealth (Stoughton, Dec. 26, 1924); *Acts of 1921*, ch. 400. Hereafter cited *Stoughton Act*.

[2] *Mansfield Act*, secs. 4–5: "All the duties now imposed by the by-laws of the town upon the finance committee, so called, and not inconsistent with the duties required by this act, shall be performed by the selectmen."

[3] *Ibid.*, secs. 9–14, 17–19.

town government and town officers would once more apply to the community.

The Middleboro act followed the provisions of the Mansfield plan relative to arrangements for a finance committee — that is, invested its selectmen with appropriate authority.[1] The town treasurer who was also the collector of taxes was to be elected. Other major officers including the clerk, assessors (subject to confirmation by the State commissioner of corporations and taxation), library trustees, overseers of the poor, chief of police, constables, town counsel, and chief of the fire department, were to be appointed by the selectmen. Section eighteen provided for the town manager. As in previous acts he was to be appointed by the selectmen, was subject to their direct supervision and was removable at their pleasure. The powers given him were the usual ones and varied little from the requirements of preceding legislation. The act also contained a "Revocation of Acceptance," as in the Mansfield legislation. The Stoughton act likewise contained no serious innovations. It did, however, provide for a finance committee of five members to be elected by the town, and to act also as a town-planning board, but save for this additional function its duties followed very closely the Norwood provisions. Under "Appointive Town Officers" receiving their tenure from the selectmen were listed the town treasurer and collector, three assessors, town clerk and auditor, six library trustees, and a town manager — the position and functions of the latter differing in no essential from his prototype in the preceding charters.[2]

---

[1] *Acts of 1920*, ch. 292. Hereafter cited *Middleboro Act.*

[2] Legislation approved February 13, 1929 (*Acts of 1929*, ch. 38), and

It is difficult to appraise any political framework in practice as excellent *per se*. The written records of charters, minutes and reports are suggestive in theories, but they are likely to be barren of those human elements that give life and fervor to political methods. They are, as it were, black-line sketches of physical qualities whose true character is often recorded in far less tangible sources. Tax rates, per capita charges, comparative expenditures, have too often proved notoriously deceiving. Inquiry elicits various responses — many of them, plainly based upon dogma and personalities. Yet there are certain facts that become apparent as political machinery operates which offer a basis for reflection, if not for the more precise methods of inductive analysis.

First, there is the manager. The four towns that have experimented with this official have, to date (May, 1928), had ten among them — Norwood four,[1] Mansfield four, Stoughton one, and Middleboro one. Their individual terms have varied extensively — from a few months to seven years — but the aggregate of some thirty-seven years that the plans have been in operation makes the average tenure between three and four. Of the ten managers who have thus served, four are still in service, three were practically forced to resign because of factional troubles, two left to fill more remunerative positions in other communities, and one held only a temporary appointment of a few months.

The qualifications that these men brought to their work have, for the most part, represented both maturity

accepted by the town of Orange, provides a town manager for this community — the smallest (5,141) to adopt the plan. Provisions of the act differ in no essential from the others.

[1] More accurately, four changes but only three managers.

and municipal experience. They have varied very much in age — the average would probably be a little over forty at the time of his appointment. All had had some form of engineering training (usually in municipal service) but only one had held a position as town manager previous to undertaking the work in these communities. Their salaries have varied from three thousand to five thousand dollars a year. With the exception of a temporary appointment in Mansfield, none were residents of the communities preceding their employment as managers, and only one of them who has left the service of his respective town has consistently followed community management as a profession.[1]

None of the original acts has been amended. Middleboro by a two-to-one vote in 1925 decided to retain the present provisions. The "Revocation of Acceptance" in the Mansfield act was never invoked, and the six years provided as a limitation having elapsed, there seems, at present, little desire for alterations. Norwood (mainly to remove minor imperfections of administrative responsibility pertaining to the five health and building departments) inserted an article in the town warrant for a special meeting in December, 1927 that read:

To see if the Town will vote to appoint a committee of nine to consider whether the present Town Charter affords the best and most efficient method of administration of its affairs; said committee to make such recommendations as it may deem to be for the Town's best interests, and to take any other action in the matter.[2]

[1] Changes of the past few months would alter this statement in minor detail, but it remains substantially true as originally written.

[2] *Norwood Town Report* (1927), p. 19. The committee has not yet reported, but there seems no prospect of anything more than recommendations to alter one or two details of administration.

At the meeting, it was explained that the town government did not seem to be functioning in all respects in accord with the original plan, and the proposed committee was merely to suggest what might seem to be necessary improvements.

It is the town meeting that makes the manager plan somewhat of an anomaly in political practice. An appointive executive who is at the same time part of a constituent assembly to which he is not directly responsible is a unique relation, but it seems to have had little effect on the manager himself so far at least, as his original position under the various acts is concerned. In the first place, town meetings do not appear to have been taken quite as seriously by the voter under the new plans as under the unreformed methods. Even in Norwood, with a potential voting strength of some fifty-eight hundred, six hundred is a large attendance and close to two hundred is more usual. In the second place, New England towns, for many generations, have come to look for leadership to their selectmen, and more recently to their finance committees, and he would be a strong man, indeed, who could successfully supplant the influence of these boards. But the manager is nevertheless usually present at town meetings. He speaks to clarify disputed points that come within his knowledge, and, on occasion, even adds his voice to sponsor certain policies; but he is not a partisan, and thus far, it seems, has very largely confined himself to maintaining the place assigned to him as an administrative official.

There remain miscellaneous features of the various acts. The recall has been used but once. Mansfield attempted to apply the provision to one of its selectmen, but the effort was unsuccessful. As has been indicated, two of the acts (Norwood and Stoughton) provide for separate finance committees elected by popular vote and two (Mansfield and Middleboro) require that the selectmen serve in this capacity. The proponents of each practice claim superiority — the former, on the basis of choosing a highly qualified board of technicians free from political influence and obligations, the latter, because the needs of the community can best be served through vesting those thought to be most familiar with its requirements, with the preparation and responsibility of the budget. The relation of the manager to the selectmen has in some instances failed to work quite as intended. There has been some friction over subordinate appointments. There have been accusations of undue dominance from one side or the other and, in one instance, at least, minor matters of policy have caused the manager's resignation. But such difficulties are certainly not peculiar to this type of government, and on the whole the town manager has justified the hopes of his proponents and has not only brought an increased precision and economy to the "pick and shovel" activities of his town, but a valuable directive force in the wider fields of community planning. He is not the same figure that is known to the American city. A more limited scope and a different relation to the policy determining organ of the community place him in another position. The town meeting is an embarrassment, and unnecessary contacts with it are to be avoided — an intensely political gathering that must be faced, if at all, without the prestige and support that accompany an elective office. His title has been unfortunate. He might be called engineer, superintendent, or even supervisor with impunity, but *manager* shocks the political ethics of the New Englander — it gives an unnecessary emphasis to the gap between a cherished heritage of direct democracy and the loss of individuality that modern administrative efficiency is supposed to require.

In addition to the town manager, local communities have, for many years, attempted a more moderate consolidation of their administrative functions under various general or special acts. Boards of public works have become frequent.[1] The town of Lexington, indeed, has simply vested the selectmen with the power to act as such a board, and has instructed them to appoint a superintendent of public works.[2] Boards of survey have been created in an effort to alleviate future difficulties in matters of street planning and highway construction,[3] and town planning boards have undertaken the task of coördinating activities relative to municipal expansion and the wider policies of public welfare.[4]

The town of Walpole has recently accepted an act[5] designed to administer its increasingly complex affairs pertaining to highways and water supply and at the same time retain the voters' interest in town government. To

[1] Stoneham (*Acts of 1902*, ch. 263); Andover (*Acts of 1912*, ch. 345); Framingham (*Acts of 1914*, ch. 701); Reading (*Acts of 1921*, ch. 118), etc.
[2] *Acts of 1922*, ch. I.
[3] Stoneham (*Acts of 1907*, ch. 191); North Andover (1923), and Ipswich (1924) under *Genl. Laws*, ch. 41, sec. 73.
[4] *Genl. Laws*, ch. 41, secs. 70–72. See also the *Annual Report of the Department of Public Welfare* (1927) (Mass. Pub. Doc. No. 17), pp. 36–38. The extent of such changes as well as many more that have been sought and refused legislative sanction can be traced by reading the annual *Bulletin of Committee Work and Business of the Legislature* under the Committee on Towns.
[5] *Acts of 1924*, ch. 377, Hereafter cited *Walpole Act,*

do this, "a modification" of the Norwood plan was adopted. In a way it was not new to the community. The town, under a "gentleman's agreement," had utilized many of its provisions some months previous to the actual change, and the accepted legislation was largely in the nature of an endorsement. The act provided, in brief, for five selectmen to be paid salaries determined by the town meeting. This board was designated as the "lawful successors of certain offices"— water commissioners, park commissioners, surveyors of highways, overseers of the poor, board of health, and tree warden. Moreover, it was directed to appoint a town clerk, a town accountant, a board of relief (three members), a town counsel, and a "town engineer"— who (except as otherwise provided) was to be the administrative head of all departments of the government the conduct of which had by the general laws and the new act been vested with the selectmen of the town. His detailed duties were similar to those of the town managers of other communities.[1]

An attempt to remedy administrative difficulties without the use of special acts was made by a general statute in 1920. A year before, a committee was appointed by the General Court to complete the work of revising and

---

[1] *Walpole Act*, secs. 3, 9–12. What is thought to be the peculiar value of the arrangement is stated by one of its sponsors (Mr. H. A. Whiting, Town Treasurer of Walpole in the *Christian Science Monitor* [Jan. 6, 1925]): "We believe . . . there is one serious drawback to the town manager plan. While it centralizes government and concentrates responsibility, it encourages the tendency to 'let George do it.' The voters get the idea that at last they can lay down the reins and let the town run itself. Now we believe this is the wrong idea. We think there is strength in the town meeting form of government up to a point where the size of the town prevents it, and it has been our purpose to retain it in its essential features."

codifying the laws relating to towns.[1] It recommended numerous changes of importance, and although the committee complained of lack of time to give adequate consideration to the improvement of town government, it did propose certain remedies.[2] To the many acts that the State had from time to time enacted in an effort to guide and unify local political practice,[3] the committee recommended six others, the most important of which provided for the extensive consolidation of town departments.[4] As finally accepted by the General Court the act provided for the consolidation of functions in the hands of the selectmen, who, in turn, were empowered to appoint supervisors to administer the various services intrusted to them. Thus, if the town voted to have its selectmen act as a board of health, as overseers of the poor, or as water and sewer boards, the selectmen were thereupon empowered to appoint, respectively, an inspector of health, a superintendent of the poor, and a superintendent of the water and sewer department, to "assist" them in the performance of their duties, and in a similar manner, a complete consolidation of administrative functions might be brought about.

[1] A previous committee had been appointed in 1918 (*Resolves of 1918,* ch. 47).

[2] Massachusetts General Court, Senate no. 2 (1919), *Report of the Commission to Complete the Work of Revising and Codifying the Laws Relating to Towns,* p. 6. Hereafter cited *Report of the Commission.*

[3] Massachusetts has followed this policy of permissive legislation — similar to the adoptive acts of the English system. The committee lists thirty-three such acts before 1902 and thirty-seven since that time (*Report of the Commission,* pp. 43–45). Towns are constantly making use of their provisions. Lists of such acts accepted yearly are published in the annual report of the Secretary of the Commonwealth. It is one of the most hopeful methods for solving the vexatious problems of over-centralization.

[4] *Ibid.,* p. 17. For the subsequent act based upon the work of the committee, see *Acts of 1920,* ch. 591.

But no town has as yet taken full advantage of the statute. In the first place, it really means a form of commission government applied to towns, and this has not been extensively received nor particularly successful in Massachusetts. Of six cities· that have undertaken it, five have abandoned the plan, and one appears to be dissatisfied.[1] It tends, moreover, to place increased responsibilities in a practically unreformed board of selectmen — an already very much overworked group. And, last, it permits and therefore encourages degrees of consolidation, that, with the temper of the Massachusetts townsman, is quite likely to preclude extensive reform.

As has been indicated frequently in the last few pages, many of the larger towns of the Commonwealth have resorted to the expedient of a finance committee. In smaller communities, the selectmen serve in this capacity, but the embarrassments that have accompanied urban conditions have made impossible so informal a procedure. The origin of the device is obscure. It has been thought that the idea was first applied in Quincy.[2] For half a century, Brookline has utilized a "committee of twenty-one" whose principal duty is to serve in an advisory capacity to the town on matters of finance. North Andover and North Attleboro have used a similar

---

[1] Commission government has existed in Massachusetts since 1909, when Gloucester and Haverhill began the movement. In 1910, Lynn was added, Lawrence and Lowell in 1911, and Salem in 1912. The optional charter law was enacted in 1915 (*General Acts of 1915*, ch. 267 [pt. 4]) and Plan C provided for commission government. No city has so far accepted this plan, and all cities (except Lawrence) that have operated under commission government have abandoned it. For a full discussion see *Massachusetts Constitutional Convention Bulletins* (1917) (2 vols., Boston, 1917), vol. 1, bull. 12, pp. 17–30.

[2] A. D. Chandler, "Brookline: A Study in Town Government" in the *New England Magazine* (August, 1893), p. 788.

expedient for close to forty years. Many other communities such as Hudson, Ipswich, Saugus, Stoneham, Reading, Uxbridge, Walpole, Ware, Wellesley, Westboro and Winchester report at least twenty years experience, and, within the last decade, practically all communities exceeding six thousand inhabitants have established and utilized finance committees of one kind or another.

It was not until 1910, however, that the General Court made definite provisions pertaining to the movement. It was then enacted that:

A town may by by-law provide for the appointment and duties of appropriation, advisory, or finance committees, who may consider any and all municipal questions for the purpose of making reports and recommendations to the town; and such by-laws may provide that committees so appointed may continue in office for terms not exceeding three years from the date of appointment.[1]

In 1923, a further step was taken. The establishment of a finance committee was made compulsory in towns whose valuation for the purpose of apportioning the state tax exceeded one million dollars. The new provisions were amendatory of the former sections and read:

Every town whose valuation for the purpose of apportioning the state tax exceeds one million dollars shall, and any other town may, by by-law provide for the appointment and duties of appropriation, advisory or finance committees, who shall consider any or all municipal questions for the purpose of making reports or recommendations to the town; and such by-laws may provide that committees so appointed may continue in office for terms not exceeding three years from the date of appointment.[2]

[1] *Acts of 1910*, ch. 130; *General Laws*, ch. 39, sec. 16.
[2] *Acts of 1923*, ch. 388. Where special provision is made — as in Norwood, Middleboro and Walpole — the committee is still elected.

The legislation, however (as is so frequently the case), did little more than approve and clarify a practice that had become widely used.

It is in the by-laws of the larger towns that the structure, duties, and responsibilities of these committees are most adequately described. They go under various names — advisory committees, finance committees, warrant committees, or appropriation committees. The appointing authority is usually the moderator, although the selectmen are sometimes designated to perform this service. The committees vary in number — from six to fifteen seems the usual size. It is almost uniformly required that they be a continuous body, an equal number of the personnel (usually a third) being assigned each year. Qualifications for membership are simple—a voter of the town who holds no elective office, and sometimes, as well, no appointive position for which he receives pay, with an occasional resident requirement when the committee is composed of district members.

Provision is likewise made for organization. The first meeting is frequently called at the instance of regular town officials — the moderator, selectmen, or even the town clerk, but further procedure is usually left to the committees which choose their officers, adopt their rules and fill vacancies in their membership for unexpired terms. Their powers and duties are described in some detail. They are ordinarily charged to consider all questions of town finance pertaining to appropriations, expenditures and indebtedness; to examine the methods of administration employed by the various officers and departments of the town; to investigate the books, accounts, and records of any such officers, and to report

their findings in these matters to the town meeting.
In actual operation, however, the activities of a finance
committee are usually confined to considering the articles in the warrant. In small towns, meetings are infrequent — sometimes, indeed, but a single session is held
immediately preceding the town meeting. On such occasions, town officers appear before the committee to explain and justify their budget plans for the ensuing year,
and upon the results of this procedure is based the recommendations that follow financial articles in the warrant. In larger places, however, the committee is quite
likely to be far more extensively occupied, and to meet
at frequent intervals throughout the year. It not only
considers the more apparent and recurring needs of the
community but may even formulate extensive fiscal programs involving not only large financial expenditures,
but important matters of town policy, as well. Preceding
the town meeting, it may hold public "hearings" on certain articles to which all interested citizens are invited;
and occasionally, joint meetings with other town agen-
cies — the selectmen, board of public works, school committee or special committees of various kinds.

The part that the finance committee plays in the town
meeting has been briefly alluded to in another connection[1] and while, as has been emphasized, actual participation varies greatly among the different towns, its
recommendations are always taken with great serious-
ness, and only on rare occasions does a town act against
its advice. Its authority, indeed, seems to be steadily
increasing. The policy of confining recommendations to
strictly financial questions is rapidly giving way to one

[1] See *supra*, ch. VI, pp. 137 *ff.*, 149 *ff.*

demanding the examination of every article in the warrant whether it carries an appropriation or not, and even requests to endorse or reject programs contained in the reports of other town authorities are frequently made. The committees, moreover, seem to be fortunately constituted for this increased service. Whatever their deficiencies, they are rarely accused of playing politics. Their personnel is generally composed of able, fair-minded business men. The moderator is an effective appointing authority — an honored, non-political but quietly influential officer. He can usually be depended upon to choose their membership intelligently through an intimate knowledge of the community life. There is every incentive (both structurally and politically) to be independent, non-partisan and judicious. It is perhaps not too much to say that from a limited advisory function designed both to relieve and to supplement the board of selectmen, the finance committee is on its way to become (as in some places it has already become) the decisive factor in town policies.

There is no doubt of the growing unrest that is manifested in the Massachusetts town pertaining to its form of government. Since Boston became a city over a century ago the same discontent has been in evidence. It was seventy-five years, however, before the Commonwealth numbered thirty-three cities.[1] The first twenty-seven years of the new century have added but six others. Each of these municipalities, when incorporated,

[1] Including, however, Roxbury and Charlestown annexed to Boston in 1868 and 1874 respectively, both of which had formerly been cities, there were a total of thirty-five cities existing before 1900 (Massachusetts General Court, *A Manual for the Use of the General Court* [1927–1928] [Boston, 1927], p. 207).

contained over sixteen thousand inhabitants, and one, Revere, over twenty-five thousand. The same period has witnessed fifteen towns, that, arriving at a population incompatible with the old order, have temporized with representative government, and turned to new expedients rather than relinquish entirely the town-meeting form. Seven smaller communities have made pronounced administrative changes, and many others have adopted less extensive devices — but each of these has left its constituent assembly untouched. There can be no doubt, however, that an old and distinguished institution is passing away. There are sixty-two communities in the Commonwealth exceeding twelve thousand inhabitants. They include the thirty-nine cities, twelve of the fifteen limited town meetings, and one of the town managers. Within this group there remain but ten others, more than half of which have shown some indication of a change.

Framingham is the largest — over twenty-one thousand — larger, indeed, than eight cities in the State. For more than fifteen years, agitation for a change has periodically disturbed the community. In March, 1925 a city charter (Plan A of the optional charter system, with slight modifications) was rejected by almost a two-to-one vote. Another committee (the third since 1912) was appointed in 1926, and its report to the town meeting in March (1927) disposed of the subject in a few noncommittal paragraphs:

It seemed wise to approach the problem on the theory that, unless some plan distinctly better than the present could be found, it would be unwise to abandon a system of government which has met the needs of the town since its incorporation.

After very thorough and careful consideration, the Committee is unanimous in its conclusion that, for the present at least, it is unwise to recommend any other form of government.[1]

The second largest community to retain the unlimited town meeting is Wakefield, while Southbridge, Milford, Clinton, Adams and Webster follow in descending order. After several years agitation, Wakefield, in March, 1926, rejected legislation that provided a limited town meeting for the community. Southbridge, on the contrary, seems to have evinced little interest in a change. Clinton, Adams, and Webster have shown similar disinclination. Milford, however, appointed a committee several years ago to consider the matter — especially the limited town meeting — but no steps were taken.

Braintree, Plymouth, and Natick are the remaining towns that exceed twelve thousand in population. A few years ago, Braintree appointed a committee to inquire concerning the town-manager plan but nothing was done, and at present there seems to be no change contemplated. Plymouth as a town has taken no action, but the selectmen appointed a committee to "make a study of representative forms of town government with the idea that sometime such a change will be necessary." There seems, however, to be no interest in the project and the committee is not working. The town of Natick appointed a committee to report at the March meeting in 1926, but when proposals for a change were inserted in the warrant, the article was indefinitely postponed.

As has been indicated, the constitutional amend-

---

[1] *Framingham Town Report* (1928), p. 191.

ment of 1926 threw the limited town meeting open to forty-six additional communities — *i.e.*, those between six thousand and twelve thousand inhabitants. Among these are four town managers (Mansfield, Middleboro, Stoughton, and Orange), as well as Lexington and Walpole, that have made less extensive but important administrative changes, and Dartmouth, Swampscott and Winchester that have recently accepted the limited town meeting. At least a third of those remaining in this group either have or are at present considering alterations in their form of government — many of them seeming to favor the limited town meeting. In Amesbury there is no committee at work, but agitation for a change has extended over several years. In Andover, a committee was appointed previous to the passage of the constitutional amendment of 1926 to investigate the limited town meeting. With the passing of the amendment, the question of accepting the plan was inserted in the warrant but was defeated by the town. In Athol, as early as 1915, a committee was appointed, and two years later submitted a report favoring a town manager, but no definite recommendations were made. In 1922, the committee was reorganized and enlarged, but no report was printed and the work was apparently dropped. In 1924, Canton appointed a committee to investigate the town-manager plan, but a report in favor of adopting such a form was not accepted by the town. There is at present an "Improvement Committee" charged with the duty of investigating local civic needs.

The town of Chelmsford seemed to be very near to becoming a limited town-meeting community. In 1924, a committee was appointed to study the "Brookline system," and while local sentiment appeared to favor the change, the population of the town at that time was less than the required number, but with the recent amendment it would not be surprising to see interest renewed and, possibly, favorable action taken. At a recent annual town meeting (1927) Great Barrington appointed a committee on change of town government, but no action has yet resulted. Ludlow now has a committee at work. Needham has had no real agitation towards a change, but a committee has been appointed to report on the advisability of a board of public works. The town has once rejected such a proposal, and once received an adverse report from its committee.

At a special election in 1922, North Attleboro refused a town-manager charter by a four-to-one vote. Reading (1924) appointed a committee on "Consolidation of Town Offices," and it reported to the town meeting in March of the following year. The recommendations embraced a board of five selectmen in which was to be consolidated numerous major town functions and, in addition, the appointment of assessors, a purchasing agent and a town accountant. But the town voted to lay the recommendations on the table, and while the report was subsequently referred to another committee, no further action has as yet been taken. Uxbridge has informally discussed the limited town meeting, but has no committee at work. In 1921, Wellesley appointed a committee of three to act with the selectmen in investigating a limited town meeting. The committee (in view of the fact that Wellesley was under twelve thousand population) offered no definite recommendations, but outlined the principal features of the limited town meeting, and recommended that its organization be continued and a report rendered at a later date. At the same annual meeting, a previous committee appointed in 1919 on "Change in Town Government" reported, recommending consolidation under the commission plan of government outlined above[1] and although the report was accepted and the committee discharged, no further action was taken.

There remain some twenty towns of upwards of six thousand population that have made little effort towards a change in their local government. Many, indeed, have given the matter no consideration whatever. In still smaller communities, there is discernible no desire (except for electoral adjustments) to alter the existing order in its essential features — indeed, proposals for a representative government such as characterize the fourth and fifth class "cities" of many of our western States would be incredible to the Massachusetts townsman. In urban areas, increased numbers have been the outstanding Nemesis of the old methods; in smaller places, state centralization has worked havoc with functions long accepted as community prerogatives. But both of these influences work through rural districts with comparative slowness, and the town meeting will undoubtedly be with us in form for many years to come. Yet whatever its failure (or more properly, its present inadequacies), the days of its pristine vigor left an indelible mark on the political thought and practice of America, and to those who have felt the embarrassments of more recent

[1] *Acts of 1920*, ch. 591. Most of the above material has been obtained through correspondence with practically all towns exceeding six thousand in population, and while constantly changing developments may lead to inaccuracies in detail, the general and persistent agitation is unmistakable.

municipal methods there is a solacing finality in the praise of Jefferson that the town meeting was

. . . the wisest invention ever devised by the wit of man for the perfect exercise of self-government, and for its preservation.

# IX

## PAST AND PRESENT

THE real value of the local institutional history of
Massachusetts lies in the fact that rarely has there
been such an opportunity to see the social process so
completely. Not only were early conditions simple and
remedies largely unrestrained by meddling legislators,
but among the colonists themselves were many cultured
and penetrating minds who perpetuated the day-by-day
experiences in carefully prepared private accounts and
public records. Perhaps nowhere in history is there so
complete and compact an unfolding of constitutional development as in the records of the Massachusetts Bay
Colony. In few instances of the past have men kept
from the beginning those frequent summaries of community thought and practice that compose the Massachusetts town record; and rare, indeed, are continuing
sources in which so intimate and thorough a knowledge
of the problems of living together find such meticulous
expression.

It is both a demonstration and analysis of these features that is justification for the historical chapters of
this book. The purpose becomes, therefore, three-fold:
to show the possibilities for institutional research that lie
hidden in these materials, to analyze the motives and
methods in which the local communities of the Commonwealth are grounded, and to indicate the pressures that

increased numbers and administrative complexities have brought to the simple machinery of another day.

The structure of an institution cannot be fairly considered irrespective of its purpose. As a practical matter, a mechanism is good or bad according to the degree of success with which it performs the task for which it was built. It may, moreover, go through many adjustments before being allowed to produce without further alteration, and in the course of time is quite likely to be discarded because, on the one hand, its product demands new refinements or, on the other, is no longer needed. But whatever the final disposition, it was originally built for a purpose — a purpose that in its wider implications may have a complicated metaphysical basis, but that in its immediate aims is appallingly finite.

Such was the rise and "fall" of the town meeting. A group of scattered settlers became engulfed in the vigorous colonization of a commercial company. Communities were established on propitious sites, selected for no other reasons than physical and social convenience. At first attempting a restraint similar to that of the directors of an economic enterprise over its persons and properties, the company subsequently found itself involved in the widest political questions that caused the rapid and involuntary expansion of its trading charter into the constitution of a Commonwealth.

In the face of such a condition, political theory was almost dumb. It was not at all a philosophy of self-government that stimulated the people of Dorchester to meet "every Mooneday before the Court by eight of the Clocke in the morning . . . to settle (and sett down) such orders as may tend to the generall good." It was the hard fact of maintaining community harmony that an increasing and diverse population was making necessary. For two hundred years there was no formal attempt to eulogize the device. Not only would philosophic definition have made necessary an unwelcome explanation to a puzzled Mother Country, but the town meeting was a perfectly apparent and workable method that had little attraction beyond its utility, and the records are searched in vain for that fervid commendation that marked the emotional references of the "middle period." The time was to come when it epitomized a theory of political development and operated as a powerful political machine that would have amazed its founders, for it not only served to exemplify extreme democracy in all its demands, but in the absence of more modern methods of communication was a most effective means of stirring the people to action.

So the town meeting emerged from the charter period almost unnoticed as a palladium of liberty, but quite capable of perpetuating itself in spite of changing charters and governors. It was exceedingly well adapted to frontier conditions as they existed in Massachusetts. The nucleus was always present in the original proprietors, it permitted the easy absorption of newcomers on a basis of equality in the common property, it assured (so far as a structure could) the choice of men most likely to express the aspirations of the community, and its isolation from the seat of colonial government for two centuries when intercourse was difficult, fostered an independence that led to the dual heritage of conservatism within the community and distrust of authority from without.

To read the acts of the Province period is to see a

growing supervision that as a paper record presages a distinct decline from the old freedom. But the futility of compelling or even expecting the fulfillment of many demands of the central government was seen in the various political subdivisions that led only gradually to full municipal life. Peculiar, plantation, district and parish were after all no more chance creations than the town itself. They were, on the contrary, official recognition of the necessity of cutting the powers to fit the need — a device well known to the modern legislator who is, however, more impelled to arrange his hierarchy on the basis of population than the more practical eighteenth century one of function.

To the Revolutionary War, town meeting government underwent few developments that were not in evidence from the first decade of settlement. Here is another sign of the stability of local institutions and of the precision with which communities with a developed political heritage adopt a device that will give effective response to their needs and that can be attuned at intervals to the quickening tempo of functional expansion. Most of the political changes that have a place in the records of the Colony, received their initial impetus from the towns themselves — indeed, much of the legislation is merely the authorization and regulation of practices long before utilized. Whatever may be the political influence from "the top" that modern methods have made possible, the vast majority of local regulations that hold over from the eighteenth century and before (as well as many of more recent origin) are merely the reflection of local practices that have found their fruition but not their beginning in legislative acts. Modern theories of centralization may justify, condemn and even guide the process, but it is very largely the slow adjustments and experiments of perplexed communities that have brought about the multiplicity of statutes pertaining to themselves. Not that state legislators are mere copyists — they regulate, adjust and stimulate — but neither are they always originators.

It was not until Alexis de Tocqueville looked at us in the early thirties, that town meetings were given anything like a formal attention. Their active part in the Revolutionary War (largely popularized by the stirring events in Faneuil Hall) had clothed them with a kind of national sanctity that served to further solidify their structure. The eulogy of the clever Frenchman did more, however, than to substantiate this position — it called attention to an institution that was the exemplification of Jacksonian democracy. Early notice was (like de Tocqueville's) largely a matter of surmise as to its origin and unstinted praise of its results, but when a younger generation of students applied the "new methods" that English, French and German scholars found so fascinating in their search for institutional origins, an added precision was given to the work.

But the conclusions were quite as varied as those that had marked the fragile hypotheses of earlier writers. Some gave emphasis to early Germanic influences and talked extensively of "survivals" and "revivals." Others urged the importance of the common law English parish of the sixteenth century with local modifications due to the social and geographic conditions of the New World. Some propped the early congregational influences with documentary supports or sought in the local governments of Massachusetts a conscious imitation of the colony's charter, and even exalted the towns themselves as "primordial cells" from which sprang the Commonwealth and eventually the Federal State.

The whole controversy was a small but vigorous eddy in the back waters of a European maelstrom that did much to refine both methods and issues. French, German and English scholars had expended much thought and energy in tracing the history of their own institutions, and if they failed to settle the difficult details, nevertheless they influenced and even destroyed many of the American conclusions. One by one the theories fell. When a group of eager economists (mainly English and French) showed that early village communities were far from the untrammelled democracies that the historians had thought but quite plainly existed, on the contrary, in a condition of serfdom under manorial lordship, they rather lost caste as ancestors of the Massachusetts town.

American scholars hastened to clarify their own conclusions. Ecclesiastical influences were vigorously modified. The first six years of settlement were found practically devoid of local records, and when documents first appeared a common terminology was about all that remained to connect town meeting government with English antecedents. The importance of charter influences faded with the others. Documentary evidence needed much unnatural twisting to show the adoption of a system with which the local governments were in constant friction. When the residue was finally examined it seemed most nearly to approximate Professor Edward Channing's conclusion that the towns were based on no models whatever, but "grew by the exercise of English common sense combined with the circumstances of the place."

In spite of the feeling that so simple an explanation is a feeble reward for such extensive effort, the discussion had merits that lifted it well beyond the scope of a mere intellectual exercise. Aside from attempting to mark the well-springs of our present heritage, and to give thereby a new appreciation of present viewpoints, the movement placed early institutional history on a documentary basis, emphasized the unity of its development, and tended to dwarf the proposals of overzealous reformers in a sobering array of historical precedents. It was not that the riddle of origins was answered, but it was thoroughly explored, and in the continual prodding of what was once a barren waste of faded manuscripts, relics were discovered that formed a surprising mosaic of "influences" that make our local constitutional pattern.

Nor is such a study devoid of more practical results. There are some thirty-eight city managers in Michigan, thirty in Florida, twenty-seven in Texas, and twenty-two in California. In Massachusetts there is only one, and the reason is very largely an historical matter. It is not possible to reconstruct a local government without attention to those common feelings and traditions that have been the results of long continued practices, and it is asking much of a Massachusetts community to abandon a town meeting for a "manager" — a term that falls harshly after three hundred years of direct democracy. To address a local Rotary Club on the merits of a town manager will require arguments quite different from those that would impress a similar group in a younger country, whose political history is a matter of short duration and often, also, of local chagrin. It is not that history "repeats itself" in terms of sequential causes and events, but the unfolding of local records teaches a steadying lesson in the continuity of motives as well as in the limits of legitimate political change.

But an essay on local government cannot always be exclusively historical — there is a realistic presentation that is often a necessary capstone to an institutional study. This approach tends to minimize the strictly historical and philosophic, and places main reliance on first, description — the delineation of legal and structural features — and second, a pragmatic analysis — the justification of existing practices by their consequences, and their improvement through experience. It is in this way that the methods of applied scholarship attempt to aid the practical politician in solving the immediate problems of popular government. In the field of the town meeting such studies have been scant and infrequent—indeed, in some one hundred years there has been no serious attempt to picture the popular assemblies of New England as "going concerns." The connotation that "mere description" arouses to the student of government is blighting enough, but contamination with practical politics is all but ruinous to scholastic preferment. The historian may excuse such lapses as "reactions" to a too severe antiquarianism; the metaphysician as the application of scholastic talents to somewhat sordid ends, and the politician (if he reads it at all), as a prosy way of approaching a very simple problem — but it is forgiveness rather than absolution.

While an institution, like an individual, can never be completely divorced from the past, its heritage is forced to act and react on a constantly changing environment, and it is here that the contemporary picture — or more accurately, perhaps the current cross section—becomes useful. A vast amount of confusion in modern political thinking is due to applying the axioms of a former time to empty shells from which the life has long since fled, and there are few more cooling antidotes for this insidious habit than to superimpose the contemporary reality on its progenitor of a past century. Increased numbers, narrowed interests, precinct voting, official ballots and public technicians are far more than mere facts and devices of town government — they are inexorable pressures that are relentlessly forcing an outworn structure into a new mold, and the work of the observer is to realize, facilitate and guide the process.

It is to this matter of guidance that the committees on change of town government first look — what is the path that the law has marked to aid the community in making the inevitable adjustments? First, any town in the Commonwealth exceeding twelve thousand people may become a city. This may be done in two ways: (1) the adoption of one of the four plans outlined in the optional charter law,[1] a course that makes it unnecessary for the

[1] *Genl. Laws,* ch. 43 (also issued in pamphlet form with amendments through 1917). This act was first passed in 1915 (*Acts of 1915,* ch. 267), and provides that any city except Boston may upon a petition signed by at least ten per cent of the registered voters at the state election preceding the filing of such petition, pass at the polls upon the question of adopting one of the four plans contained in the law. This, however, applies only to cities. Should a town desire to adopt such legislation, or should a city desire a special charter, formal application must be made to the General Court in accordance with rules prescribed for such a procedure. See the state Constitution, Amendments, Art. II (*Genl. Laws,* xxvii); *Genl. Laws,* ch. III, sec. 5 as amended by *Acts of 1926,* ch. 107, sec. 1; House Rule 32, Senate Rule 25, Joint Rule 9 (Massachusetts General Court, *Manual for the Use of the General Court* [1927–1928], pp. 587–588, 557, 625).

community to apply for original legislation; or (2) application may be made to the General Court for a special charter. If the former course is accepted, the town will have the choice of four plans of city government—Plan A (the "strong mayor plan" as in Quincy), Plan B (the "old mayor-council plan" as in Cambridge, Fitchburg, Lowell, Newburyport, Salem and Waltham), Plan C (the "commission plan" as in Lawrence) and Plan D (the "city manager plan," recently accepted in Fall River).[1] If the latter method is chosen, a special charter must be drafted, and as a practical matter the choice would probably be restricted to combinations or modifications of the optional charter proposals.[2]

Second, a town may desire less extensive changes that fall short of representative government, and (aside from local adjustments requiring no special authorization), this would probably mean one of three things: (1) a limited town meeting (if the town exceeds six thousand inhabitants);[3] (2) a town manager; or (3) minor administrative or electoral alterations through either special legislation or the acceptance of permissive statutes.

Insofar as adopting city government is concerned, the towns of the Commonwealth have (as has been indicated) uniformly undertaken such a change with great hesitancy and outspoken regrets. After a generation of debate, Boston adopted a representative government in 1822, but the succeeding century added but thirty-eight

[1] Waltham accepted Plan D of the optional charter system at the state election November 6, 1917 (*Ms. Letter*, City Clerk to Secretary of the Commonwealth [Waltham, November 9, 1917], and abandoned it to accept Plan B, November 7, 1922 [*ibid.*, Waltham, November 8, 1922]).

[2] Merely because these plans with modifications represent all distinct forms of city government generally used in the United States.

[3] Constitution, Amendments, Art. LXX (1926); *Acts of 1927*, p. 494.

others. For the most part their governments have been on the "old mayor-council plan," but six cities have at one time or another operated under commission government, several (including Boston) under the "strong mayor plan," and two have experimented with a city manager. It is not practicable to undertake an analysis of these forms of municipal government, especially as local conditions so often vitiate the force of theoretical criticism,[1] but from the student's standpoint, the "old mayor-council plan" (Plan B) is probably considered the least likely and the "city manager plan" (Plan D), the most likely to give responsibility and efficiency to the administrative services of the community. Commission government (Plan C) has proved to be merely a step in the development of the city manager, and is steadily losing ground both in favor of its successor as well as of older forms of local control. Plan A (the "strong mayor plan") is historically a remedy for the abuses of the "old mayor-council" arrangement that became particularly notorious in the decades following the Civil War; and while in principle it still dominates the larger cities of the country, a growing recognition of expert services in municipal government, as well as tendencies towards machine politics that an elected mayor with wide appointing powers must almost necessarily engender, is steadily retarding its extension.

So far as devices short of complete representative government are concerned, the limited town meeting is foremost. It has proved itself both adaptable and accept-

[1] Thorough criticism with collateral readings may be found in William Anderson's *American City Government* (N. Y., 1925), ch. XIII, and W. B. Munro's *Government of American Cities* (4th ed., N. Y., 1926), chs. XIV-XVII.

able. It fits well with the traditions of New England. It provides for popular participation in local policy. It offers opportunity for administrators to make their influence felt, and it tends to stimulate an interest in a more effective citizenship. The next few years will undoubtedly see additional towns in Massachusetts of upwards of six thousand population added to the steadily growing list, and other New England states are showing interest in the plan.

In its structure there are, however, elements that will bear watching. While it has both the origin and stability of a representative assembly, it misses classification as a city council largely because it preserves the influence of the average voter, admits administrative officers to its ranks, and lacks certain features that mark the conventional assembly — i.e., it rarely operates through standing committees, it lacks rigid procedural requirements, it has no responsibility toward any executive, and it is constantly sitting in the presence of its constituents.

But it offers an opportunity for partisan organization that the old town meeting lacked. Its personnel is known and stable, and depends for its position on basically the same conditions that all elective officers are subject to. Politics has rarely been able to depend on the average voter to do more than protect his individual or group interest, and it is well known that this is more surely secured through party organization than through public declamation.

There is still another matter. Dispatch and precision on the one hand and efficiency, economy and technical knowledge on the other will emphasize more and more the need of administrative services responsive to a more flexible representative body or better still, responsible to a single administrative officer. There has been as yet no attempt to combine the principles of the limited town meeting with that of the town manager, but this may well be done before the present experiments are complete. It would probably be an improvement, and under favorable conditions might ward off the "bogey" of city government for some time to come.

Massachusetts (as well as all New England) has been slow to accept extensive administrative reform in its local communities. In spite of the fact that Plan D of the Massachusetts optional charter system provides for a city manager, and Plan C for a commission government, and chapter 591 of the *Acts of 1920*, a similar arrangement for towns, only two cities have accepted the first and no communities the second and last. Only four towns, moreover, have had experience with a town manager, although a fifth has recently joined the group. Adoptive acts and special legislation have led to minor adjustments in structure, but interest has centered more on the reform of an overflowing town meeting than on the less observable need of precision and economy in administration.

The town must, however, come to accept it. The manager is no longer an experiment, and whatever may be his position in the political framework of the future, he is in one form or another an essential to every modern municipality whose community economy is out of the family stage. Wise men have always insisted on the need of a trained and responsible personnel in government. The manager offers a means to this end, and there is much to warrant the belief that the plan is the most hopeful, the most understandable, and the most in harmony with our institutions that has yet been tried.

In brief conclusion there are several general points that it is necessary to accept before any political problem in local government can be seen correctly, and collectively they form an attitude of mind that approaches realities in a broad and human way but that is nevertheless alive to the inflexible lessons that history has to teach. In the first place, the study of government offers no formula that will upon mere application remove the political difficulties under which a municipality may rest. There is, moreover, no political framework that will upon adoption automatically turn a bad government into a good one. There is no single form of government that is essentially democratic as opposed to all other forms, and in spite of much fervor to the contrary, the citizen will judge good government almost entirely by its results. And finally no method of government can be isolated and judged irrespective of local history and tradition or without regard to the environment in which it is to be applied, and it is very probable that the success of a new proposal will depend more upon the character of the local support that it receives than upon the theoretical excellences of the plan itself.

On the contrary, there are definite contributions that the study of government can make to aid patient committees who feel the futility of abstractions in the face of hard local sentiment and vested political interests. Historical and comparative methods can bring to light the innumerable devices through which communities of the past and present have attempted to solve local problems of recurring perplexity. While it is true that there is no political structure that will, upon application, turn a bad government into a good one, there are undoubtedly some that make it easier for able men to give effective service and for unscrupulous men to be controlled than others offer, and although no single form carries exclusively within itself the mechanical refinements of popular control, there are tests which students apply to estimate democratic potentialities—namely, that the electoral process so far as the choice of officers is concerned be confined almost wholly to policy determining officials; that the voter be given a practical method of making his influence felt; that the control of the representative assembly extend over the whole field of government; that administrative officers be qualified for their positions, that they work through a properly correlated and integrated system under personnel, budgetary and purchasing conditions that modern industry has found to be successful.

America has been a nation of charter tinkerers, and at the first "miss" in its political engines, eager citizens are under the hood with pliers in hand to remove the offending element. As a pen and ink sketch of municipal functions the Massachusetts town is a sprawling mass of unrelated services, but as a "going concern" it has a long record of sustained accomplishment based on fundamentals of citizenship which have been the despair of more "scientific" methods. In the presence of an orderly chart it is easy to forget the value of those basic but intangible qualities that Mill placed at the foundation of any plan aspiring to political permanence:

The people for whom the government is intended must be

willing to accept it . . . They must be willing and able to do
what is necessary to keep it standing.   And they must be
willing and able to do what it requires of them to enable it to
fulfill its purposes.[1]

[1] J. S. Mill, *Considerations on Representative Government* (London, 1861),
p. 5.

# INDEX

# INDEX

Acton, resolution of town meeting on independence, 97.

Adams, C. F., "The Genesis of the Massachusetts Town and the Development of Town-Meeting Government," 61–62; "Massachusetts Charter Theory," 63, 64, 224; on decline of town meeting (1830–1840), 111–112.

Adams, H. B., "The Germanic Origin of New England Towns," 56–57, 223.

Adams, no change of town government, 214.

Akagi, R. H., *The Town Proprietors of the New England Colonies*, 68n, 84n.

Alfred, resolution of town meeting on independence, 97.

Amesbury, proposed changes, 215.

Andover, proposed changes, 215.

Andrews, C. M., "The Beginnings of the Connecticut Towns," 61; "The Theory of the Village Community," 61.

Andros, Sir Edmund, attitude toward towns, 78–79; royal instructions of, 79, 79n, 80; overthrow of, 80–81.

Arlington, limited town meeting, 175–177; precincts, 179; town meeting membership, 180–181; referendum in, 185.

Assessors, early functions, 82n; penalty for neglect to provide, 83; selection and duties, 159.

Athol, proposed changes, 215.

Bacon, John, on towns in Commonwealth (1820), 105.

Ballots, early use, 45n; "official," 130; officers elected by, 135; preparation and use in town meetings, 145–146.

Barnstable, settlement and incorporation, 24; early records, 26.

Belmont, limited town meeting, 179; quorum in, 183.

Body of Liberties, moderator first mentioned, 43n; local privileges in 45; "prudential affairs" in, 45–46; Nathaniel Ward as author of, 46; provision for participation in town meetings in, 48–49.

Boston, first settled, 11; Dudley's account, 14; naming, 19; early attempts to incorporate, 71, 113–115; town meeting (18th century), 95–96; as "hotbed of sedition," 97; Boston Port Bill, 98; population (1820), 105; decline of town meeting in, 112–113; city government adopted in, 115; early precedent for limited town meeting in, 166; early changes rejected, 167; "strong mayor plan" in, 229.

Bradford, William, Plymouth charter of, 4, 22; opposed to expansion, 23; on towns in Plymouth Colony (1640), 24–25n.

Braintree, early settlement, 5–6; typical town record of (1708), 41; proposed changes in, 214.

Brookline, limited town meeting, 168–169; town meeting (1915), 169–170; attempts at improvements, 170–171; accepts limited town meeting (1915), 171–172; limited town meeting act (1915), 172–173; precincts, 179; town

237

70
71
72
74
75
76
77
79
8
83
85
88